ILLICIT ACTIVITY

For Lynsey, Angus, Su and Angus

Illicit Activity

The economics of crime, drugs and tax fraud

Edited by

ZIGGY MacDONALD
DAVID PYLE
*Public Sector Economics Research Centre,
University of Leicester*

Ashgate

DARTMOUTH

Aldershot • Burlington USA • Singapore • Sydney

Published by
Dartmouth Publishing Company Limited
Ashgate Publishing Ltd
Gower House
Croft Road
Aldershot
Hants GU11 3HR
England

Ashgate Publishing Company
131 Main Street
Burlington
Vermont 05401
USA

Ashgate website: http://www.ashgate.com

British Library Cataloguing in Publication Data
Illicit activity : the economics of crime, drugs and tax
    fraud
    1.Crime - Economic aspects 2.Crime - Social aspects 3.Drug
    abuse - Social aspects 4.Tax evasion
    I.MacDonald, Ziggy II.Pyle, David J., 1947-
    364

Library of Congress Cataloging-in-Publication Data
Illicit activity : the economics of crime, drugs, and tax fraud / [collected by] Ziggy MacDonald and David Pyle.
        p. cm.
    Includes bibliographical references.
    ISBN 0-7546-2047-6
    1. Crime--Economic aspects. I. MacDonald, Ziggy. II. Pyle, David J.

HV6171 .I55 2000
338.4'7664--dc21

                                                        00-44165

ISBN 0 7546 2047 6

Printed and bound by Athenaeum Press, Ltd.,
Gateshead, Tyne & Wear.

Contents

List of Figures

List of Tables

List of Contributors

Ali al-Nowaihi   Lecturer, Department of Economics, University of Leicester, UK.

Derek Deadman   Senior Lecturer, Department of Economics, University of Leicester, UK.

Amor Diez-Ticio   Lecturer, Department of Applied Economics, University of Zaragoza, Spain and Visiting Fellow at the Public Sector Economics Research Centre, University of Leicester, UK.

Ingolf Dittmann   Research Assistant, Department of Economics, University of Dortmund, Germany and Visiting Fellow at the Public Sector Economics Research Centre at the University of Leicester, UK.

Ziggy MacDonald   Lecturer, Department of Economics, University of Leicester, UK.

Denise Osborn   Professor of Econometrics, University of Manchester, UK and Visiting Fellow at the Public Sector Economics Research Centre, University of Leicester, UK.

Stephen Pudney   Tyler Professor in the Department of Economics and Director of the Public Sector Economics Research Centre, University of Leicester, UK.

David Pyle   Professor of Applied Economics in the Department of Economics, University of Leicester, UK.

Tolga Saruc   Ph.D student in the Department of Economics, University of Leicester, UK.

1. Introduction

ZIGGY MACDONALD AND DAVID PYLE

Overview

This book contains a collection of research papers on the theme of illicit activity, all written by either members or associate members of the Public Sector Economics Research Centre in the Department of Economics at the University of Leicester. The Oxford English Dictionary defines 'Illicit' as anything which is 'unlawful; not allowed'. The work that is reported in this volume covers three broad areas of such activity, namely crime (especially property related crime), consumption of illegal substances (drugs) and income tax evasion.

Crime and drug taking, especially, are regarded as major social issues in many advanced societies. For example, the UK Prime Minister (Tony Blair) in announcing the Government's ten-year strategy on drugs in 1998 said that, life in Britain 'could be so much better if we could break once and for all the vicious cycle of drugs and crime which wrecks lives and threatens communities' (Home Office, 1998, p. 1). The Strategy Document went on to say, 'drugs are a very serious problem in the UK...(they) are now more widely available than ever before and children are increasingly exposed to them. Drugs are a threat to health, a threat on the streets and a serious threat to communities because of drug-related crime' (ibid, p. 2). In the US, President Clinton announced, in 1998, a strategy to cut the use of illegal drugs by 50 per cent by 2007. This followed a report from the National Institute of Health showing that in 1996 over 40 per cent of High School Seniors had used drugs in the last year. In the UK, the British Crime Survey 1998 showed that 31 per cent of 16-19 year olds had used drugs in the last year.

Concern about crime is widespread throughout the Western World. The 1996 International Crime Victimisation Survey (Mayhew and van Dijk, 1997) shows that in eleven OECD countries, on average 22 per cent of respondents felt unsafe when out alone after dark. In England and Wales, the proportion was as high as one-third. However, the good news is that fear of crime has fallen in Britain during the 1990s, as the crime rate has come down (British Crime Survey, 1998). The same survey shows that in eight of the 11 OECD countries included in the sample, the crime

1

victimisation rate was at least 24 per cent in 1995, with The Netherlands and England heading the league table with victimisation rates of 31 per cent. Despite this, in several countries (US, Canada and England and Wales, for example) rates of recorded crime have been falling since the early 1990s. Nevertheless, rates of recorded crime are still high by historical standards and the reasons for the decline in recent years are not entirely clear (but see Chapters Two through Six below).

For obvious reasons, the extent of income tax evasion cannot be known with any degree of certainty. However, various ingenious devices have been used by economists in order to try to measure it (see Pyle, 1989 for a survey) and it is common to see estimates of 'hidden' economic activity amounting to between ten and 15 per cent of Gross Domestic Product in a whole range of countries. This might be thought to have a number of economic consequences, the most obvious of which is the loss of tax revenue for the Government. In fact, loss of tax revenue is not obvious, provided tax evaders buy goods and services from others, which will generate income for the providers and tax receipts for the Government. However, tax evasion will certainly distort macroeconomic indicators such as unemployment statistics and measures of national income and output. Such distortions may cause governments to make totally inappropriate macroeconomic interventions. Also, tax evasion may distort resource allocation, if the opportunities to evade are greater in certain occupations than others. This may lead some individuals to choose an occupation that is in their own financial interest, but not in the best interests of society (for example, university professors may prefer to become self-employed odd job people, if by doing so they can avoid paying a great deal of income tax).

In response to evidence of increasingly widespread engagement in illicit activity by members of the general public, governments have been increasing their expenditure on policing, prisons, courts, and law enforcement generally. This represents a social waste, for the resources used in this way could be used for more productive purposes. For example, in the UK, expenditure on the criminal justice system increased in real terms from £8.6 billion in 1988-9 to £11.3 billion in 1997-8, i.e. by about 30 per cent over nine years (Social Trends, 1999).

What have economists got to say about such phenomena? Most people's view (if they have any view at all) is that economists examine either issues such as unemployment, inflation, and interest rates or the structure and performance of firms and industries and the role of markets. In other words, economists focus upon what can be described as narrowly economic and financial issues. Nothing could be further from the truth.

Over the last 30 years or so, an increasing number of economists have been applying economic methods to analyse all kinds of social phenomena, including activities such as crime, drug taking, marriage and divorce.

There are two aspects of illicit activity to which economists can contribute. First, in dealing with the problems which illicit activity creates, government agencies use a great deal of resources and it is an economic issue about how much resource should be put into dealing with these problems and how best to allocate that resource amongst competing areas and policies. For example, should we spend more on police (prevention and detection) or prisons (punishment), say, as a way of reducing theft? Should we spend more on education and rehabilitation programmes for drug users than on catching and punishing drug dealers? If we had additional resources should we use them to reduce tax evasion or allocate them to burglary prevention programmes instead? This kind of analysis is meat and drink to an economist. Second, the decision to engage in illicit activities can be viewed as an economic one about how individuals allocate their time to competing activities, some of which are risky i.e. you might get caught and punished. Economists are used to analysing decisions of this type e.g. labour supply decisions, choice in risky situations, etc. What distinguishes the economic approach to criminal participation is the assumption that individuals engaged in such activity are rational decision makers who attempt to optimise some welfare function. In this volume you will see a number of papers that explore the implications of this approach for modelling participation in illicit activity.

The economic approach to participation in illicit activities was first advanced by the American economist Gary Becker. In fact, Becker applied the economic approach to a much wider range of 'social' issues, such as crime, marriage and divorce, discrimination, drug addiction and religion. Somewhat modestly, Becker attributes his interest in applying economics to 'social' problems to advice given to him by the Chicago economists Milton Friedman and Theodore Schultz when he was a young graduate student (see Tommasi and Ieurelli, 1995).

This collection of papers has a unifying theme, which is the approach that the contributors have adopted to the study of their subject. The approach adopted at PSERC to analyse illicit activity is primarily empirical, although it is quite broad. It encompasses aggregate time-series studies, micro (cross-sectional and panel data) analysis, and mathematical simulation. Members of PSERC have been at the forefront of the application of economic methods to the study of illicit activity in the UK and this volume reflects the breadth of the work that is being undertaken by them. Members of PSERC have recently published articles outlining this research in a number of academic journals. Whilst the papers contained in this volume are based upon that published work, they have been specially written for this book.

In the rest of the Introduction we outline the contents of each chapter. We have grouped this discussion under three headings, which are crime, drugs and tax evasion.

Crime

In recent years research into crime at PSERC has focussed upon an economic explanation of criminal activity. In particular much analysis has been undertaken of the relationship between the incidence of crime, especially property crime, and the state of the nation's economy. In simple terms this work confronts the question whether there is any evidence that when the economy is in recession property crime increases and that when the economy enters a boom property-related crime diminishes. This work has concentrated upon the experience in England and Wales using aggregate, annual time-series data. Chapters Two to Four report some of that work. In Chapter Five Denise Osborn, a Visiting Fellow at PSERC examines the relationship between crime and the economy using quarterly aggregate data. In Chapter Six, Amor Diez-Ticio, another visitor to PSERC, applies the underlying technique to data for the US. Chapter Seven, written by another visiting scholar at PSERC (Ingolf Dittmann) presents a theoretical analysis of the reasons why States tend to use both fines and imprisonment as alternative forms of punishment for the same crime.

In Chapter Two, Derek Deadman and David Pyle begin by presenting a theoretical model of criminal participation, which treats involvement in crime as a labour supply decision. This is the essence of the economic approach to crime, which treats potential criminals as rational individuals who respond to incentives. They conclude that the amount of time someone will spend engaged in criminal activity will then depend upon 'wage rates' in both legitimate and criminal activity, the probability of being caught and convicted of committing a crime, the size of the punishment if caught and the probability of being unemployed in legitimate activity. The bulk of Deadman and Pyle's chapter is devoted to applying the economic approach outlined earlier in their chapter to data on residential burglaries in England and Wales between 1950 and 1995. They use aggregate national level data (i.e. data for the whole of England and Wales). This model contains a number of deterrence, economic and 'taste' variables, which are the probability of being convicted, the conditional probability of being imprisoned, the number of police officers, the expected length of imprisonment, the number of males aged 15 to 24 years, the unemployment rate, and per capita real personal consumption. Deadman and Pyle provide a discussion of some of the issues, which confront this type of analysis e.g. measurement error in the crime variable (their research uses recorded crime data, which are notoriously error prone. This is issue is addressed more fully in Chapter Three) and possible simultaneity between the dependent and explanatory variables. They also discuss a major problem in modelling time series aggregate data, which are the time-series properties of their data. This is an important issue for regression analysis, because both crime and economic data in post-war England are dominated by time trends and meaningful regression results can only be found when the data are freed of these trends. This has proved a controversial issue, which is explored in several chapters in this volume. Turning to their results, Deadman and Pyle find that the majority of the explanatory variables, and especially the deterrence and economic variables, are statistically significant and have their expected signs. Deterrence seems to work, especially in the short term, in lowering crime and economic variables have both short and long term effects upon the rate of residential burglary (this is explored more fully in Chapter Four).

In Chapter Three, Derek Deadman, Stephen Pudney and David Pyle address the issue of measurement error in recorded crime. Recorded crime data are well known to be error prone (data from the British Crime Survey suggests that perhaps only one third of all crime is reported to and recorded by the police). Unfortunately, there is insufficient time-series victimisation data available to enable the estimation of a model of the type reported in Chapter Two. Deadman *et al.* investigate whether the use of recorded crime data can lead to erroneous conclusions being drawn about the influence of both economic and deterrence variables upon the 'true' crime rate. Their theoretical analysis indicates that the effect of measurement error in an economic model could be quite complex, particularly where one of the explanatory variables (the conviction rate) is measured by the ratio of convictions to recorded crime. As recorded crime is an underestimate of the true amount of crime, the estimated conviction rate will overstate its true value. This will tend to impart a negative bias to the effect of the conviction rate upon crime. However, the real situation is even more complex than that, because of the presence in the time-series model of lagged values of variables. As a result, it becomes virtually impossible to assess the likely impact of measurement error. Deadman *et al.* address this issue by incorporating extraneous information on the reporting of crime to the police, which comes from the British Crime Survey (BCS) and the General Household Survey (GHS). These are two household surveys, which include questions about respondents' experience of crime and whether incidents were reported to the police. Deadman *et al.* focus upon residential burglary and use Monte Carlo simulation to examine whether the parameter estimates in a time series economic model of residential burglary are affected by the presence of measurement error. They find that whilst this does lead to biases in parameter estimates, these are not particularly serious and would not lead a 'naïve' investigator to draw incorrect conclusions.

The relationship between the incidence of crime, especially property crime, and the state of the economy is something which has received a great deal of attention from economists and criminologists in the UK in recent years. Derek Deadman and David Pyle have played a leading role in that discussion and in Chapter Four they both review that debate and offer some fresh results on the short- and long-term nature of the relationship. In 'theory' the direction of the link between crime and economic activity is not immediately obvious, because of the conflicting effects of 'opportunity' and 'motivation'. This uncertainty may explain the often unclear conclusions that emerged from early (1970s) empirical work that examined the link between crime and unemployment. In the 1990s, British economists began to examine the link between crime and other economic variables, especially real consumption expenditure and Gross Domestic Product (GDP). Deadman and Pyle pioneered the adoption of modern time series econometric methodology in this area. This enabled them to build dynamic models of crime which separate out the short term and long-term effects upon crime of the different variables. The results of this kind of work show that there is a much stronger link between recorded crime and economic indicators than had been thought in the early 1980s. In particular there is evidence that when the economy enters a recession (manifested by lower real consumption spending and higher unemployment) then the incidence of property crime increases. In the longer term, crime increases with increases in real consumption and unemployment. In Chapter Four, Deadman and Pyle report estimates of such a model for residential burglary in England and Wales between 1950 and 1995 and find exactly these effects.

In Chapter Five, Denise Osborn offers some further analysis of the time-series relationship between recorded crime and economic factors in England and Wales. She uses quarterly data between 1975 and 1993 to model separately the series for burglary, theft and handling of stolen goods, criminal damage and personal crime (crimes of violence and sex offences). She also models the series for all property crime, i.e. the first three series listed above. The choice of quarterly data restricts the number of explanatory variables and, unlike Deadman and Pyle, Osborn does not include deterrence and demographic variables in her model. In modelling the long-term relationship between crime and economic variables, she concludes that there is stronger evidence of a relationship between crime and consumption than there is between crime and GDP and that unemployment is not cointegrated with crime in the long run. Even the addition of unemployment to the crime–consumption relationship weakens the evidence for the existence of cointegration between crime and economic variables. Therefore, she dismisses any role for unemployment in explaining long-run changes in crime in England and Wales. In fact, she is unable to find any economic explanation for the rise in personal crime in England over the 20-year period of her data. However, Osborn does find that changes in unemployment appear to have a role in explaining short-term changes in personal crime. She also concludes that there is little role for changes in consumption and unemployment having any role in determining short-term movements in property crime, although there is some evidence that unemployment has an asymmetric (i.e. ratchet) effect. A rise in unemployment leads to an increase in property crime that does not disappear when unemployment falls again.

In Chapter Six Amor Diez-Ticio applies the modelling approach suggested by Deadman and Pyle in Chapter Four to time–series data for the US. This is an interesting comparison, for there is now a great deal of evidence from both recorded crime statistics and victimisation data that crime in the US has been falling for considerably longer than it has in the UK. For example, the burglary rate in the US has been on a downward trend for almost 20 years and is now one half of what it was in 1980. Indeed, with the exception of homicide (murder) statistics, crime rates in the US (whether recorded or 'real') are often lower than in England and Wales (see Langan and Farrington, 1998). Diez-Ticio analyses annual time–series data for the period 1950 to 1996 for three separate crime groups: burglary, robbery and auto-theft. Explanatory variables are the clear up rate for the crime itself, the unemployment rate, real personal consumption per capita, the proportion of the population aged between 15 and 24 years and a measure of income inequality (the share of income received by the poorest 20 per cent of the population relative to the richest 20 per cent). She finds evidence that economic variables have a role in explaining the behaviour of US crime rates, although that role may be different across crimes and between the short-term and the long-term. For example, both unemployment and real consumption have long-term influences upon robbery rates, but only unemployment has a short-term effect. For burglary, unemployment has a long-run effect and consumption has a short-term effect. Only unemployment affects auto-theft rates, both in the short-term and the long-term. Perhaps somewhat controversially, she finds that the effect of unemployment on crime rates in the long-term is negative, which is contrary to the findings of Deadman and Pyle for English and Welsh data. For robbery, she also finds that the inequality variable has both a short and long-term effect, although it is not significant for other crimes.

The focus of Chapter Seven, by Ingolf Dittmann, is upon punishment and in particular whether an economic model of punishment can explain why sometimes the same crime is punished by either a fine or a sentence of imprisonment. Becker's seminal article (Becker, 1968), and the subsequent literature on the economics of punishment, suggests that the use of fines is more efficient than imprisonment because fines are cheaper in social cost terms. For example, they do not lead to the loss of output which imprisoning someone implies, the capital costs of prison building and the recurrent costs of employing prison warders. Only if the size of the fine is limited by the level of an individual's wealth should imprisonment be used. Dittmann explores a number of recent attempts to reconcile the prescription of the economic model that punishment should take the form of a fine with the observed use by the courts of both fines and imprisonment (and a host of other forms of punishment) for the same type of offence. He shows that these approaches can explain the use of fines and imprisonment as alternative methods of punishing the same offence. However, only his model can explain the existence mandatory sentences of imprisonment, i.e. situations in which judges have no discretion but to impose a gaol term no matter how rich the offender. He posits a model in which citizens vote for mandatory imprisonment for some offences (the more serious ones) in order to limit the power of the government to maximise revenue from fines. If punishment was always by fines, a government interested solely in revenue could lower the detection probability by spending less on police but raise the size of the fine for those who are caught. Where the crimes are serious this would not be in the citizens' interests.

England and Wales has one of the highest rates of household burglary in the OECD. Chapters Two through Four have presented a series of econometric models of the domestic burglary rate in England. In Chapter Eight, Ziggy MacDonald and Stephen Pudney address a related issue, which is the distributional impact of household burglary. In order to do this they examine burglary victimisation data reported in the GHS in 1985, 1986, 1991-2 and 1993-4. In all some 30,000 cases are explored. First, they model the probability that a household would be the victim of a burglary using a probit analysis (in probit analysis the dependent variable takes the value one or zero depending upon whether an event has occurred or not.) The results of this analysis are of interest in themselves and show that a household is more likely to be burgled if its head is either Black or Asian, is unemployed, and is living in rented accommodation. On the other hand, the probability of being burgled is lower if the head of household is retired and/or married. They also find that middle-income households are less likely to be burgled than either poor or rich households. They then estimate the financial losses associated with burglary including the costs of damage from forced entry. These results are then used to simulate the distributional impact of burglary by calculating the expected annual rate of loss for each household. They find that expected annual losses are highest for the lowest household income group and decline until about the 25th income percentile, after which they rise modestly and steadily. Their results show that burglary losses are highly regressive, in that as a percentage of household income losses decline with income. In addition they also show that losses for Black and Asian households are larger than for White households at the same income level.

In Chapter Three Deadman *et al.* examined the impact which measurement error had upon the parameter estimates of a typical economic model of crime. In Chapter Nine, Ziggy MacDonald examines the so-called 'dark figure' of crime (i.e. unreported crimes) from a different perspective. Here the focus is upon individuals' decisions to report crimes that have been committed against them and how those decisions are determined by individual characteristics and the attributes of the crime. One of MacDonald's findings is that individuals are less likely to report a crime committed against them when they are unemployed. At the aggregate level this suggests that the extent of under recording may vary with the phase of the economic cycle, which would have some implications for the analysis of the relationship between crime and economic activity. MacDonald examines information on reporting of residential burglary contained in the British Crime Surveys (BCS) of 1994 and 1996. This covers some 35,000 individuals altogether, of whom about eight per cent were the victims of crime. In the BCS, individuals are asked whether they have reported the crime to the police. This information is used to construct a binary variable (reported/not reported), which is then regressed upon a number of explanatory variables. The factors that make individuals more likely to report a crime include being female, being Asian, age, if the crime took place at night or at the weekend, if the victim was injured during the course of the crime, if the victim was worried about crime in the area and if the burglary resulted in a financial loss. Individuals were less likely to report a burglary if they were unemployed and if they felt that the police do a very poor job.

Drugs

Drugs have become a major social issue in the last ten years or so in many Western societies. The incidence of drug use (by which we mean consumption of drugs such as cannabis, cocaine, heroin, ecstasy etc) has increased substantially amongst young people. For example, the BCS reveals that 40 per cent of respondents under the age of 25 admit to having tried drugs at some point in their lives. The UK government is committed to reducing the prevalence and incidence of drug misuse and in 1998 it launched a ten-year strategy for tackling the problem. However, relatively little objective evidence is available about the characteristics of drug users, let alone the reasons why they consume such substances. In recent years there has been some work by economists looking at ways in which drug consumption can be reduced by operating on either the supply side or the demand side of the 'markets' for such drugs. There has also been some analysis of the reasons for government intervention in this situation (Stevenson, 1994).

In Chapter Ten, Ziggy MacDonald considers the more fundamental question 'who actually consumes drugs?'. In order to answer this question, he analyses data drawn from the BCSs of 1994 and 1996. The BCS asks three questions about drug use, which are basically 'have you ever taken drug X...?', 'have you taken drug X in the last twelve months?' and 'have you taken drug X in the last month?'. MacDonald highlights the limitations of the BCS questions for obtaining information on drug consumption and shows that a simple reordering of the existing questions in the survey would generate much more useful information than is available at present. The bulk of MacDonald's chapter is devoted to an analysis of some 22,000 individual responses, which are modelled as a binary variable. Logit analysis is then carried out using a series of explanatory variables measuring individuals' characteristics. Drug use in the past (i.e. at least twelve months before) and now (i.e. within the last month) are separately analysed, as are the consumption of 'soft' and 'hard' drugs. MacDonald's analysis shows that the factors influencing soft and hard drugs consumption are remarkably similar. To illustrate, he finds that a young, single male, living in the inner city and who is unemployed and a frequent drinker has a probability of about 0.57 of being a current soft drug user. On the other hand, the probability that a 30 something Asian woman who is married and belongs to a religious group being a current soft drug user is only 0.003. MacDonald's chapter goes on to consider the relationship between drug use and income, drug use and alcohol consumption and whether there is any evidence of escalation from soft to hard drugs. In all of these areas it is found that the current BCS data are somewhat limited, especially in being unable to tell us anything about the intensity of drug use.

One of the arguments often mounted for government interference with an individual's decision to consume drugs is that drug users become ill and as a consequence are absent from work, possibly lose their job, and society bears the cost of this lost output. In Chapter Eleven Ziggy MacDonald and Stephen Pudney investigate whether the consumption of hard and/or soft drugs affects the probability of a drug user being unemployed and, if they are employed, their occupational achievement (measured by their wage in a job). In order to answer these questions, they analyse data from the British Crime Surveys of 1994 and 1996, in which individuals report whether they have used drugs in the past or currently, whether they are unemployed and, if employed, what occupation they follow. Separate analyses are undertaken for men and women and for those aged 16 to 25 years and 26 to 50 years. The empirical analysis is in two stages. First, there is an analysis of individuals' past use of drugs and then the joint estimation of current drug use, unemployment and occupational attainment. The results of the impact of drug use on labour market outcomes shows that past hard drug use is associated with higher unemployment in all cases (except women aged 26-50 years), there is little effect of soft drug usage on unemployment, and there is no evidence of a negative impact of hard drugs consumption upon occupational attainment, except for women aged 16-25 years. The effect of soft drug usage on occupational attainment is positive for women aged 26-50, but negative for men aged 26-50.

Income Tax Evasion

The third strand of work covered in the volume relates to income tax evasion. Chapter Twelve, written by Ali al-Nowaihi and David Pyle, examines the economic model of the decision to under-declare income to the tax authority, whilst in Chapter Thirteen Stephen Pudney, David Pyle and Toga Saruc undertake some empirical analysis of the tax declaration decision using data drawn from a number of tax experiments carried out in Turkey.

After setting out the basic economic model of tax declaration, al-Nowaihi and Pyle devote the rest of their chapter to an exploration of one of the more peculiar predictions of economic analysis. In the literature on income tax evasion, it has been shown that if individuals aim to maximise expected utility, which depends solely upon income, and that the penalty for unsuccessful tax evasion is related to the amount of unpaid tax, then an increase in the rate of income tax leads individuals to declare more, not less, income to the tax authority. This theoretical prediction is wildly at odds with known evidence on the effect of the income tax rate upon tax declarations, whether this comes from audits of taxpayers' affairs or from tax experiments. Al-Nowaihi and Pyle explore one way in which the theoretical model can be adapted in order to make it consistent with the evidence. The route they choose is to incorporate stigma into the individual's decision calculus, so that utility depends not just upon income, but also upon the amount of income that is declared to the tax authority. In this formulation individuals suffer pangs of conscience (i.e. loss of utility) when they fail to declare income and the more that they under-declare their income the greater is their suffering. Of course, they have to compare this suffering with the financial gains from reduced income taxation, from which they derive positive utility. Al-Nowaihi and Pyle then use a particular functional form (Cobb-Douglas) of the utility function in order to simulate the effect of a change in the rate of income taxation upon the amount of income declared to the tax authority. They are able to show that for realistic values of the tax rate, the penalty rate etc. and a wide range of values of the probability of detection, an increase in the income tax rate will lead individuals to declare less of their income.

In the final chapter of the volume, Stephen Pudney, David Pyle and Tolga Saruc explore some evidence on the determinants of the decision to evade and the extent of income tax evasion. In this area evidence is particularly hard to find. Some empirical work has been conducted in the past based upon the results of so-called tax experiments in which groups of individuals (normally university students) are put into a hypothetical situation and asked to make an income tax declaration. In theses games, the participants are given a level of income and are informed about the income tax rate, the penalties for under declaration of income and the probability of being audited by the tax authority. In successive rounds of these experiments, the values of some of these parameters are changed in order to observe the effect upon the amount of income declared. A striking feature of much of the experimental work that has been undertaken in this area is that it has normally involved small numbers of students (15-20 is a typical number) participating in a classroom environment. The data used by Pudney *et al.* come from a much larger set of experiments involving some 270 individuals, most of whom are people in work (principally professional groups). The experiments were also conducted over a longer time period, which enabled the participants to obtain advice about their tax declaration. In other words the experiments made a real effort to mimic the real life situation facing income taxpayers. The authors use a two stage empirical methodology in order first to examine the decision to declare or not and then to explain how much income is declared. At each stage the dependent variable is related to a number of individual characteristics (such as age, marital status, occupation) of the participants and to the tax rate, audit rate and the penalty for undeclared tax. Pudney *et al.* find that an increase in the rate of income tax encourages under declaration and that an increase in the expected penalty for income tax evasion discourages evasion.

References

Becker, G.S. (1968) 'Crime and Punishment: An Economic Approach', *Journal of Political Economy*, vol. 76, 169-217.

Home Office (1998), *Tackling Drugs to Build a Better Britain: The Government's Ten-Year Strategy for Tackling Drugs Misuse*, HMSO, London.

Langan, P.A. and Farrington, D.P. (1998), *Crime and Justice in the United States and in England and Wales, 1981-96*, US Department of Justice, Washington DC.

Mayhew, P. and van Dijk, J. (1997), *Criminal Victimisation in Eleven Industrialised Countries*, Dutch Ministry of Justice, The Hague.

Pyle, D.J. (1989), *Tax Evasion and the Black Economy*, Macmillan, Basingstoke.

Stevenson, R. (1994), *Winning The War on Drugs: To Legalise or Not?*, Hobart Paper 124, Institute of Economic Affairs, London.

Tommasi, M. and Ieurelli, K. (1995), *The New Economics of Human Behaviour*, Cambridge University Press, Cambridge.

2. An Economic Model of Criminal Activity

DEREK DEADMAN AND DAVID PYLE

Introduction

Crime is a major social problem in many western, liberal democracies. Surveys suggest that, in many of the OECD countries, between 25 per cent and 30 per cent of individuals are the victims of criminal acts each year (Criminal Statistics England and Wales, 1997, Table 10.10). Much of this criminal activity is property related. For example, in England and Wales about 70 per cent of all recorded crime falls into the categories of burglary and theft, whilst another 20 per cent of recorded offences are cases of fraud or criminal damage. Recorded crime has shown a marked upward trend during the post-war period. In England and Wales it increased by a factor of about ten between 1946 and 1996 (see Figure 2.1). Similar trends have occurred in other countries. In response to this, public expenditure on the criminal justice system has grown substantially; in the UK by more than 50 per cent in real terms in the last ten years, so that now more is spent on law enforcement than on the whole Higher Education system. Similar observations could be made about most advanced, industrialised nations.

In the last 30 years, following Becker's seminal contribution (Becker, 1968), economists have devoted a considerable amount of time to the study of criminal activity. In particular, much effort has gone into estimating empirical models that try to explain the incidence of crime by reference to deterrence, economic and socio-demographic variables. Examples of such work will be reported later in this chapter.

From the standpoint of criminal justice policy, it is important, first of all, to estimate the quantitative effects which different variables, especially detection, conviction and imprisonment, have upon the crime rate. If such effects can be measured with a reasonable degree of confidence, it should then be possible to rank the cost effectiveness, in terms of crime reduction, of an extra pound spent on each of these actions.

In this chapter we explore the economists' model of criminal participation. This model is based upon the premise that criminals are rational agents who respond to incentives, which include the punishments associated with unsuccessful attempts at criminal activity. Also, we will briefly review previous attempts to test the predictions of the economic models, particularly in relation to the effectiveness of deterrence variables. Much of this literature has relied upon recorded crime statistics in order to determine the deterrent effects of various criminal justice measures. However, there are a number of methodological issues, which need to be addressed in relation to the use of error prone, recorded crime statistics. We will discuss these issues here, although a more detailed analysis is contained in Chapter Three.

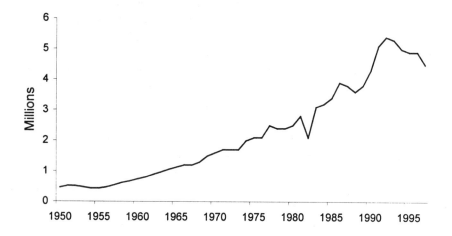

Figure 2.1   Recorded crime in England and Wales 1950-1997

Finally, a major part of the chapter will be devoted to an attempt to test the economic model of crime. This is done by estimating a model of residential burglary for England and Wales, using annual time-series data for the period 1950 to 1995. Time series data can present particular difficulties for statistical analysis when the series are dominated by strong time trends, which post-war UK data on crime and economic variables are. We discuss these issues and how to resolve them. Analysis of aggregate data raises another issue, which is the direction of causality between crime and the criminal justice variables, i.e. is crime caused by the conviction and imprisonment probabilities, say, or are they caused by crime or does causality run in both directions. We examine this issue and find that for UK data causation runs in one direction only and that is from the criminal justice variables to the crime variable.

The Economic Theory of Criminal Participation

The economic approach to criminal involvement rests on the assumption that most potential criminals are rational people who respond to incentives. Becker (1968) argued that individuals will commit a crime if the benefits (expected utility) from doing so exceed those derived from legitimate activity. In Becker's model no account is taken of the disutility (qualms of conscience) which individuals might incur by engaging in criminal activity (for an attempt to incorporate such moral scruples see Block and Heineke, 1975).

For the purposes of economic analysis, an important aspect of criminal activity is that it is inherently risky. You might get caught and punished, which would reduce the expected utility from engaging in criminal acts. As a result, Becker claimed that potential criminals will be deterred from committing crimes by increases in (i) the probability of being caught and punished and (ii) the amount of punishment if caught, because each of these events reduces expected utility.

A Simple Model of Criminal Activity

In Becker's model individuals are treated as if they are gambling with a part of their wealth, but it might be more helpful to consider crime as a labour intensive activity, for the planning and carrying out of a burglary or robbery may take time which is then diverted from legitimate pursuits. In effect this means that criminal participation should be treated as a labour supply decision, which is influenced by factors such as earnings in legitimate work, returns to criminal activity and the probability of unemployment in legitimate activity.

Below we set out a highly simplified model in which individuals choose how to allocate their time (T) between legitimate activity (t_l) and crime (t_c) in order to maximise their utility (U). The wage rates in the two forms of activity are fixed and given by W_l and W_c, respectively. If caught, offenders are punished by a penalty (f) that is related to the amount of time they spend in criminal activity (judges are assumed to know this or at least are able to infer it!). What income level the individual enjoys will depend upon whether or not he or she is caught and convicted. Call these income levels I_u (for unsuccessful in evading detection for criminal activity) and I_s (for successful). Hence

$$I_s = W_1 t_1 + W_c t_c$$
$$I_u = W_1 t_1 + W_c t_c - f t_c = I_s - f t_c$$

with associated utilities $U(I_s)$ and $U(I_u)$. If someone devotes all of her time to legitimate activity, then her income will be the same whether or not she is caught, so that

$$I_u = I_s = W_1 T.$$

On the other hand if she spends all of her time engaged in criminal activity, then

$$I_u = (W_c - f)T$$
$$I_s = W_c T.$$

We draw the opportunity locus in Figure 2.2. At point A the individual specialises in legitimate activity, i.e. $t_1 = T$, whereas at point B the individual specialises in criminal activity and $t_c = T$. Points between A and B represent non-specialisation in either legitimate or criminal activity. For example, at C (the mid point of the line AB) the individual devotes half of her time to each form of income generating activity. The closer someone is to A, then the less time they devote to criminal activity, whereas the closer they are to B the more time they spend in criminal activity. The opportunity locus is linear because we have assumed that W_c, W_1 and f are all constants. Expected utility is given by:

$$EU = pU(I_u) + (1 - p)U(I_s).$$

Note that we have assumed that p (the probability of detection) is independent of t_c. The preferences define a set of indifference curves and along each indifference curve expected utility is held constant. As both I_u and I_s are desirable in their own right (they are both income), the indifference curves will be negatively sloped and convex to the origin.[1] A typical indifference curve is drawn in Figure 2.3.

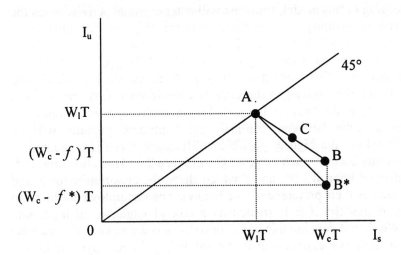

Figure 2.2   The opportunity locus

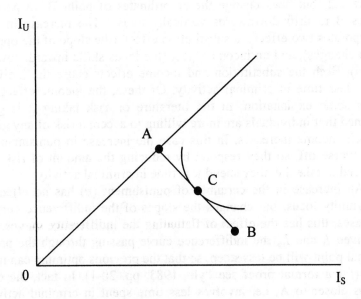

Figure 2.3   Optimum criminal activity

According to this model, someone will enter criminal activity when the slope of the opportunity locus is flatter than the slope of the indifference curve passing through A in Figure 2.2. It can be shown that this will arise when $W_c - W_l > pf$ (for a formal proof see Pyle, 1983, pp. 19-20). That is when the increased financial return ($W_c - W_l$) from spending a unit of time in criminal activity outweighs the expected punishment (pf) arising from such involvement. For those individuals for whom this applies, an optimum allocation of time between criminal and legitimate pursuits will be established where the highest possible indifference curve is tangential to the opportunity locus – such as point C in Figure 2.3. This allocation (t_c^*, t_l^*) will depend upon W_l, W_c, and f, which shape the opportunity locus and p, which shapes their preferences (see below). The unemployment rate can be added to this list if it is treated as a risk of engaging in legitimate activity. We do not develop this point formally in order to keep the analysis simple. An intuitive explanation is the following. Unemployment lowers the return from legitimate activity and so an increase in the unemployment rate, *ceteris paribus*, makes criminal activity more attractive. As a result, a rational criminal will devote a larger proportion of her time to crime.

Briefly we will look at the effect of changes in f and p. An increase in the severity of punishment (f) does not affect the co-ordinates of point A in Figure 2.2, but does change the co-ordinates of point B. In particular it causes B to drift downwards vertically to B*. The increase in f clearly incorporates two effects: a substitution effect, (the slope of the opportunity locus changes), and an income effect (the locus shifts inwards towards the origin). Both the substitution and income effects cause the individual to spend less time in criminal activity. Of these, the income effect perhaps needs some explanation. In the literature on risk taking it is generally assumed that individuals are more willing to accept a risk of any given size as their income increases. In this case the increase in punishment makes them worse off, so they respond by reducing the amount of risk they are prepared to take, i.e. they spend less time in criminal activity.

An increase in the certainty of punishment (p) has no effect on the opportunity locus, but changes the slopes of the indifference curves. If p increases, this has the effect of flattening the indifference curves. That is, for given I_s and I_u, the indifference curve passing through the previously optimal point will be less steep, so that the previous optimum can no longer hold (for a formal proof see Pyle, 1983, pp. 20-1). In fact, the optimum moves closer to A, i.e. involves less time spent in criminal activity (see Figure 2.4).

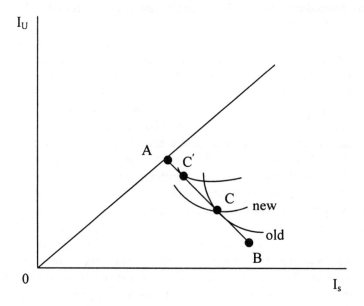

Figure 2.4   An increase in certainty of punishment

Clearly this point was not understood by Dau-Schmidt (1990) who argued that '... economists analyse only the opportunity-shaping method of affecting individual behaviour, assuming that individual preferences are exogenous and immutable' (p. 5).

Evidence on Deterrent Effects

From the standpoint of criminal justice policy, it is important to know, quite precisely, the quantitative effects that the criminal justice variables have upon crime. As a result of Becker's original theoretical contribution, economists have devoted a great deal of research effort to the estimation of what are called crime 'supply' equations. Surveys and critiques of that work can be found Pyle (1983), Cameron (1988) and Ehrlich (1996). Here we present only a brief résumé of the more important methodological issues confronting that work, as well as reporting a representative sample of estimates of deterrence elasticities.

Most of the empirical testing of the relationship between crime and deterrence variables has analysed data on recorded crimes using standard statistical procedures, normally multiple regression analysis. Three basic types of study can be distinguished. These are (i) cross section comparisons of areas, such as provinces or counties in a particular year; (ii) analyses of a particular area (a region or country) over a period of time and (iii) longitudinal studies of individuals, usually released prisoners. The use of recorded crime statistics might be thought to present some difficulties. We will discuss these problems in some detail in Chapter Three, so we will present only a short account of the problem here. It is well known that recorded crime statistics are error prone and so this raises questions about the reliability of results of statistical modelling, which make use of such statistics. The problems are further compounded if one of the deterrence variables, e.g. the conviction rate, is obtained by dividing the number of convictions by the number of recorded crimes.[2]

Measurement error in the recorded crime variable will bias the conviction rate upwards and impart a negative bias to the observed relationship between the recorded crime rate and the certainty of punishment (see Chapter Three for a full discussion of this). Despite this, measurement error may not be quite as big a problem as it appears. In Chapter Three of this volume Deadman *et al.* report the results of a study, which has used data from the General Household Survey and the British Crime Survey on the reporting of burglary offences to examine the impact of measurement error in a generic model of crime. That study has used simulation experiments that show that the general nature of measurement error biases in economic models of crime tends not to be particularly serious. The conclusion is that studies which have ignored measurement error problems may still produce meaningful conclusions. In the light of this finding, it may be safe to accept the results of earlier empirical studies as having some validity.

Many econometric studies have adopted a 'single-equation' approach. The variable to be explained is the crime rate. The explanatory variables include the detection/conviction rate, the probability of being sent to prison if found guilty, the expected length of prison sentence, economic factors (unemployment, consumers' expenditure), demographic factors, such as the age structure of the population and so on. The implication of this approach is that the criminal justice variables cause recorded crime and not the other way around. Only if this is the case will the coefficients of the estimated equation properly measure the deterrent effects of the policy variables. However, one can envisage a situation in which the crime rate might influence the criminal justice variables. For example, high levels of crime could bring forth an increased use of imprisonment or longer prison sentences, as judges and politicians 'get tough on crime'. Therefore, it is important to investigate the possibility of feedback between the criminal justice variables and the level of recorded crime. This chapter considers this issue and concludes that for UK data at least, there is no statistical evidence that criminal justice variables have been endogenously determined along with recorded crime.

The empirical literature attempting to assess the deterrent effect of punishment is now vast. Most of the estimated economic models of crime have used data for the US and only a few studies have used data for other countries, e.g. England and Wales, Canada and Finland. Much of the published work lends support to the view that crimes are deterred by increases in both the likelihood and the severity of punishment. However, there is rather less consensus about the size of any deterrent effect. This can be seen from Table 2.1, which presents estimates of deterrent effects from a sample of studies. In Table 2.1 we report estimates of the elasticities of crime (particularly property crime) with respect to variables such as the conviction rate, the imprisonment rate and sentence length.[3] The variation in the reported sizes of the deterrence elasticities may be due to different data sets. However, it may also be caused by differences in model specification. For example, it is clear that some studies of deterrent effects have omitted variables to measure the impact of positive incentives such as employment and earnings opportunities (Ehrlich, 1996).

An Economic Model of Residential Burglary in England and Wales

In this chapter we present results obtained from estimation of an empirical model of residential burglary in England and Wales, using annual time-series data for the period 1950 to 1995. The selection of the explanatory variables has been based upon the theoretical analysis of the earlier section of this chapter, previous empirical modelling and an examination of the criminology literature (see also the discussion in Chapter Four). The explanatory variables used are the probability of conviction (*convict*), the conditional probability of imprisonment (*prison*), the number of police officers (*police*), the expected length of imprisonment (*senten*), the proportion of males aged 15 to 24 years in the total population (*youths*), the unemployment rate (*unemp*) and the level of per capita real personal consumption (*consum*). The exact definitions of the variables and data sources are given in the Appendix to this chapter. A dummy variable (taking the value zero for the years up to 1968 and one thereafter) has been incorporated to allow for the structural break in the residential burglary series, which occurred following the Theft Act, 1968.

Table 2.1   Estimated deterrence elasticities

Author	Type of Offence	Conviction	Prison	Sentence Length	Data Set
Avio and Clark (1978)	Break and Enter	-1.01	-	-0.17	Ontario Canada, cross-section census divisions 1971
Carr-Hill and Stern (1979)	All offences	-1.05 (clear up)	-0.21	-	England and Wales, cross-section, counties 1971
Ehrlich (1973)	All offences	-	-0.99	-1.12	USA, cross-section, States 1960
	Burglary	-	-0.72	-1.13	
Koskela and Viren (1993)	Auto Theft	-1.0 to -1.5 (short-run) -2.0 (long-run)	-	-0.05 (short-run) -0.05 (long-run)	Finland, time-series 1958-1990
Pudney *et al.* (2000)	Residential Burglary	-0.89	-0.70	-0.97	England and Wales, time-series 1950-1995
Pyle (1989)	Burglary	-	-1.12	-0.89	England and Wales, time-series/cross-section counties 1977/1978
Reilly and Witt (1996)	Burglary	-0.25 (clear up)	-	-0.39	England and Wales, pooled cross section/time series 1980-1991
Willis (1983)	Theft	-0.43	-0.30	-	England and Wales, cross-section counties 1979
Wolpin (1978)	Burglary	-0.62	-0.59	-0.17	England and Wales, time-series 1894-1967
	All offences	0.08	-0.84	0.03	

The empirical model is set out in equation (2.1) below (where ln stands for the natural logarithm of the variable it precedes and t is a time subscript):

$$\ln burglary_t = \theta_0 + \theta_1 \ln convict_t + \theta_2 \ln prison_t + \theta_3 \ln senten_t$$
$$+ \theta_4 \ln unemp_t + \theta_5 \ln consum_t + \theta_6 \ln youths_t \qquad (2.1)$$
$$+ \theta_7 \ln police_t + \theta_8 dummy_t + \varepsilon_t$$

In this chapter we are particularly interested in the effects of changes in the criminal justice/deterrence variables upon recorded crime. In other words, we are concerned with the sizes of the coefficients θ_i ($i = 1, 2, 3$ and 7) in equation (2.1). As the equation is written in terms of the natural logarithms of the variables, then the estimated coefficients are also elasticities. In order to determine the sizes of these coefficients we would estimate equation (2.1) using Ordinary Least Squares (OLS). However, in the modelling which follows, we will use time series data in which many of the variables are dominated by strong time trends. In such a situation the straightforward application of OLS to equation (2.1) may produce biased estimates of the coefficients. Modern approaches to time-series econometric modelling can surmount this problem, and we explain how this is done in the next section.

Time-Series Modelling

Variables exhibiting systematic patterns of change (such as strong time trends) are termed 'nonstationary'.[4] Conventional regression analysis requires that the variables included in a regression equation are stationary. If regression equations are estimated with nonstationary data, meaningless results may be obtained.

Recently, econometricians have developed techniques to achieve stationarity of data series. These techniques involve removing the trends from the series. Often this can be achieved by simply calculating the change in the value of a variable from one period to the next referred to as first 'differencing'). However, sometimes it may be necessary to take second differences in order to make a series stationary. Second differences are merely the differences in the first differences. Where a variable can be made stationary by taking first differences it is referred to as being 'integrated of order one'. If it requires second differencing in order to achieve stationarity, then the variable is said to be 'integrated of order two'. And so on.

The first stage of the statistical analysis is to determine the orders of integration of the variables in equation (2.1). Determining the order of integration of a variable is normally straightforward, although sometimes the results can be ambiguous. Testing is by the so-called Dickey-Fuller (DF) or augmented Dickey-Fuller (ADF) test (Dickey and Fuller, 1979, 1981). For example, if we wish to test whether a variable, y_t, is either integrated of order zero (i.e. is I(0)) or is integrated of order one (i.e. is I(1)), then we estimate the following regression equation:

$$\Delta y_t = \alpha + \mu t + \beta y_{t-1} + \sum_{i=1}^{k} \gamma_i y_{t-i} + \varepsilon_t \qquad (2.2)$$

where α, μ, β and γ_i ($i = 1, \ldots, k$) are coefficients. The inclusion of a constant (α) and/or a time trend (t) is in itself a problem in integration testing (see Charemza and Deadman, 1997, Chapter 5). Equation (2.2) is that for the ADF test in which k lagged dependent variables are included in the estimated equation to take account of autocorrelation in the error process. The DF test excludes these lagged dependent variables from the right hand side of the equation.

If β is found to be negative and significantly different from zero, then y_t is taken as being I(0). However, if we cannot reject the hypothesis that β is different from zero, then y_t is at least I(1) and may be integrated of a higher order still. Testing for higher orders of integration is explained in detail in Charemza and Deadman (1997).

If the variables are found to be I(1), they can be made stationary by first differencing and the relationship between them can be estimated in this form. However, estimating models in differences, in order to overcome the problems of nonstationarity, means that some of the information contained in the long-run relationship (equation (2.1)) is lost. Modern econometrics attempts to overcome this by estimating so-called error correction models, which incorporate aspects of both long-run and short-run behaviour.

Suppose there is a long-term relationship between two variables (say, *X* and *Y*, which are both integrated of order one), of the form:

$$Y = \alpha + \beta X \qquad (2.3)$$

The short-run discrepancies, given by

$$u_t = Y_t - \alpha - \beta X_t \qquad (2.4)$$

should not show any tendency to increase over time. If they do not, and more precisely, if u_t in (2.4) is stationary, the variables Y and X are described as being cointegrated (one method used to test for cointegration involves estimation of the postulated long-run model and testing whether the residuals from this model are stationary).

There are alternative views about how static long-run relationships should be estimated, although if the variables are cointegrated, direct estimation by ordinary least squares may retain some desirable properties despite the nonstationarity of the variables (see Banerjee *et al.*, 1993, p. 158). In more extensive models involving more than two variables, there may be possible simultaneity problems between the variables. This issue is considered later.

If the variables can be accepted as being cointegrated, there is an error correction representation of the relationship between them. An error correction model is a short-run model, which incorporates a mechanism which restores a variable to its long-term relationship from a disequilibrium position. For the simple model given in equation (2.3), if Y and X are cointegrated, then an error correction depiction of the relationship between them would be of the form:

$$\Delta Y_t = \theta_1 \Delta X_t + \theta_2 (Y_{t-1} - \alpha - \beta X_{t-1}) + \varepsilon_t \qquad (2.5)$$

The bracketed term in (2.5) is the error correction mechanism. If θ_2 is negative and less than one in absolute terms, then if Y is 'above' its 'equilibrium' level for a given value of X (given by the long-term relationship), the error correction mechanism will reduce the value of Y in the following period to below what it would otherwise have been, so that there is a tendency to restore Y towards its long-run relationship with X.

Methodology

The model described by equation (2.1) includes explanatory variables representing both deterrence and motivational/opportunity factors. The deterrence variables are (i) the probability of conviction; (ii) the conditional probability of imprisonment given conviction; (iii) the expected length of prison sentence imposed by the courts and (iv) the number of police. The motivational/opportunity variables are (i) unemployment; (ii) the level of real personal consumption and (iii) the proportion of young males in the population. All variables are measured in natural logarithmic form, which means that the coefficients may be directly interpreted as elasticities. Unemployment is used as an indicator of social deprivation that might drive some individuals to commit crime, while consumption could be interpreted as a 'lure' for potential criminals. Young males are widely seen as the demographic group having the strongest inclination towards crime.

The statistical series on residential burglaries per 1,000 members of the England and Wales population for 1950-95 is plotted in Figure 2.5. The most striking features are the strong upward trend, together with an obvious break in the series in the late 1960s. The break is due to the Theft Act of 1968, which led to revisions in the way recorded crimes were allocated to classes of offences, resulting in major alterations from 1969 in the recorded crime figures. It is impossible from published series and definitions to construct series for recorded residential burglaries based on a consistent definition throughout the period. Yet, to base econometric analysis on either the pre or post 1968 data alone would severely curtail the degrees of freedom available. Our strategy is to use the full sample period, allowing for the discontinuity by means of a dummy variable taking the value zero up to 1968 and one thereafter.

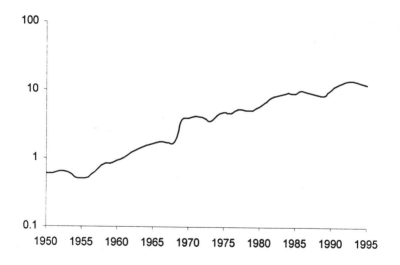

Figure 2.5   Residential burglaries per capita, England and Wales 1950-1995

It is extremely important to determine the existence and nature of the non-stationarity of the data. The order of integration of the dependent variable is a contentious issue in the literature on crime. Pyle and Deadman

(1994) found that the crime variables they investigated were integrated of order two. Later authors (Hale, 1998a, 1998b; Osborn, 1995; Pudney *et al.*, 2000) have argued that the crime series are integrated of order one. If one performs Augmented Dickey-Fuller (ADF) unit root tests separately on the pre and post-1968 samples for the residential burglary variable, the results are ambiguous. For the pre-break data, the series appears non-stationary in levels irrespective of whether an intercept or intercept and trend are included in the test regression. First differences of the series over this period also appear non-stationary. Whether or not one can reject the null hypothesis of non-stationarity for the second differences of the series depends on whether a linear trend is included in the test regressions. For the post-break sample, the same analysis indicated non-stationarity of levels, stationarity of first differences (provided a trend term was included) and stationarity of second differences. Thus from split samples, it appears that the series is either I(1) or I(2), but the shortness of the series used for the tests makes a firm decision problematic.

The use of the full sample to determine the order of integration of this series is ruled out on similar grounds to those usually advanced for the testing of series subject to a structural break. It is known (Perron, 1990) that in such cases Dickey-Fuller tests are biased towards non-rejection of the non-stationary null hypothesis. One can argue that Perron-type tests are not appropriate here, however, as the break is the effect of a change in the definition of the series, rather than a change in the underlying stochastic character of the series under investigation. The best solution is perhaps to adjust the recorded crime series for the effect of the break. A linear trend was fitted to the (log) series for 1950 to 1968. This was then used to forecast the value of the series for 1969. The jump in the series due to the Theft Act was assumed to be the difference between the observed and forecast values for 1969. This difference was then subtracted from all observed values from 1969 to 1995 to form an adjusted series. As the series is in logarithmic form, this adjustment is equivalent to assuming that the growth in those crimes newly involved in the definition of residential burglary after 1968 grew at the same rate over the post 1968 period as those under the original definition. Unit root tests on the adjusted series were then performed. Stationarity of the series in levels could be rejected, but stationarity of first differences could not. This was so irrespective of whether intercept or intercept and trend were included in the test regressions. No augmentation was required in either case. On the basis of these results, the residential burglary series has been taken as I(1) in the modelling which follows, subject only to shift dummies to account for the break in 1968.

Determining the order of integration of the other variables in the study (none of which were affected by the Theft Act) was generally straightforward, using ADF tests on the logarithm of the variables. All explanatory variables (except the 1968 dummy) were found to be I(1).

As all the variables (except the dummy) are non-stationary, the straightforward estimation of a static regression in the form of Equation (2.1) by OLS would be expected to produce spurious results. All of the variables are I(1) and so can be made stationary by first differencing. However, estimating equation (2.1) in first differences removes valuable long-run information. One way of preserving this information is to estimate an Error Correction Model (ECM) if the long-run relationship between levels of crime and levels of the explanatory variables is a cointegrating relationship. This would give the following regression equation:

$$
\begin{aligned}
\Delta \ln burglary_t =\ & \beta_1 \Delta \ln convict_t + \beta_2 \Delta \ln prison_t + \beta_3 \Delta \ln senten_t \\
& + \beta_4 \Delta \ln unemp_t + \beta_5 \Delta \ln consum_t + \beta_6 \Delta \ln youths_t \\
& + \beta_7 \Delta \ln police_t + \beta_8 \Delta dummy_t + \beta_9 \Delta \ln burglary_{t-1} - \beta_9 \theta_0 \\
& - \beta_9 \theta_1 \ln convict_{t-1} - \beta_9 \theta_2 \ln prison_{t-1} - \beta_9 \theta_3 \ln senten_{t-1} \\
& - \beta_9 \theta_4 \ln unemp_{t-1} - \beta_9 \theta_5 \ln consum_{t-1} - \beta_9 \theta_6 \ln youths_{t-1} \\
& - \beta_9 \theta_7 \ln police_{t-1} - \beta_9 \theta_8 dummy_{t-1} + \varepsilon_t
\end{aligned}
\tag{2.6}
$$

Equation (2.6) is a peculiar mixture of variables in levels and first differences, i.e. variables which are either I(0) or I(1). However, it has been shown that the estimated coefficients of such a model have standard asymptotic properties (Sims *et al.*, 1990). Simulations reported by Pudney *et al.*, (1997) confirm this.

From equation (2.6), it is possible to determine both short run and long run influences of the explanatory variables upon the rate of residential burglary. The short run effects (elasticities) are given by the β_i's ($i = 1, 2, \dots 8$), whilst the long run effects are found by calculating $(\beta_9 \theta_i)/\beta_9$ (also for $i = 1, 2, \dots 8$).

Estimation problems may be compounded if it is not possible to treat all of the explanatory variables as exogenously determined. In other words, if some of them depend upon the upon the crime variable itself. If that is the case, then there is a simultaneous relationship between the variables. We have already described a possible scenario for such feedback to exist between the crime and criminal justice variables. *A priori*, it would seem that the economic and demographic variables (real personal consumption, unemployment and the proportion of young males in the population) are unlikely to be affected by the level of crime. However, we need to test for the existence of feedback between the criminal justice variables and in the following section we discuss how that has been done.

Endogeneity and Criminal Justice Variables

Of the variables in equation (2.1), the potentially endogenous ones are the number of recorded residential burglaries per capita, the probability of conviction, the conditional probability of imprisonment and the length of sentence for residential burglary, and the number of police officers.

The approach we have adopted follows that of Pesaran and Pesaran (1997) and uses the postulated breakdown of variables into endogenous and exogenous categories in order to build a co integrating VAR (Vector Autoregressive) model linking these variables. First, the number of cointegrating vectors is established using a variety of test statistics. Of these, the maximum eigenvalue and trace statistics are perhaps the most familiar (see Charemza and Deadman, 1997). In this case, both indicate that there is only one cointegrating vector. Second, error-correction equations for each of the potentially endogenous variables are computed. If there is only a single cointegrating vector, we would expect only one of the error-correction equations to be well determined, and this is the case. The equation in point is that for residential burglary. In none of the equations for the probability of conviction, the conditional probability of imprisonment, sentence length or police numbers is the error-correction term statistically significant. Moreover, there are no statistically significant coefficients at all in the equations for the conviction rate and number of police, and only marginally significant coefficients for the exogenous variables in the equations for probability of imprisonment and sentence length. Therefore, it seems reasonable to proceed with single equation estimation of the residential burglary series in which feedback within the rest of the set of criminal justice variables is excluded.

This conclusion finds support from research carried out in the United States. Using a traditional VAR approach to estimating the simultaneous relationship between crime, employment and deterrence variables in New York City, Corman *et al.* (1987, p.700) conclude that their results '...strongly confirm the often reported finding that arrests do deter crime. Moreover, criminal behaviour is more sensitive to changes in sanctions than law enforcement agencies are to changes in crime'.

Results

Table 2.2 reports the results of estimating equation (2.6) using annual time-series data for England and Wales between 1950 and 1995. Definitions of the variables used are given in the Appendix to this chapter.

It is clear from examination of Table 2.2 that many of the explanatory factors are statistically significant and the coefficients have their expected signs. The deterrence variables (*convict, prison, senten* and *police*) all have negative coefficients in both the short and long-term, and, except for *convict* and *prison* in the long term only, they are all statistically significant. Overall, these findings suggest that the criminal justice system may be capable of delivering significant reductions in residential burglary in England and Wales, both in the short and long-term. The model predicts that the proportion of young males (i.e. those aged between 15 and 24 years) in the population has a significant effect upon residential burglary in the long run, but not in the short run. However, the effect could be substantial. The model predicts that a one per cent increase in the proportion of young men in the population would increase the rate of residential burglary by about three per cent.

The economic variables (*unemp* and *consum*) are both statistically significant in the short and long-term. Increases in unemployment raise rates of residential burglary in both time periods. However, changes in consumption have different effects in the short-term (a negative coefficient) and the long-term (a positive coefficient). In the short term, burglary increases in response to a fall in consumption, whilst it increases in the long-term in response to rising consumption. This confirms an effect reported by Field (1990), which is explored more fully in Chapter Four. Put simply, the explanation is that in the short-term a motivational effect dominates. Falling consumption indicates a fall in living standards, which generates more crime. In the long-term, rising consumption provides increased opportunities (targets) for would-be criminals. In this sense, both motivational and opportunity theories of crime receive some support from the findings reported here. Finally, the changes to the way in which the residential burglary series are defined, following the Theft Act, 1968, is reflected in the statistically significant (positive) dummy variable.

Table 2.2   **OLS estimates of the determinants of residential burglary***

	Coefficient	|t| value
$\Delta \ln convict_t$	-0.366	2.446
$\Delta \ln prison_t$	-0.251	2.008
$\Delta \ln senten_t$	-0.360	1.904
$\Delta \ln unemp_t$	0.267	4.132
$\Delta \ln consum_t$	-1.701	3.276
$\Delta \ln youths_t$	0.662	0.687
$\Delta \ln police_t$	-1.509	1.705
$\Delta dummy_t$	0.460	5.839
$\Delta \ln burglary_{t-1}$	-0.260	2.798
$\ln convict_{t-1}$	-0.154	0.966
$\ln prison_{t-1}$	-0.104	0.774
$\ln senten_{t-1}$	-0.639	2.838
$\ln unemp_{t-1}$	0.110	1.960
$\ln consum_{t-1}$	0.929	2.923
$\ln youths_{t-1}$	0.842	3.008
$\ln police_{t-1}$	-1.717	2.838
$dummy_{t-1}$	0.150	2.229
intercept	-1.993	0.766
R^2	0.924	
F	19.198	
Serial correlation χ_1^2	0.059	

* Dependent variable = $\Delta \ln burglary_t$

Conclusion

In this chapter we have introduced the economic approach to the modelling of criminal behaviour. This approach owes its origins to the path breaking work of the Chicago economist Gary Becker, who was awarded the Nobel Prize for Economics partly for his innovative work in this area. The distinctive feature of this approach is its reliance upon the assumption that criminals are rational individuals who respond to incentives.

We presented a simple version of the model in which individuals choose how much of their time to allocate to criminal and legitimate activity. They do this in response to signals such as wages rates in legitimate activity, potential illegal gains and the expected costs of engaging in criminal activity (the probability of being caught, the punishment if caught and convicted and so on). This model predicts that criminals will be deterred by increases in both the certainty and severity of punishment, i.e. by so-called deterrence factors. However, and this has often been overlooked in the discussion of the model, it also predicts that criminals will be 'deterred' by increases in wage rates and reductions in the probability of unemployment in legitimate activity. In other words, they respond to positive incentives, too.

The chapter provides a brief review of previous empirical work in this area. Inevitably this review is highly selective. However, the studies reported are representative of the many hundreds of empirical papers that now exist in this area. Many of these papers claim to provide evidence in support of the economic model's predictions, especially concerning the deterrent effects of punishment.

The main part of the chapter was devoted to reporting the estimation of an economic model of residential burglary for England and Wales, using annual time series data from 1950 to 1995. Time-series data present particular problems for estimation and we discussed these issues and how they can be overcome. We also addressed the problem of possible simultaneity between the crime rate and the criminal justice variables in the model, although it would appear that this is not a real issue for the model presented here. The estimates reported in the chapter provide further support for the view that criminals do respond to incentives, whether positive or negative, and that these effects can be both short and long-term.

Notes

1. In fact, convexity requires the assumption of risk aversion. See Pyle, 1983, p. 19.
2. Exactly the same problem would arise if, instead of the conviction rate, investigators had used the arrest rate (the number of arrests divided by the number of recorded crimes) or the clear up rate (crimes cleared up divided by the number of recorded crimes).
3. For those unfamiliar with the concept, elasticity is a measure of the response of one variable to changes in another. To be precise, it is the percentage change in one variable resulting from a one per cent change in another variable. In this case, it is the percentage response of crime to a one per cent change in, say, the conviction rate.
4. Systematic changes in either the mean, the variance or even the auto-covariances of a variable over time would constitute nonstationary behaviour.

References

Avio, K.L. and Clark, C.S. (1978), 'The Supply of Property Offences in Ontario: Evidence on the Deterrent Effect of Punishment', *Canadian Journal of Economics*, vol. 11, pp. 1-19.

Banerjee, A., Dolado, J., Galbraith, J.W. and Hendry, D.F. (1993), *Cointegration, Error Correction and The Econometric Analysis of Non-stationary Data*, Oxford University Press, Oxford.

Becker, G.S. (1968), 'Crime and Punishment: An Economic Approach', *Journal of Political Economy*, vol. 76, pp. 169-217.

Block, M.K. and Heineke, J.M. (1975), 'A Labor Theoretic Analysis of Criminal Choice', *American Economic Review*, vol. 65, pp. 314-25.

Cameron, S. (1988), 'The Economics of Crime and Deterrence: A Survey of Theory and Evidence', *Kyklos*, vol. 41, pp. 301-23.

Carr-Hill, R.A. and Stern, N.H. (1979), *Crime, the Police and Criminal Statistics*, Academic Press, London.

Charemza, W.W. and Deadman, D.F. (1997), *New Directions in Econometric Practice*, second edition, E. Elgar, Cheltenham.

Corman, H., Joyce, T. and Lovitch, N. (1987), 'Crime, Deterrence and the Business Cycle in New York City: A VAR Approach', *The Review of Economics and Statistics*, vol. 69, pp. 695-700.

Dau-Schmidt, K. (1990), 'An Economic Analysis of Criminal Law as a Preference-Shaping Policy', *Duke Law Journal*, vol. 1990, pp. 1-38.

Dickey, D.A. and Fuller, W.A. (1979), 'Distributions of the Estimators for Autoregressive Time Series with a Unit Root', *Journal of the American Statistical Society*, vol. 74, pp. 427-31.

Dickey, D.A. and Fuller, W.A. (1981), 'Likelihood Ratio Statistics for Autoregressive Time Series with a Unit Root', *Econometrica*, vol. 49, pp. 1057-72.

Ehrlich, I. (1973), 'Participation in Illegitimate Activities: A Theoretical and Empirical Analysis', *Journal of Political Economy*, vol. 81, pp. 521-64.

Ehrlich, I. (1996), 'Crime, Punishment and The Market for Offences', *Journal of Economic Perspectives*, vol. 10, pp. 43-67.

Field, S. (1990), *Trends in Crime and Their Interpretation. A Study of Recorded Crime in Post-War England and Wales*, Home Office Research Study no. 119, Home Office, London.

Hale, C. (1998a), 'Crime and the Business Cycle in Post-War Britain Revisited', *British Journal of Criminology*, vol. 38, pp. 678-98.

Hale, C. (1998b), 'The Labour Market and Post-War Crime Trends in England and Wales', in P. Carlen and R. Morgan (eds) *Crime Unlimited: Questions for the Twenty-First Century*, MacMillan, Basingstoke.

Koskela, E. and Viren, M. (1993), 'An Economic Model of Auto Theft in Finland', *International Review of Law and Economics*, vol. 13, pp. 179-91.

Osborn, D.R. (1995), *Crime and the UK Economy*, Robert Schuman Centre, Working Paper 95/15, European University Institute.

Perron, P. (1990), 'Testing for a Unit Root in a Time Series with a Changing Mean', *Journal of Business Economics and Statistics*, vol. 8, pp. 153-62.

Pesaran, M.H. and Pesaran, B. (1997), *Working with Microfit 4.0 Interactive Econometric Analysis*, Oxford University Press, Oxford.

Pudney, S., Deadman, D. and Pyle, D. (1997), *The Effect of Under-Reporting in Statistical Models of Criminal Activity: Estimation of an Error Correction Model with*

Measurement Error, Discussion Paper in Public Sector Economics 97/3, Department of Economics, University of Leicester.

Pudney, S., Deadman, D.F. and Pyle, D.J. (2000), 'The Relationship Between Crime, Punishment and Economic Conditions: Is Reliable Inference Possible When Crimes are Under-Recorded?', *Journal of the Royal Statistical Society Series A (Statistics in Society)*, vol. 163, pp. 81-97.

Pyle, D.J. (1983), *The Economics of Crime and Law Enforcement*, MacMillan, London.

Pyle, D.J. (1989), 'The Economics of Crime in Britain', *Economic Affairs*, vol. 9, pp. 6-9.

Pyle, D.J. and Deadman, D.F. (1994) 'Crime and the Business Cycle in Post-War Britain', *British Journal of Criminology*, vol. 34, pp. 339-57.

Reilly, B. and Witt, R. (1996), 'Crime, Deterrence and Unemployment in England and Wales: An Empirical Analysis', *Bulletin of Economic Research*, vol. 48, pp. 137-55.

Sims, C.A., Stock, J.H., and Watson, M.W. (1990), 'Inference in Linear Time Series Models with Some Unit Roots', *Econometrica*, vol. 58, pp. 113-44.

Willis, K.G. (1983), 'Spatial Variations in Crime in England and Wales: Testing an Economic Model', *Regional Studies*, vol. 17, pp. 261-72.

Wolpin, K.I. (1978), 'An Economic Analysis of Crime and Punishment in England and Wales, 1894-1967', *Journal of Political Economy*, vol. 86, pp. 815-40.

APPENDIX 2.1

Definitions of variables and sources of data

1. Residential burglary (*burglary*):

Recorded offences in England and Wales. *Up to and including 1968*: category 29: Housebreaking; *1969 and after*: categories 28 and 29: Burglary and Aggravated Burglary.

Source: Criminal Statistics, England and Wales (various).

2. Conviction rate (*convict*):

The number of convictions divided by the number of recorded offences. The number of convictions is the number of persons found guilty in all courts. After 1970 this includes the number of offenders who were cautioned for an offence.

Source: Criminal Statistics for England and Wales (various).

3. Prison (*prison*):

The proportion of those convicted of offences of residential burglary who were sentenced to immediate imprisonment.

Source: Criminal Statistics for England and Wales (various).

4. Sentence (*senten*):

The average length of prison sentence (in months) given to those sentenced to imprisonment for residential burglary offences.

Source: Criminal Statistics for England and Wales (various) and unpublished data provided by the Home Office.

5. Youths (*youths*):

Numbers of Males aged 15 - 24 years as a proportion of the total population of England and Wales.

Source: Population Trends (various).

6. Consumption (*consum*):

UK real personal consumption per capita, £ billion, 1985 prices.

Source: Economic Trends (various).

7. Unemployment (*unemp*):

Numbers of people registered as unemployed in the UK, excluding adult students, per capita.
Source: Economic Trends (various).

8. *Police*

Numbers of police officers. Actual strength at the end of the year, excluding special constables.

Source: Annual Abstract of Statistics.

9. *Dummy*

We also include a variable *dummy* to capture the effect of the Theft Act, 1968.

3. Measurement Error in Economic Models of Crime

DEREK DEADMAN, STEPHEN PUDNEY AND DAVID PYLE

Introduction

In Chapter Two we reported estimates of a time-series econometric model, which linked the incidence of crime to various criminal justice, demographic and economic variables. This model indicated that measures of both the certainty and severity of punishment as well as economic indicators such as unemployment and real consumers' expenditure appeared to exert significant influences upon the incidence of residential burglary in England and Wales during the post-war period. However, modelling of this kind has been criticised by criminologists and sociologists, who argue that such studies make use of official statistics of recorded crime, which are well known to be error prone. If the crime data are riddled with measurement errors, how can the results obtained by using such data produce reliable judgements about the determinants of crime and the effectiveness of criminal justice policies? Is statistical modelling using crime data a complete waste of time? (for general discussions of crime data see Coleman and Moynihan, 1996; Jupp, 1995; Maguire, 1994).

It is generally accepted that official statistics of crime (or recorded crime, as it is sometimes called) measure only a proportion of all crimes that take place each year (see Table 3.1). It has been argued that underreporting can happen for a number of reasons. For example, victims may fail to report crimes to the police; either because they think that the police will do nothing about them or even if they did there is little prospect of ever regaining their property. Alternatively, the police may decide not to record as crimes acts that are reported to them by members of the public, because they feel that either there is little prospect of catching the offender or the offence is so minor that it would be a waste of their time to investigate it. In effect, the police may feel that if they record the crime they would be at best wasting their time or at worst causing their performance in league tables of detection rates to deteriorate. As a consequence of these perverse 'incentives', official crime statistics are often regarded by criminologists to be a gross distortion of reality. Some observers even claim that such statistics tell us more about the activities of the police than they do about the activities of criminals.

Table 3.1   Percentages of offences reported to the police in England and Wales, 1997*

Offence	Percentage
Theft of a vehicle	97
Burglary (with loss)	85
Robbery	57
Burglary (no loss)	50
Wounding	45
Theft from a vehicle	43
Theft from a person	35
Vandalism	26

* Source: Mirrlees-Black *et al.* (1998).

By comparison, economists who have ventured into the study of crime have used recorded crime statistics as if they were perfectly accurate indicators of the extent of criminal activity (for a survey of research which has adopted such an approach see Pyle, 1995). This heroic assumption could be justified if reporting/recording rates were constant either over time or across areas of the country (depending upon whether time-series or cross-section data are being analysed).[1]

However, one suspects that reporting/recording rates are unlikely to remain constant (Maguire, 1994). If that is the case, then how reliable can economists' models of criminal activity be? Such models usually find evidence of the existence of significant deterrence effects of both certainty and severity of punishment and some find evidence of the influence of economic factors upon crime, but if these results are obtained by using suspect data can we really trust these findings?

In this chapter we examine how information about the extent of under-reporting of crime can be incorporated into a generic economic model of criminal activity (similar to that reported in Chapter Two) and test the robustness of that model's conclusions in the presence of measurement error. The model has been estimated using data on residential burglaries committed in England and Wales each year between 1950 and 1995. The reason for choosing residential burglary for analysis is that there exists good extraneous information on the reporting of such offences. This information comes from the British Crime Survey and the General Household Survey.

This chapter addresses only one of the criticisms which criminologists level against the use of official criminal statistics. This is the argument that criminal statistics can tell us nothing useful about the incidence of crime. We do not concern ourselves with issues surrounding the relationship between criminal statistics and social processes (the so-called 'institutionalist approach') or how criminal statistics represent the outcome of particular power (class) relationships within society (the so-called 'radical approach'). We adopt what has been called a 'positivist-realist' approach to the use of criminal statistics. This approach is predicated on the assumption that statistics can be used to explain criminal activity and in particular their relationship with economic factors and deterrence variables, provided that they are adjusted so as to reflect more accurately the 'true' crime figures.[2]

Measurement Error and the Modelling of Criminal Activity: An Intuitive Introduction

In order to illustrate the potential problems created by measurement error, in this section we will use a highly simplified economic model of criminal behaviour, which incorporates some of the ideas from the economics of crime literature. This is to provide a motivation for the later sections of the paper, which deal with more complex issues.

Following the work of Becker (1968) and Ehrlich (1973), economists have generally accepted an economic model of criminal participation in which an individual's involvement in criminal activity is determined by, amongst other things, the probability of being caught/convicted, the severity of punishment if caught/convicted, employment/earnings prospects in legitimate activity and the rewards from engaging in criminal activity (for an introduction to the economic theory of criminal participation see Chapter Two). In order to simplify the discussion of this section we will focus upon two explanatory variables only - (i) the probability of conviction (labelled as p) and (ii) prospective returns from legitimate economic activity (labelled as E). In order to test the economic model, economists would like to estimate (by regression methods) a relationship like the following:

$$\ln C^* = \alpha + \beta \ln p^* + \gamma \ln E + \varepsilon \qquad (3.1)$$

where C^* is the number of crimes committed, p^* is the proportion of crimes resulting in a conviction, E is a measure of economic activity (such as unemployment, or real consumers' expenditure - see Chapter Two) and ε is a random error.[3] The term 'ln' in front of a variable indicates that the natural logarithm of that variable has been used in the regression equation.[4]

On the whole, empirical work in this area has used data at a relatively high level of aggregation, i.e. at the level of the city or county or even the nation. The theoretical model of criminal participation is clearly based upon the microeconomic analysis of individual behaviour. However, empirical work has rarely used data on individuals (Pyle, 2000, includes a review of a number of such studies, most of which derive their data from the post-release activities of prison inmates). We do not deal with the aggregation problem in this chapter, but focus instead upon the problems created by measurement error in aggregate crime data.[5]

In empirical work, economists have proxied C^* by the number of crimes recorded by the police (C^R). The economic theory of crime is couched in terms of the 'true' number of crimes committed and not the number recorded. What difference does it make to the estimates of the effect of punishment (p) and the economy (E) upon crime if empirical work uses data on the dependent variable which contains an amount of measurement error? Suppose that measurement error is of the form:

$$\frac{C^R}{C^*} = R \tag{3.2}$$

where R is a constant (this means that a constant fraction of all crimes is reported to the police authorities). This can be rewritten as:

$$\ln C^* = \ln C^R - \upsilon \tag{3.3}$$

where υ is ln R. In this case, measurement error will impart little or no bias to the estimates of the parameters β and γ in the economic model (3.1).[6] To see this we replace ln C^* in (3.1) by ln C^R - υ to obtain:

$$\ln C^R = (\alpha + \upsilon) + \beta \ln p^* + \gamma \ln E + \varepsilon \tag{3.4}$$

The effect of measurement error is to alter the intercept term, which becomes $(\alpha + \upsilon)$ so that the estimates of β and γ remain unbiased estimates of their true values.

Clearly, the model we have suggested is highly simplified. It is hardly a surprise to realise that if a constant proportion of all crime is recorded, then changes in the level of recorded crime will exactly mirror changes in the true level of crime and so models which use recorded crime statistics will not cause us to be misled about the determinants of crime. Consider an alternative depiction of the recording process in which the recording rate (proportion) fluctuates randomly around R. This would lead to the following:

$$\frac{C^R}{C^*} = \mathrm{Re}^u \tag{3.5}$$

where u is a random disturbance term, having zero mean and a constant variance. Taking natural logarithms of (3.5), we obtain:

$$\ln C^R = \ln C^* + \ln R + u \tag{3.6}$$

If we use (3.6) to solve for $\ln C^*$ and substitute into (3.1) we obtain the following estimating equation:

$$\ln C^R = (\alpha + \ln R) + \beta \ln p^* + \gamma \ln E + (u + \varepsilon) \tag{3.7}$$

Again, the parameters β and γ are entirely unaffected by the fact that only a proportion of all crimes is recorded. Only the intercept $(\alpha + \ln R)$ and the error term $(u + \varepsilon)$ are altered. As both u and ε are random variables, then so is their sum, so that the error term in this estimating equation is also random and the parameter estimates will be unbiased estimates of their true values.

It would appear, from the preceding analysis, that measurement error is a relatively trivial matter. However, we have investigated only two simple cases of the way in which the reporting rate may be determined. The matter may be further complicated by the way in which the conviction rate (p^*) is constructed. In practice the conviction rate is often measured as the proportion of recorded crimes which result in a conviction:

$$p^r = \frac{A}{C^R} \tag{3.8}$$

where A is the number of convictions. If C^R is subject to measurement error, then the measured conviction rate will be a biased estimator of the 'true' conviction rate. The 'true' conviction rate is clearly given by A/C^*, whereas the observed conviction rate is given by (3.8). The more that crimes are under recorded then the more the conviction rate will be overstated. This 'systematic' component of measurement error would appear to impart a negative bias to the estimate of the deterrent effect of punishment, in the sense that if C^R is lower than C^*, then p' will be larger than p^*. As a result, measurement error in the crime variable may make it appear that either there is a negative relationship between crime rates and conviction rates when in fact there is no such relationship or make the relationship between the two variables appear to be stronger than it is in reality. This result is illustrated in Figure 3.1. This statistical artefact is potentially of much greater significance than any problems caused by random measurement error and could potentially undermine attempts to estimate the deterrent effect of punishment, which has been a major preoccupation of economic models of crime.

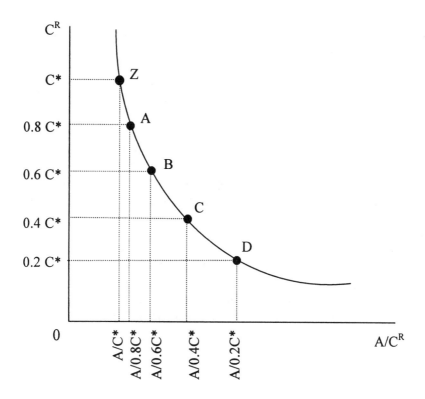

Figure 3.1   Effect of measurement error in the crime variable

This problem has been recognised in the econometric literature on crime (see, for example, Klein *et al.*, 1978; Taylor, 1978) and has even featured in the more quantitative criminological literature (see, for example, Gibbs and Firebaugh, 1990; Zedlewski, 1983). However, the findings of these researchers are fairly inconclusive. For example, Taylor has argued that '...measurement error can cut both ways' (p. 64) and '...what is generally thought to be a spurious negative correlation could then turn out to be a spurious positive correlation' (p.65).[7]

Later, Gibbs and Firebaugh concluded that '...there is no definitive way to demonstrate whether the negative correlation between the crime rate and the objective certainty of punishment reflects deterrence or merely measurement error' (p. 347).

The Nature of Measurement Errors: A Theoretical Analysis

In the last section we presented a highly simplified analysis of the impact of measurement error in an economic model of crime. Despite its simplicity we realised that the effect of measurement error could be quite complex. In this section we offer a rather more rigorous analysis of the likely impact of measurement error and particularly how it would impact upon an economic model similar to that described in Chapter Two (the model is given by equation (3.21) below). We begin by describing the essence of the reporting/recording process.

Consider first a single period, and for the sake of clarity suppress the time subscript. We will consider explicitly only the probability of conviction, although a similar analysis applies to the probability of imprisonment given conviction (however, we do not expect this variable to be subject to significant measurement error).

The number of crimes committed is C. For each individual crime $i = 1$ ... C, define the following:

x_i = a set of characteristics of the ith crime,
r_i = 1 if the crime is reported and recorded, and 0 otherwise;
$R(x_i)$ = $E(r_i \mid x_i)$ = recording probability;
R = $E(R(x_i))$ = mean recording probability over all crimes;
p_i = 1 if a conviction is (or would be) obtained if the crime is reported, and 0 otherwise;
$\Pi(x_i)$ = $E(p_i r_i \mid x_i)$ = the criminal's probability of being convicted;
Π = $E(\Pi(x_i))$ = mean probability of conviction over all crimes.

Note that the recording probability R is the joint probability that a crime is both reported to the police by the victim and then also recorded by the police. Define the following variances:

$$\sigma_1^2 = E[\text{var}(r_i \mid x_i)] = E[R(x_i)(1 - R(x_i))] \tag{3.9}$$

$$\sigma_2^2 = E[\text{var}([p_i r_i - (\Pi / R)r_i] \mid x_i)) \tag{3.10}$$

The number of recorded crimes is $C_i = \sum_{i=1}^{C} r_i$ and the proportion of recorded crimes resulting in a conviction is:

$$\tilde{\Pi} = \sum_{i=1}^{C} r_i p_i (\sum_{i=1}^{C} r_i)^{-1} \tag{3.11}$$

The observed variables $\tilde{C}$, and $\tilde{\Pi}$ are then used as proxies for the unobservable variables C_t and Π_t. If we condition on the true number of crimes, C, and their characteristics $x_1, \ldots, x_c$ in period t, it is possible to derive the distributions of the proxies. Note that the number of crimes is large (typically several hundreds of thousands). Thus, for $\tilde{C}_t$, a simple application of the central limit theorem gives the following approximation:

$$\tilde{C}_t \sim C_t \times N(R_t, \sigma_{1t}^2 / C_t) \tag{3.12}$$

A Taylor series expansion of the ratio (3.11) defining the conviction rate, followed by an application of the central limit theorem, then gives the following approximate distribution for the measured conviction rate:

$$\tilde{\Pi}_t \sim R_t^{-1} \times N(\Pi_t, \sigma_{2t}^2 / C_t) \tag{3.13}$$

We have added a time subscript in the approximations (3.12) and (3.13), to allow the possibility that the recording and conviction probabilities may change over time. There are two distinct elements of the measurement problem embodied in (3.12) and (3.13).

The first is a systematic downward bias in $\tilde{C}_t$ and upward bias in $\tilde{\Pi}_t$ due to the terms R_t and $1/R_t$ respectively. Superimposed on this is the random variation described by the two normal distributions.

The important feature of (3.12) and (3.13) is that the variance in each case has the form of a small value σ_{1t}^2 or σ_{2t}^2 divided by the number of crimes. Thus the measurement error variances are $O(C_t^{-1})$ and therefore negligible for all practical purposes, since C_t is so large. The approximations (3.12) and (3.13) then reduce to the following proportionalities:

$$\tilde{C}_t \approx R_t C_t \tag{3.14}$$

$$\tilde{\Pi}_t \approx R_t^{-1} \Pi_t \tag{3.15}$$

In this sense, it is only systematic misrecording (i.e. deviation of R_t from unity) that matters. However, R_t is not directly observable, so it is necessary to use some stochastic model to capture the movements over time in the mean recording rate R_t. To model R_t some external source of information on reporting and recording practices is required.[8]

As we have shown above, if the rate of under-recording is constant over time, the measurement error problem is essentially negligible. In the model described by equation (2.6) in Chapter Two (a version of which will be used later to simulate the effects of measurement error), the conviction rate and crime variables appear in logarithmic form and if R_t is constant, the multiplicative biases in $\tilde{C}_t$ and $\tilde{\Pi}_t$ become additive terms that are absorbed into the intercept. In the more realistic case where the recording rate R_t evolves over time according to some stochastic process, bias is introduced into the model by the presence in the residuals of time-varying measurement error correlated with the measured crime and conviction rate variables. In this case, since the contaminated residual will be correlated with three of the explanatory variables (ln *burglary*$_{t-1}$, Δ ln *convict*$_t$, and ln *convict*$_{t-1}$) in a complex way, it is difficult to assess the possible size of the measurement error bias in the coefficients of a model like that described in Chapter Two. The following sections use a simulation-based approach to examine these biases. In order to undertake this work we need information about the extent of under-recording of crime.

Survey Data on the Reporting of Crimes

For a number of years, sample survey data have been collected which reveal something of the extent of measurement error in reported/recorded crime statistics. In England and Wales there are two sources of such information - the British Crime Survey (BCS) and the General Household Survey (GHS). The BCS is a rather more general source of information about the reporting of crime, whilst the GHS is concerned only with the reporting of burglary offences. The BCS considers a variety of crimes against individuals and their property and so covers most thefts, residential burglaries and robberies.

The first BCS was published, by the Home Office, in 1982 and since then six further surveys have been published - in 1984, 1988, 1992, 1994, 1996 and 1998. Each survey refers to the year before publication. Until the 1994 survey, the panel for the BCS consisted of between 10,000 and 11,000 individuals aged over 16 years, but in 1994 the sample size was increased to some 14,500 individuals. Information on crime reporting is obtained by face to face interviews, in which individuals are asked whether they have been the victim of crime(s) during the past year and whether those crimes have been reported to the police. For more detail on the sampling procedures see Hales and Stratford (1997).

Coverage of the BCS and police crime statistics is different. The BCS includes some offences, e.g. common assault and threats, which are not included in 'notifiable offences' in the Criminal Statistics. On the other hand, the BCS does not cover crimes against organisations, such as the crimes of fraud, shoplifting, and burglary in commercial premises. Nor does it include offences such as drug taking or crimes against children. Another difference between the BCS and police crime records is that whereas the police try to determine whether an offence has taken place, the BCS treats information from 'victims' at more or less face value. However, the BCS investigators do attempt to determine whether an incident reported to them can in fact be classified as a crime.

Whilst, there may be a *prima facie* argument that BCS data may be more accurate than police data on crimes, the BCS record is not without possible measurement error itself. Respondents may make errors in recalling crimes committed against them. For example, they may forget that a crime has occurred, or they may have mis-remembered the date when it occurred, or they may prefer not to mention something (e.g. domestic violence) or they may fail to realise that something was indeed a crime. Some may even make something up. However, for many major offences e.g. residential burglary, car theft and so on, the BCS respondent is likely to have a very good recall of the date of the event, have little reason to hide the incident from the interviewer and be quite clear that the act was indeed a crime. Also, respondents are likely to be well aware of whether they reported the incident to the police. So, for crimes of this kind, the BCS is likely to have low measurement error and produce reliable information on the extent of the reporting of crime to the police.

The GHS is an annual sample survey conducted by the Office of Population Censuses and Surveys of about 10,000 households in England and Wales. Questions on the incidence of burglary were first included in 1972 and have been repeated in the Surveys of 1973, 1979, 1980, 1985, 1986, 1991 and 1993. Unfortunately, the BCS and the GHS data on burglary are not strictly comparable. For example, the BCS definition of household burglary includes unsuccessful attempts to gain entry, whereas before 1985, the GHS asked only questions about incidents where the burglar gained entry to the premises. Furthermore, in the GHS there are no supplementary questions included to check whether an incident described by a respondent met the criteria for the definition of a burglary.

Information on the proportion of offences of burglary reported to the police by respondents to the GHS and BCS is given in Table 3.2. There are three characteristics of recording rates that matter for the analysis. First, any systematic trend in R_t may be proxied by the explanatory variables, thus imparting bias to their coefficients. Second, autocorrelation in R_t will alter the time-series properties of the measured burglary series, thus distorting the estimated dynamic structure of the model. Third, unsystematic random variation in R_t over time will lead to a standard errors-in-variables bias relating to the conviction rate and lagged burglary variables, which are measured with random error.

Inspection of the reporting frequencies in Table 3.2 suggests that they are rather stable over time, with a moderate degree of variation. It is unclear whether the survey estimates of reporting rates display a systematic upward trend or are untrended but highly autocorrelated. The most obvious potential source of trend is the increasing rate of insurance coverage. Information on insurance coverage has been obtained from the Family Expenditure Survey (FES), which reports the proportion of households in its sample which have household contents insurance (often a condition of payment by insurance companies for losses incurred as a result of burglary is that the loss is reported to the police). We have smoothed these data, using a three-year moving average, in order to minimise the effects of sampling fluctuations. The coverage rate z_t rises from around 65 per cent in the early 1960s, when it first appears in the FES, to around 75 per cent in the 1990s. For the years prior to 1961, we have assumed the coverage rate was constant at its 1961 level.

Table 3.2   **The proportion of burglaries reported to the police***

Year	GHS	BCS
1972	0.76	-
	(0.024)	
1973	0.76	-
	(0.026)	
1979	0.75	-
	(0.025)	
1980	0.81	-
	(0.023)	
1981	-	0.85
		(0.025)
1983	-	0.87
		(0.022)
1985	0.87	-
	(0.020)	
1986	0.87	-
	(0.021)	
1987	-	0.86
		(0.021)
1991	0.86	0.92
	(0.018)	(0.015)
1993	0.86	0.87
	(0.016)	(0.017)
1995	-	0.84
		(0.017)

* Approximate standard errors are given in parentheses.

Since there is insufficient data to estimate a very detailed model of recording behaviour, we work with a simple model. Combining both trend and autocorrelation elements, our recording model is:

$$\lambda_t = \mu_0 + \mu_1 z_t + \rho \lambda_{t-1} + \omega \eta_t \qquad (3.16)$$

where $\eta_t \sim N(0,1)$ is a random error and ω the corresponding scale parameter. The term λ_t is the logit transformation of the reporting rate, i.e. $\lambda_t = \ln [R_t/(1 - R_t)]$. The logit transformation is used here to ensure that the reporting rate R_t remains within the plausible range $(0,1)$. Note that we are defining R_t to be the reporting rate multiplied by the police recording rate for burglaries reported to them. A comparison of police statistics on

recorded burglaries per capita and BCS statistics on reported burglaries per capita for the available years within 1979-1993 gives an estimated police recording rate that fluctuates around a mean of 0.716 (General Household Survey, 1993). We therefore, use this factor to convert GHS and BCS reporting rates into approximate estimates of the gross reporting rate R_t.

It is difficult to estimate this model from the sparse data available, owing to the gaps in the observations on R_t. However, we can derive the joint distribution of those observations that we do have as a function of the parameters μ_0, μ_1, ρ and ω (further detail of how this has been done can be found in Pudney *et al.*, 2000). For estimation, we have used both the BCS and GHS series, treating them as independent estimates of the same underlying realisation R_t. A test of this assumption was made by allowing a different intercept (μ_0) for the GHS and BCS series, and the homogeneity hypothesis was not rejected. The final estimation results for four alternative versions of the recording model (3.16) are as follows (standard errors in parentheses).

$$\lambda_t = 0.410 + 0.144\eta_t \qquad\qquad (3.17)$$
$$(0.039) \quad (0.027)$$

$$\lambda_t = -0.357 + 1.295z_t + 0.025\eta_t \qquad\qquad (3.18)$$
$$(0.253) \quad (0.341) \quad\;\; (0.004)$$

$$\lambda_t = 0.056 + 0.860\lambda_{t-1} + 0.073\eta_t \qquad\qquad (3.19)$$
$$(0.037) \quad (0.088) \qquad\;\; (0.016)$$

$$\lambda_t = -0.084 + 0.218z_t + 0.837\lambda_{t-1} + 0.071\eta_t \qquad\qquad (3.20)$$
$$(0.125) \quad (0.216) \qquad (0.123) \qquad\;\; (0.017)$$

Monte Carlo Simulation of the Measurement Error Bias

We have used Monte Carlo simulation to examine the coefficient biases that are introduced by the process of under-reporting and the results of that exercise are reported in this section. The four alternative measurement error assumptions are used: the serially-independent processes ((3.17) and (3.18)), and the autoregressive processes ((3.19) and (3.20)), both estimated with and without an insurance effect. In these simulations, the process given by equation (3.21) below (with ε_t assumed to be an IID normal sequence) is treated as the true data generating process (this is a slightly simplified version of the model reported in Chapter Two, which has been published in Pudney *et al.* (2000)).

$$\Delta \ln burglary_t = \beta_1 \Delta convict_t + \beta_2 \Delta \ln prison_t + \beta_3 \Delta \ln senten_t$$
$$+ \beta_4 \Delta \ln unemp_t + \beta_5 \Delta \ln consum_t + \beta_7 \Delta dummy_t$$
$$+ \beta_8 \Delta \ln burglary_{t-1} - \beta_8 \theta_0 - \beta_8 \theta_1 \ln convict_{t-1} \qquad (3.21)$$
$$- \beta_8 \theta_2 \ln prison_{t-1} - \beta_8 \theta_3 \ln senten_{t-1} - \beta_8 \theta_4 \ln unemp_{t-1}$$
$$- \beta_8 \theta_5 \ln consum_{t-1} - \beta_8 \theta_6 \ln youths_{t-1} + \varepsilon_t$$

We use the OLS estimates of equation (3.21) as the 'true' model parameters, in order to generate 5000 independent realisations of the burglary series (each of length $T = 50$). For convenience, these parameter estimates are reproduced in Table 3.3 below under the column headed 'true' coefficients. On each of these simulated 'true' series we superimpose a simulated sequence of recording errors (R_t), and then apply the OLS estimator to the contaminated data. We have implemented this simulation approach in two alternative ways: (i) conditional on the exogenous explanatory variables by using the same sample values for them in each replication; and (ii) unconditionally, by generating at each replication a fresh sample on the exogenous variable from a set of autoregressive processes in first difference form with cross-correlated residuals, estimated from the sample data. The Monte Carlo results were similar in each case, and Table 3.3 shows only those from experiment (ii).

The outcome of the simulation experiment is summarised in Table 3.3, which compares the true coefficients with the outcome of the OLS estimator, averaged over the 5000 replications. The effect of measurement error is clearly not very serious in general. The coefficient biases are statistically significant, but in most cases negligible for all practical purposes. The largest biases (which are away from, rather than towards, zero as in the classical static errors-in-variables case) are in the estimated short and long-run effects of the conviction rate. However, even there, given the inherent estimation uncertainty indicated by the OLS standard errors in the 'true' model (contained in brackets underneath the 'true' coefficient given in column two of the table), the applied researcher would not be seriously misled as a result of measurement error bias.

Table 3.3   **The effect of measurement error bias: mean OLS estimates (5000 replications, simulation standard errors in parentheses)**

Variable	'True' Coefficient	$R_t = 1$	(5)	(6)	(7)	(8)
$\Delta \ln unemp_t$	0.178	0.179	0.173	0.178	0.177	0.176
	(0.050)	(0.001)	(0.001)	(0.001)	(0.001)	(0.001)
$\Delta \ln consum_t$	-1.408	-1.411	-1.381	-1.405	-1.401	-1.394
	(0.526)	(0.001)	(0.001)	(0.001)	(0.001)	(0.001)
$\Delta \ln convict_t$	-0.443	-0.441	-0.743	-0.493	-0.537	-0.606
	(0.152)	(0.002)	(0.001)	(0.002)	(0.002)	(0.002)
$\Delta \ln senten_t$	-0.256	-0.264	-0.192	-0.255	-0.240	-0.227
	(0.177)	(0.002)	(0.002)	(0.002)	(0.002)	(0.002)
$\Delta \ln prison_t$	-0.327	-0.328	-0.328	-0.329	-0.327	-0.327
	(0.111)	(0.002)	(0.002)	(0.002)	(0.002)	(0.002)
$\Delta dummy_t$	0.555	0.553	0.550	0.552	0.552	0.551
	(0.065)	(0.001)	(0.001)	(0.001)	(0.001)	(0.001)
$\ln burglary_{t-1}$	-0.251	-0.258	-0.257	-0.258	-0.257	-0.256
	(0.079)	(0.001)	(0.001)	(0.001)	(0.001)	(0.001)
Constant	3.530	3.450	3.015	3.250	3.270	3.087
	(1.278)	(0.016)	(0.018)	(0.017)	(0.017)	(0.018)
$\ln unemp_{t-1}$	0.063	0.067	0.062	0.067	0.065	0.063
	(0.044)	(0.001)	(0.001)	(0.001)	(0.001)	(0.001)
$\ln consum_{t-1}$	0.272	0.267	0.274	0.268	0.269	0.272
	(0.177)	(0.001)	(0.001)	(0.001)	(0.001)	(0.001)
$\ln convict_{t-1}$	-0.160	-0.164	-0.288	-0.187	-0.205	-0.234
	(0.124)	(0.002)	(0.002)	(0.002)	(0.002)	(0.002)
$\ln senten_{t-1}$	-0.465	-0.479	-0.412	-0.474	-0.456	-0.446
	(0.170)	(0.002)	(0.002)	(0.002)	(0.002)	(0.002)
$\ln prison_{t-1}$	-0.197	-0.204	-0.203	-0.205	-0.202	-0.201
	(0.132)	(0.002)	(0.002)	(0.002)	(0.002)	(0.002)
$\ln youths_{t-1}$	0.311	0.308	0.314	0.306	0.310	0.314
	(0.214)	(0.005)	(0.006)	(0.005)	(0.006)	(0.006)

(Model of recording error spans columns (5), (6), (7), (8).)

Joint estimation of the crime and recording models

The Monte Carlo simulations reported in Table 3.3 suggest that even a large degree of under-recording is unlikely to lead to large biases under realistic conditions. However, the simulation experiment reported there is necessarily dependent on a particular set of assumed parameter values, and it is desirable to confirm the results using an alternative approach. Pudney, *et al.* (2000) have provided a new estimator which attempts to remove the asymptotic bias present in the OLS estimates. In this section we report their results only and leave it to the interested reader to decide whether to obtain further information on the estimation method used, details of which are contained in their article.

It is not a simple matter to estimate the crime model taking account of the time series data and the survey-based reporting frequencies. Derivation of a correct likelihood function, for instance, involves starting from the joint distribution of all relevant variables and then integrating out those that are not observed. This process must take account of the fact that the survey-based reporting rates are themselves subject to non-negligible sampling error. The basic variables are the true number of burglaries per capita and the recording rate, but neither is observable. Instead, we observe the recorded crime variable for each year and the intermittent series of reporting frequencies contained in the BCS and GHS. There is a complication with the GHS reporting rates; interviews are conducted uniformly throughout the year, and the burglary question relates to the 12 months preceding the interview, rather than a particular calendar year. However, provided interviewing and non-response is evenly distributed throughout the year, and we treat response rates as constant within years, it can be shown that the measured response rate is an unbiased estimate of the average of r_t in the GHS year and the one preceding it. There is a further complication, since the GHS switches from a calendar year basis to a financial year basis in 1991. This is taken account of in our estimation procedure.

Thus we observe either $R_t^{GHS} = (R_t+R_{t-1})/2 + \upsilon_t^{GHS}$ or $R_t^{BCS} = R_t + \upsilon_t^{BCS}$ (or both) in each of the $K = 14$ survey years $t \, \varepsilon \{\tau_1...\tau_k\}$, where υ_t is the sampling error for the survey in question, whose distribution we assume to be normal, with mean zero and standard deviation as given by the standard errors in Table 3.2. Note that we use both GHS and BCS reporting rates, and these overlap, giving (independent) sample information on the years 1991 and 1993.

The problem of computing the likelihood function is only tractable if we use simulation rather than integration to eliminate the unobservables. For a detailed description of the simulation process see Pudney *et al.* (2000). The simulated maximum likelihood (SML) estimator is asymptotically equivalent to true maximum likelihood provided the number of replications increases sufficiently rapidly with the sample size (see Gourieroux and Monfort, 1991). We use 200 replications, together with antithetic variance reduction. For all practical purposes, this is almost identical to true maximum likelihood.

The results are reproduced in Tables 3.4 and 3.5, which give the SML estimates for two variants of the measurement error process (3.16): one which includes the insurance variable and one which excludes it. Of these two specifications, the unrestricted model (i.e. that for which $\mu_1 \neq 0$) gives noticeable differences from the OLS estimates in the coefficients of $\Delta \ln consum_t$, $\Delta \ln convict_t$ and $\Delta \ln senten_t$. For the restricted model ($\mu_1 = 0$), there are noticeable differences for the coefficients of $\Delta \ln consum_t$, $\Delta \ln convict_t$, $\ln burglary_{t-1}$, $\ln convict_{t-1}$, $\ln senten_{t-1}$ and $\ln prison_{t-1}$. However, in both cases, these differences are not large in relation to the degree of estimation uncertainty associated with this type of regression model.

It is reassuring that, in line with our earlier Monte Carlo results, a 'naive' statistician relying on orthodox estimation methods and ignoring the measurement error problem would not be seriously misled. There seems to be no serious bias imparted by relying on the simple OLS estimates, rather than using the theoretically more appropriate (and more complex) SML estimator. Indeed, the main outcome of estimating the crime and measurement models jointly is to give better estimates of the latter. Comparing the estimates in Table 3.5 with those in equations 3.19 and 3.20, statistical precision increases considerably for ρ.

Table 3.4   OLS and SML estimates of joint burglary/recording model 1950-95: burglary coefficients

Variable	OLS	SML ($\mu_1 = 0$)	SML ($\mu_1 \neq 0$)
$\Delta \ln unemp_t$	0.178	0.178	0.184
	(0.050)	(0.042)	(0.039)
$\Delta \ln consum_t$	-1.408	-1.055	-1.148
	(0.526)	(0.431)	(0.399)
$\Delta \ln convict_t$	-0.443	-0.529	-0.482
	(0.152)	(0.119)	(0.104)
$\Delta \ln senten_t$	-0.256	-0.208	-0.165
	(0.177)	(0.141)	(0.141)
$\Delta \ln prison_t$	-0.327	-0.315	-0.314
	(0.111)	(0.095)	(0.087)
$\Delta dummy_t$	0.555	0.538	0.593
	(0.065)	(0.056)	(0.053)
$\ln burglary_{t-1}$	-0.251	-0.302	-0.244
	(0.079)	(0.068)	(0.062)
Constant	3.530	3.383	3.180
	(1.278)	(1.246)	(0.874)
$\ln unemp_{t-1}$	0.063	0.069	0.060
	(0.044)	(0.036)	(0.035)
$\ln consum_{t-1}$	0.272	0.243	0.263
	(0.177)	(0.157)	(0.119)
$\ln convict_{t-1}$	-0.160	-0.241	-0.156
	(0.124)	(0.102)	(0.100)
$\ln senten_{t-1}$	-0.465	-0.536	-0.418
	(0.170)	(0.132)	(0.142)
$\ln prison_{t-1}$	-0.197	-0.279	-0.204
	(0.132)	(0.115)	(0.104)
$\ln youths_{t-1}$	0.311	0.328	0.239
	(0.214)	(0.173)	(0.180)
σ	0.054	0.045	0.042
	(0.005)	(0.005)	(0.004)

Table 3.5   SML estimates of joint burglary/recording model 1950-95: recording coefficients

Variable	SML ($\mu_1 = 0$)	SML ($\mu_1 \neq 0$)
μ_0	0.022	-0.003
	(0.006)	(0.009)
μ_1	-	0.404
		(0.208)
ρ	0.948	0.925
	(0.019)	(0.044)
ω	0.096	0.076
	(0.018)	(0.016)

Conclusion

Measurement error is an important issue in the statistical modelling of crime, since the under-reporting and under-recording of crime is thought to be particularly serious. We have investigated the impact of measurement error on estimates of a simple but representative time-series model of the determinants of residential burglary, for which there is relatively good external information on reporting practices. The model is of the error correction type, and rests upon preliminary unit root testing to determine the order of integration of the dependent and explanatory variables (see Chapter Two). The nature of measurement errors is inferred from extraneous survey information on reporting practices, and is modelled as an autocorrelated process with a trend imparted by rising insurance coverage. There are two main conclusions.

Firstly, an argument based on the central limit theorem shows that, in the case of reporting errors for crime, measurement errors are in a sense necessarily systematic. Their effect is multiplicative and influences both the crime and conviction rate variables. If reporting practices vary over time, measurement error generates dynamically complex biases.

Secondly, we have found that the general nature of measurement error biases in an Error Correction Model of crime is not particularly serious. Monte Carlo simulations reveal coefficient biases that are statistically significant, but in most cases negligible for all practical purposes. The most serious biases (which are away from zero, rather than towards zero as in the classical static errors-in-variables case) are in the estimated short and long-run effects of the conviction rate, as the earlier simple theorising had predicted. We have developed a new simulated maximum likelihood estimator to correct these biases by combining extraneous survey data with the official crime series. However, the results differ from simple OLS estimates by amounts that lie well within the usual degree of statistical uncertainty surrounding the estimates. Thus, the statistician who chooses to ignore the under-recording problem completely would not be seriously misled to any important degree. This is a very reassuring conclusion.

Notes

1. Just such an assumption was made by the so-called 'moral statisticians', such as Quetelet, in the nineteenth century and by the Chicago School (of criminologists) in the 1920s and 1930s (see Coleman and Moynihan, 1996).
2. For a more detailed discussion of the various views about official statistics of crime see Coleman and Moynihan (1996), Chapter One or Jupp (1995), Chapter Three.
3. Sometimes the number of crimes is deflated by population size. We will ignore the issue of whether the observed conviction rate, p, adequately reflects the individual criminal's assessment of the subjective probability of being caught.
4. Estimation of so-called 'double logarithmic' regression equations has been a common practice in the literature on the economics of crime. There are several reasons for estimating relationships in such a form. One, which is often cited, is that one can then easily interpret the parameters β and γ as elasticities.
5. It could be argued that analysis of the criminal activities of a random sample of the population might solve the problems of both the measurement error and aggregation simultaneously. However, this would require self-report survey data on the extent of criminal activity to be perfectly accurate. There are good reasons to believe that this is unlikely to be the case.
6. Presumably υ is constrained to be greater than zero, unless we allow for the possibility of 'over-recording' of crime, caused by for example insurance fraud.
7. Using a simple model of the form, $\ln C = \alpha + \beta \ln p + \varepsilon$, Taylor (1978) has shown that least squares estimates of β will, in the limit, converge to $\beta(M/M+\sigma^2)-(\sigma^2/M+\sigma^2)$, where M is the variance of p and σ^2 is the variance of υ, the measurement error. It is clear that measurement error has two effects upon the parameter estimate and these work in opposite directions. Assuming that the true value of β is negative, then the first, a multiplicative element which is less than one, tends to bias the estimate of β towards zero, whilst the second, an additive element, will tend to enlarge the estimate of β in absolute terms. However, if M is large relative to σ^2, then measurement error need not impart a major bias to the parameter estimate of β. One can only confidently predict the effect of measurement error if one knows whether β is greater than or less than one. As a result, even in a simple model, it is almost impossible to say in which direction measurement error will bias the estimated coefficient. In a more complicated multiple regression model it is impossible to derive simple conditions showing the impact of measurement error on the estimated coefficients.
8. Exactly the same analysis applies to the probability of imprisonment: random fluctuations of the imprisonment rate around the true probability are negligible, because the denominator (the number of convictions) is large. However, there is no significant

problem of systematic under-recording for the imprisonment rate, since the number of convictions is recorded with great accuracy by the criminal justice system.

References

Becker, G. (1968), 'Crime and Punishment: An Economic Approach', *Journal of Political Economy*, vol. 76, pp. 169-217.

Coleman, C. and Moynihan, J. (1996), *Understanding Crime Data: Haunted By The Dark Figure*, Open University Press, Milton Keynes.

Ehrlich, I. (1973), 'Participation in Illegitimate Activities: A Theoretical and Empirical Investigation', *Journal of Political Economy*, vol. 81, pp. 521-64.

Gibbs, J.P. and Firebaugh, G. (1990), 'The Artefact Issue in Deterrence Research', *Criminology*, vol. 28, pp. 347-67.

Gourieroux, C. and Monfort, A. (1991), 'Simulation Based Inference in Models with Heterogeneity', *Annales d'Economie et de Statistique*, vol. 20/21, pp. 69-108.

Hales, J. and Stratford, N. (1997), *1996 British Crime Survey (England and Wales): Technical Report*, SCPR, London.

Jupp, J. (1995), *Methods of Criminological Research*, Routledge, London.

Klein, L.R., Forst, B.E. and Filatov, V. (1978), 'The Deterrent Effect of Capital Punishment: An Assessment of the Estimates', in A. Blumstein, J. Cohen, and D. Nagin (eds), *Deterrence and Incapacitation: Estimating the Effect of Criminal Sanctions on Crime Rates*, National Academy of Sciences, Washington D. C.

Maguire, M. (1994), 'Crime Statistics, Patterns, and Trends: Changing Perceptions and Their Implications', in M. Maguire, R. Morgan and R. Reiner (eds), *The Oxford Handbook of Criminology*, Clarendon Press, Oxford, pp. 233-91.

Mirrlees-Black, C., Budd, T., Partridge, S. and Mayhew, P. (1998), *The 1998 British Crime Survey, England and Wales*, Home Office Statistical Bulletin 21/98, Home Office, London.

Pudney, S., Deadman, D.F. and Pyle, D.J. (2000), 'The Relationship Between Crime, Punishment and Economic Conditions: Is Reliable Inference Possible When Crimes are Under-Recorded?', *Journal of the Royal Statistical Society Series A (Statistics in Society)*, vol. 163, pp. 81-97.

Pyle, D.J. (1995), *Cutting The Costs of Crime: The Economics of Crime and Criminal Justice*, Hobart Paper No. 129, Institute of Economic Affairs, London.

Pyle, D.J. (2000), 'Economists, Crime and Punishment' in N. Fielding, A. Clarke and R. Witt (eds), *Economic Dimensions of Crime*, Macmillan, forthcoming.

Sims, C.A., Stock, J.H. and Watson, M.W. (1990), 'Inference in Linear Time-series Models with some Unit Roots', *Econometrica*, vol. 58, pp. 113-44.

Taylor, J.B. (1978), 'Econometric Models of Criminal Behavior' in J.M. Heineke (ed), *Economic Models of Criminal Behavior*, North Holland, Amsterdam.

Zedlewski, E.W. (1983), 'Deterrence Findings and Data Sources: A Comparison of the Uniform Crime Reports and the National Crime Surveys', *Journal of Research in Crime and Delinquency*, vol. 20, pp. 262-76.

4. Crime, Deterrence and Economic Factors

DEREK DEADMAN AND DAVID PYLE

Introduction

The idea that the incidence of crime may be related to the state of the economy, and particularly to the level of unemployment, has caused considerable debate, both amongst academics and politicians. This chapter examines the association between crime and economic activity in an attempt to resolve this important policy issue. We begin by considering possible reasons why crime might be related to the economy, before surveying the evidence from previous studies linking crime to economic circumstances. Finally, we present some results, obtained using annual data for England and Wales, concerning the relationship between economic factors and the incidence of residential burglary.

The Link Between Crime and Economic Circumstances

Many different theories of criminal behaviour suggest that economic hardship might induce some individuals to resort to crime.[1] If these views are correct then one would expect the incidence of property crimes (i.e. burglaries, thefts and robberies; crimes which may be committed largely for financial gain) to increase during a recession and fall, or perhaps increase less rapidly, during a boom.

Box (1987) argued that young males, and especially those who have been unemployed for a long period of time, are those most likely to turn to crime. He claimed that this group has been encouraged to be competitive but was not yet conditioned to passivity. As a result, they are likely to react to their plight in an active and indignant manner. Those who have been unemployed for only a short period of time may think that risking the acquisition of a criminal record is too heavy a price to pay for avoiding what may be only a temporary period of economic hardship.[2]

Cantor and Land (1985) argue that '... traditional criminogenic theories are incomplete ... because they concentrate only on the effects of the unemployment rate on the prevalence of motivated offenders' (p. 318). Developments in criminal-opportunity theory (see Cook and Zarkin, 1985; Cantor and Land, 1985) suggest two reasons why a positive association between crime and unemployment may not be observed in practice. First, during a recession there is less property available for thieves to steal (the so-called system activity effect). Second, with more workers unemployed there will be more people at home during the day, so that surveillance of residential premises is increased (the guardianship effect).

Clearly there are conflicting theories linking crime and economic forces (unemployment). One set (motivational theories) predicts that property crime should increase in times of economic hardship, whilst the other (opportunity theories) predicts that property crime may fall during a recession. Of course, both theories may be correct, in which case two quite different sets of factors pull the crime rate in opposing directions. In fact, Cantor and Land (1985) argue that this is the reason why many empirical studies have reached conflicting (and sometimes indeterminate) conclusions concerning the effect of unemployment upon crime. In the next section we consider the evidence from a number of studies, which have examined this issue.

A Review of Earlier Empirical Studies

The idea that crime and economic conditions may be linked is hardly new. For example, Adam Smith observed that 'The establishment of commerce and manufactures ... is the best police for preventing crimes' (Smith, 1763). Neither is it an insight that has been revealed only to economists. Wilhelm Bonger (1916) reports attempts, mainly by French statisticians during the nineteenth century, to test the link between crime and economic circumstances, measured for example by unemployment, wages and inflation. Later studies include those by Thomas (1927) and Henry and Short (1954), both of which used time-series data on recorded offences and tried to correlate changes in the levels of offending with variations in the level of economic/business activity using the then standard measures of the reference cycle.

Thomas, in analysing the relationship between crime and the business cycle in England and Wales between 1857 and 1913 found that 'Burglary, house breaking and shop-breaking and robbery ... show a definite tendency to increase in a business depression and to decrease with prosperity' (p. 139). Henry and Short used a similar technique to relate burglary and robbery offences to a standard business cycle indicator for the USA between 1929 and 1949. They also report similar exercises for six cities. They found '... a strong and persistent tendency for robberies and burglaries to fall in prosperity and rise during depression' (p. 179).

Following Becker (1968), there was a great deal of interest amongst economists in estimating so-called 'supply of offences' functions. Part of this literature attempted to relate crime to labour market conditions, particularly unemployment. Some years before Becker's theoretical contribution, Belton Fleisher (1963) had undertaken some *ad hoc* and fairly primitive modelling of the relationship between juvenile delinquency and unemployment using data for three US cities. However, his work had not led to any further empirical analysis of the relationship between crime and unemployment. Reading the literature now it is clear that few economists were aware of the work of either Thomas or Henry and Short. The preoccupation with studying the relationship between crime and unemployment may have been misplaced, but it was to be another twenty years before economists were to 'rediscover' the pioneering work connecting crime to business cycle indices.

Several fairly extensive literature reviews of the relationship between crime and unemployment, written in the 1980s, concluded that the relationship was weak (Long and Witte, 1981; Tarling, 1982; Freeman, 1983; and Box, 1987).

As a whole, our survey of the literature relating economic factors to crime, provides only weak support for the simple economic models of crime which see high unemployment (and) low incomes ... as major factors causing crime... (Long and Witte, 1981, p. 135).

In all over 30 studies ... were examined. On balance rather more found no evidence of a significant relationship between unemployment and crime than found some evidence of a significant relationship (Tarling, 1982, p. 29).

... empirical analysis shows at best only a moderate link between unemployment and crime (Freeman, 1983, p. 89).

The relationship between overall unemployment and crime is inconsistent ... on balance the weight of existing research supports there being a weak but none the less causal relationship (Box, 1987, p. 96).

Chiricos (1987, p. 188) has referred to this as 'the consensus of doubt', whilst Cantor and Land (1985) argue that these findings can be explained by the countervailing effects of criminal motivation and criminal opportunity (see above). Chiricos (1987) argues that a positive relationship between crime and unemployment is more common for studies using data for the 1970s onwards, a period when unemployment was considerably higher than it had been in earlier years. Chiricos also finds stronger evidence of a positive crime-unemployment relationship in studies that have focused upon property crimes, i.e. burglaries and thefts. Another possible explanation for finding a weak relationship is that it was common for investigators to correlate crime rates with the *aggregate* unemployment rate, when the unemployment rate and the duration of unemployment amongst young males may be more appropriate causal variables.[3]

Many of the studies referred to in the surveys listed above used data from North America. Whilst studies using aggregate British data also produce mixed results, the majority have found some evidence of a positive correlation between unemployment and the incidence of crime, although the size of any effect is often quite small (see Carr-Hill and Stern, 1979; Hale and Sabbagh, 1991; Pyle, 1989; Pyle and Deadman, 1993; Reilly and Witt, 1992, 1996; Sampson and Wooldredge, 1987; Willis, 1983; Wolpin, 1978).

One criticism that has always dogged studies of the relationship between crime and unemployment using aggregate data is that evidence of a correlation between the two series does not imply anything about causation (the so-called ecological fallacy). One way of overcoming this has been to study individuals' criminal careers and employment histories. Even here, finding that criminals are more likely to be unemployed than other individuals does not prove that unemployment causes crime. The causal link may run in the other direction or both may be unrelated by-products of a third factor, e.g. personal characteristics such as IQ or education. Farrington *et al.*, (1986) have tried to overcome this problem by examining the criminal records of individuals during periods when they were employed and when they were unemployed. Their study is based upon a longitudinal survey of 411 males born in London in 1953 and draws upon interview responses obtained at the ages of sixteen and eighteen years of age. Official records of offending were compared with self-reporting of periods of unemployment. The investigators found that, '... the rate of offending during periods of unemployment was about three times as great as during periods of employment' (p. 342) and that, 'offences of material gain were committed more frequently during periods of unemployment' (p. 347).[4]

The results of Farrington *et al.* help to justify further studies of the relationship between aggregate levels of crime, especially property crime, and overall indicators of the state of the country's economy. An influential study along these lines, using annual data for England and Wales between

1950 and 1987, is that by Field (1990), who concluded that, '... economic factors have a major influence on trends in both property and personal crime' (p. 5). An interesting 'innovation' in Field's work is his attempt to turn attention away from the relationship between crime and unemployment and to consider instead the role of other economic indicators, particularly consumers' expenditure, in explaining crime. His work also marked the first stage of a return to a methodology pioneered nearly seventy years before by Thomas (1927) (see above).

Field could find little evidence of link between crime and unemployment.[5] One explanation for this may be that recorded unemployment is no longer a good indicator of the UK economy, especially following the substantial revisions to it that occurred throughout the 1980s. Also, unemployment lags behind the cycle in economic activity, by on average between six and twelve months but sometimes by as much as two years. As a consequence, when the economy turns into a recession, manifesting itself in terms of reduced overtime, part-time working and falling income, unemployment may not be rising. However, if property crime is a response to worsening economic circumstances, then it will have begun to increase, as reduced income begins to reduce living standards.[6] Therefore, one might expect other economic indicators, which are more closely related to the economic cycle than unemployment, to be better correlated with recorded crime rates.

Field's second contribution was to try to incorporate recent developments in time-series econometric methodology into the estimation of the crime-economy relationship. Both crime rates and economic variables are dominated by strong time trends in the post war period in England and Wales. Where time-series are dominated by trends it is possible to obtain entirely spurious correlations between the series (see Charemza and Deadman, 1997, Chapter Five). The preferred statistical procedure in such cases is to remove the trends from the series and, roughly speaking, to correlate the respective deviations of the series around their trends (see Chapter Two for more detail on this). Just such an approach had been pioneered by Thomas (1927).

In fact, Field correlated annual *growth rates* in crime with annual *growth rates* in other variables. He found evidence of an inverse relationship between the growth in personal consumption and the growth in property crime, but only in the short-term. In the long-run, the rate of growth of property crime shows no relationship to the rate of growth of consumption. He argues that several different factors work to produce these results. In the short-run a motivational effect dominates. The recession affects a relatively small group in society, who live at the margin between crime and legitimate economic activity. These individuals switch into criminal activities following the downturn in their economic fortunes. When the economy recovers, they drift back into legitimate occupations. In the long-run, growth in consumption increases the opportunities for crime, which tends to counteract any motivational effect of increasing consumption.

Following Field's contribution, further work on the relationship between crime and economic indicators using time-series data for the UK was undertaken by Deadman and Pyle (1997), Hale (1998a,b), Osborn (1995), Pudney *et al.*, (2000) and Pyle and Deadman (1994). This later work went much further in incorporating developments in time-series econometric modelling, in particular cointegration analysis and error-correction modelling (see Chapter Two). This approach was first applied to crime data by Pyle and Deadman (1994), who attempted to model three property crime series, i.e. the series for burglary, robbery and theft and handling of stolen goods, using annual data for England and Wales between 1946 and 1991. The model used by Pyle and Deadman was quite simple and included only three explanatory variables - the conviction rate, the number of police officers and a measure of economic activity (three alternative measures were used: real consumers' expenditure, real Gross Domestic Product and unemployment). Somewhat controversially, Pyle and Deadman concluded that the crime series were integrated of order two, but that the other variables were integrated of order one, so that the model they estimated was of the form:

$$\Delta\Delta crime_t = \beta_1\Delta E_t + \beta_2\Delta convict_t + \beta_3\Delta police_t + \beta_4(ECM)_{t-1} \quad (4.1)$$

where E represents the economic indicator (i.e. either consumers' expenditure, Gross Domestic Product (GDP) or unemployment), *convict* is the conviction rate (the number of convictions divided by the number of recorded offences), *police* is the number of police officers, *ECM* is the error correction mechanism, and t is a time subscript.

The general pattern of their results is probably of more interest than the precise coefficient estimates. First, the economic variable (whether consumers' expenditure, GDP or unemployment) is invariably significant. Increases in either GDP or personal consumption are associated with reductions in $\Delta crime$, whilst increasing unemployment leads to increases in $\Delta crime$. Second, the conviction rate is generally negative and significant, except for burglary when unemployment is the economic variable. Increases in the conviction rate tend, as expected, to reduce the rate of increase in crime. Third, the number of police officers is generally just insignificant, the only exceptions to this being burglary and theft when personal consumption is the economic variable. Finally, the error correction mechanism is invariably significant and negative, indicating that if the relationship between Δ*crime* and its explanatory factors is disturbed there is a tendency for crime to bounce back in the long-term, so that the long-run equilibrium relationship is restored. This pattern of results is remarkably consistent, both across offence groups and within groups for different measures of the economic variable.

Subsequently, Deadman and Pyle (1997) used their model to forecast the crime series for the period 1992-5. The model works quite satisfactorily in that it correctly predicts the turning points in the series for recorded theft (in 1992) and for recorded burglary (in 1993). Prediction of turning points is generally regarded as a quite severe test of any econometric model. The model performs less well in terms of predicting the actual levels of crime, but generally the 95 per cent confidence interval for the forecast encompasses the actual value of recorded crime for that year.

Pyle and Deadman's claim that the crime series are integrated of order two has been disputed by both Osborn (1995) and Hale (1998a,b), who argue that the crime series are integrated of order one. Their arguments are made partly for technical reasons (related to the methods used to test for orders of integration), but also on the grounds that it is unreasonable to accept that crime would continue to rise indefinitely even if the economy was stationary in the long-run. In addition, both Hale and Osborn found real consumers' expenditure to be a more appropriate explanatory variable than real GDP. Despite their agreement on these points, there is some disparity between their empirical results. Using quarterly data for 1975-1993, Osborn found limited evidence for an effect of macro-economic conditions (real consumption) on crime in the long run and no effect in the short-run. On the other hand, Hale (1998a), using a longer series of annual data (1950-1991), found significant effects for both consumption and unemployment in the short-run and for consumption in the long-run. Subsequently, Hale (1998b) extended his analysis to include additional criminal justice variables and to incorporate a number of labour market indicators intended to reflect changes in the structure and composition of employment. The deterrence variables were the proportion of those found guilty who were given a custodial sentence and average sentence length. Labour market variables included the proportions of employment in the manufacturing sector and women in employment, together with measures of income inequality. He concluded that there was only weak evidence of a deterrent effect for criminal justice variables, but that changes in the structure of the labour market had a significant long-run effect upon property crime.

A Time-Series Model of Residential Burglary in England and Wales

In Chapter Two we reported the results of estimating an economic model of residential burglary in England and Wales, using annual time-series data for the period 1950-1995. In that chapter we focussed on the effects of the criminal justice variables upon recorded crime. In this chapter we shall use the same model but concentrate upon the effects of the economic variables (real personal consumption and unemployment). In order to facilitate comparison with the bulk of published work in this area and to produce estimates less subject to bias, we have computed estimates of the model using a one-step regression procedure proposed by Sims *et al.* (1990) and first used in this area by Pudney *et al.* (1997). This regression equation is obtained by substituting for the error correction component from the long-run model to give:

$$
\begin{aligned}
\Delta \ln burglary_t = {} & \beta_1 \Delta \ln convict_t + \beta_2 \Delta \ln prison_t + \beta_3 \Delta \ln senten_t \\
& + \beta_4 \Delta \ln unemp_t + \beta_5 \Delta \ln consum_t + \beta_6 \Delta \ln youths_t \\
& + \beta_7 \Delta \ln police_t + \beta_8 \Delta dummy_t + \beta_9 \Delta \ln burglary_{t-1} - \beta_9 \theta_0 \\
& - \beta_9 \theta_1 \ln convict_{t-1} - \beta_9 \theta_2 \ln prison_{t-1} - \beta_9 \theta_3 \ln senten_{t-1} \\
& - \beta_9 \theta_4 \ln unemp_{t-1} - \beta_9 \theta_5 \ln consum_{t-1} - \beta_9 \theta_6 \ln youths_{t-1} \\
& - \beta_9 \theta_7 \ln police_{t-1} - \beta_9 \theta_8 dummy_{t-1} + \varepsilon_t
\end{aligned}
\tag{4.2}
$$

For a full discussion of this model see Chapter Two, and for the variable definitions see the Appendix to this chapter. At first sight, this appears to be an inappropriate equation for estimation by OLS regression, since the explanatory variables are a mixture of $I(0)$ and $I(1)$ variables. Despite this, the results of Sims *et al.* (1990) can be invoked to show that the estimated coefficients of (4.2) have standard asymptotic properties. Monte Carlo simulations presented by Pudney *et al.* (1997) for a broadly similar model confirm this and show that OLS applied to (4.2) has rather better small-sample properties than the Engle-Granger procedure. Therefore, we make use of the OLS estimator applied to (4.2). This yields the following results given in Table 4.1.

Table 4.1 **OLS estimates of the determinants of residential burglary***

	Coefficient	|t| value
$\Delta \ln convict_t$	-0.366	2.446
$\Delta \ln prison_t$	-0.251	2.008
$\Delta \ln senten_t$	-0.360	1.904
$\Delta \ln unemp_t$	0.267	4.132
$\Delta \ln consum_t$	-1.701	3.276
$\Delta \ln youths_t$	0.662	0.687
$\Delta \ln police_t$	-1.509	1.705
$\Delta dummy_t$	0.460	5.839
$\Delta \ln burglary_{t-1}$	-0.260	2.798
$\ln convict_{t-1}$	-0.154	0.966
$\ln prison_{t-1}$	-0.104	0.774
$\ln senten_{t-1}$	-0.639	2.838
$\ln unemp_{t-1}$	0.110	1.960
$\ln consum_{t-1}$	0.929	2.923
$\ln youths_{t-1}$	0.842	3.008
$\ln police_{t-1}$	-1.717	2.838
$dummy_{t-1}$	0.150	2.229
Intercept	-1.993	0.766
R^2	0.924	
F	19.198	
Serial correlation χ_1^2	0.059	

* Dependent variable = $\Delta \ln burglary_t$

In this chapter we focus upon the impact of the economic variables (*unemp* and *consum*), both of which are statistically significant in both the short and long-term. The effects of the deterrence variables (*convict, prison* and *senten*) have been discussed in Chapter Two. It is clear from inspection of Table 4.1 that increases in unemployment raise rates of residential burglary in both time periods, which is entirely in agreement with our prior expectations. However, changes in consumption have different effects in the short-term (a negative coefficient) and the long-term (a positive coefficient). In the short-term, residential burglary increases in response to a fall in consumption, whilst in the long-term it increases in response to rising consumption. This confirms an effect reported by Field (1990). In simple terms his explanation focused on the difference between motivation and opportunity. Increases in the level of real consumption provide greater opportunities for criminals to steal. Hence we observe a positive association between real consumption and residential burglary in the long-term. However, when consumption falls individuals feel worse off, because falling consumption indicates a fall in living standards. This generates more crime, as individuals resort to crime in order to increase their resources. In the short-term it would appear that the motivational effect dominates, whereas in the long-term it is the opportunity effect that is predominant. In this sense, both motivational and opportunity theories of crime receive some support from the findings reported here.

Conclusion

The notion that the incidence of (property-related) crime may be related in some way to the state of the nation's economy has a long and distinguished intellectual pedigree. However, it was not until the 1960s that this thesis was examined seriously by economists. The focus of the empirical work undertaken during the 1960s and 1970s was upon the relationship between crime and unemployment, but the results of this work were somewhat mixed. Whilst a number of studies found evidence of a positive relationship between the two variables, other studies were unable to detect any relationship. The consensus in the early 1980s was that no obvious relationship existed between crime and the economy, at least when the latter was measured by the rate of unemployment.

Since 1990, a number of British economists have changed the focus of the research on the relationship between crime and economic activity. Beginning with Field (1990), they have widened the analysis to incorporate other economic indicators, particularly real consumers' expenditure and gross domestic product. Further, by utilising developments in time-series econometrics (cointegration and error-correction modelling), they have shown that economic forces can play different roles and have different effects in the short-term and the long-term.

The model we have worked with in this chapter was intended primarily to be representative of a wide class of applied time-series crime models, rather than a new contribution to the literature. Nevertheless, the results have proved to be interesting, and they do cast further light on the nature of the relationship between property crime and the state of economic activity and criminal justice in England and Wales during the post-war period. We have found evidence of a significant short-term effect of economic conditions upon the incidence of residential burglaries, although evidence of a long-term effect is marginally weaker.

Notes

1. For example, Cantor and Land (1985) refer to strain theories, rational choice theories (or economic models of criminal behaviour), conflict/Marxist theories, labelling theory and social control theory as all pointing to a positive association between unemployment and crime.
2. This argument conjures up a picture of a super-rational youth calculating the probability that he will remain unemployed for the next T time periods and deciding between crime and legitimate pursuits on the basis of their alternative streams of expected future earnings. This is only one way (an economist's way!) of explaining the choice between crime and legitimate pursuits.
3. Although Chiricos finds little support for this thesis. This may be due, in part, to the absence of data on age-specific crime rates.
4. However, studies using individual level data will overlook the effect that the aggregate unemployment rate has upon the criminal activities of those who are not made unemployed themselves, but whose economic fortunes are adversely affected, i.e. those who because of the recession experience part-time work, low paid jobs or jobs which inadequately match their aspirations (see Allan and Steffensmeier (1989)).
5. 'Once the effect of personal consumption is taken into account, no evidence emerged, despite extensive statistical testing, that unemployment adds anything extra to the explanation of any type of crime' (p. 7). And '... if consumption growth is removed from the picture, by dropping all consumption variables from the models, a statistical relationship between crime and unemployment can sometimes be identified. But the relationship is weak' (pp. 38 - 9).
6. Allan and Steffensmeier (1989, p. 110) argue that '... for young adults the choice of legitimate over illegitimate pursuits may be influenced more by the quality of employment than the mere availability'. They find some support for this hypothesis using age-specific data on arrest rates for property crimes during the years 1977-80. The quality of employment is proxied by the percentage of the labour force who are (i) employed part-time because they are unable to find full-time work and (ii) in receipt of wages below the poverty level. Both variables are generally positively and significantly related to property crime arrest rates.

References

Allan, E.A. and Steffensmeier, D.J. (1989), 'Youth, Underemployment, and Property Crime: Differential Effects of Job Availability and Job Quality on Juvenile and Young Adult Arrest Rates', *American Sociological Review*, vol. 54, pp. 107-23.

Becker, G.S. (1968), 'Crime and Punishment: An Economic Approach', *Journal of Political Economy*, vol. 76, pp. 169-217.

Bonger, W. (1916), *Criminality and Economic Conditions*, Little Brown, Boston.

Box, S. (1987), *Recession, Crime and Punishment*, MacMillan, London.

Cantor, D. and Land, K.C. (1985), 'Unemployment and Crime-Rates in the Post-World War II United States: A Theoretical and Empirical Analysis', *American Sociological Review*, vol. 50, pp. 317-32.

Carr-Hill, R.A. and Stern, N.H. (1979), *Crime, The Police and Criminal Statistics*, Academic Press, London.

Charemza, W.W. and Deadman, D.F. (1997), *New Directions in Econometric Practice*, second edition, Edward Elgar, Cheltenham.

Chiricos, T.G. (1987), 'Rates of Crime and Unemployment: An Analysis of Aggregate Research Evidence', *Social Problems*, vol. 34, pp. 187-212.

Cook, P.J. and Zarkin, G.A. (1985), 'Crime and the Business Cycle', *Journal of Legal Studies*, vol. 14, pp. 115-28.

Deadman, D.F. and Pyle, D.J. (1997), 'Forecasting Recorded Property Crime using a Time-Series Econometric Model', *British Journal of Criminology*, vol. 37, pp. 437-45.

Farrington, D., Gallagher, B., Morley, L., Ledger, R. and West, D. (1986), 'Unemployment, School - Leaving and Crime', *British Journal of Criminology*, vol. 26, pp. 335-56.

Field, S. (1990), *Trends in Crime and Their Interpretation. A Study of Recorded Crime in Post-War England and Wales*, Home Office Research Study no. 119, Home Office, London.

Fleisher, B.M. (1963), 'The Effect of Unemployment on Juvenile Delinquency', *Journal of Political Economy*, vol. 71, pp. 543-55.

Freeman, R.B. (1983), 'Crime and Unemployment', in J.Q. Wilson (ed.), *Crime and Public Policy*, Institute for Contemporary Studies, San Francisco, pp. 89-106.

Hale, C. (1998a), 'Crime and the Business Cycle in Post-War Britain Revisited', *British Journal of Criminology*, vol. 38, pp. 681-98.

Hale, C. (1998b), 'The Labour Market and Post-War Crime Trends in England and Wales', in P. Carlen and R. Morgan (eds), *Crime Unlimited?: Questions for the Twenty-first Century*, Macmillan, London.

Hale, C. and Sabbagh, D. (1991), 'Testing the Relationship Between Unemployment and Crime: A Methodological Comment and Empirical Analysis using Time-Series Data for England and Wales', *Journal of Research in Crime and Delinquency*, vol. 28, pp. 400-17.

Henry, A.F. and Short, J.F. (1954), *Homicide and Suicide*, Free Press, Illinois.

Long, S.K. and Witte, A.D. (1981), 'Current Economic Trends: Implications for Crime and Criminal Justice', in K.N. Wright (ed), *Crime and Criminal Justice in a Declining Economy*, Oelgeschlager, Gunn and Hain, Cambridge, Massachusetts, pp. 69-143.

Osborn, D. (1995), *Crime and the UK Economy*, Robert Schuman Centre Working Paper 95/15, European University Institute.

Pudney, S., Deadman, D. and Pyle, D. (1997), *The Effect of Under-Reporting in Statistical Models of Criminal Activity: Estimation of an Error Correction Model with Measurement Error*, Discussion Paper in Public Sector Economics 97/3, Department of Economics, University of Leicester.

Pudney, S., Deadman, D.F. and Pyle, D.J. (2000), 'The Relationship Between Crime, Punishment and Economic Conditions: Is Reliable Inference Possible When Crimes are Under-Recorded?', *Journal of the Royal Statistical Society Series A (Statistics in Society)*, vol. 163, pp. 81-97.

Pyle, D.J. (1989), 'The Economics of Crime in Britain', *Economic Affairs*, vol. 9, pp. 6-9.

Pyle, D.J. and Deadman, D.F. (1993), 'Crime and Unemployment in Scotland: Some Further Results', *Scottish Journal of Political Economy*, vol. 41, pp. 314-24.

Pyle, D.J. and Deadman, D.F. (1994), 'Crime and the Business Cycle in Post-War Britain', *British Journal of Criminology*, vol. 34, pp. 339-57.

Reilly, B. and Witt, R. (1992), 'Crime and Unemployment in Scotland', *Scottish Journal of Political Economy*, vol. 39, pp. 213-28.

Reilly, B. and Witt, R. (1996), 'Crime, Deterrence and Unemployment in England and Wales: An Empirical Analysis', *Bulletin of Economic Research*, vol. 48, pp. 137-55.

Sampson, R.J. and Wooldredge, J.D. (1987), 'Linking the Micro- and Macro-Level Dimensions of Lifestyle - Routine Activity and Opportunity Models of Predatory Victimisation', *Journal of Quantitative Criminology*, vol. 3, pp. 371-93.

Sims, C.A., Stock, J.H. and Watson, M.W. (1990), 'Inference in Linear Time Series Models with some Unit Roots', *Econometrica*, vol. 58, pp. 113-44.

Smith, A. (1763), *Lectures on Justice, Police, Revenue and Arms*, Edited by Edwin Cannan, Oxford, 1896.

Tarling, R. (1982), *Crime and Unemployment*, Home Office Research and Planning Bulletin, no. 12, Home Office, London.

Thomas, D. S. (1927), *Social Aspects of The Business Cycle*, Gordon and Breach, New York.

Willis, K.G. (1983), 'Spatial Variations in Crime in England and Wales: Testing an Economic Model', *Regional Studies*, vol. 17, pp. 261-72.

Wolpin, K.I. (1978), 'An Economic Model of Crime and Punishment in England and Wales, 1894 – 1967', *Journal of Political Economy*, vol. 86, pp. 815-40.

APPENDIX 4.1

Definitions of variables and sources of data

1. Residential burglary (*burglary*):

Recorded offences in England and Wales. *Up to and including 1968*: category 29: Housebreaking; *1969 and after*: categories 28 and 29: Burglary and Aggravated Burglary.

Source: Criminal Statistics, England and Wales (various).

2. Conviction rate (*convict*):

The number of convictions divided by the number of recorded offences. The number of convictions is the number of persons found guilty in all courts. After 1970 this includes the number of offenders who were cautioned for an offence.

Source: Criminal Statistics for England and Wales (various).

3. Prison (*prison*):

The proportion of those convicted of offences of residential burglary who were sentenced to immediate imprisonment.

Source: Criminal Statistics for England and Wales (various).

4. Sentence (*senten*):

The average length of prison sentence (in months) given to those sentenced to imprisonment for residential burglary offences.

Source: Criminal Statistics for England and Wales (various) and unpublished data provided by the Home Office.

5. Youths (*youths*):

Numbers of Males aged 15 - 24 years as a proportion of the total population of England and Wales.

Source: Population Trends (various).

6. Consumption (*consum*):

UK real personal consumption per capita, £ billion, 1985 prices.

Source: Economic Trends (various).

7. Unemployment (*unemp*):

Numbers of people registered as unemployed in the UK, excluding adult students, per capita.

Source: Economic Trends (various).

8. *Police*

Numbers of police officers. Actual strength at the end of the year, excluding special constables.

Source: Annual Abstract of Statistics.

9. *Dummy*

We also include a variable *dummy* to capture the effect of the Theft Act, 1968.

5.   An Investigation into Quarterly Crime and its Relationship to the Economy

DENISE OSBORN

Introduction

The nature of any relationship between aggregate crime and the economy is of wide interest in both academic and policy-making areas. Recent empirical studies examining the issue in the UK context include Field (1990), Reilly and Witt (1992), Dickinson (1993), Pyle and Deadman (1994), Deadman and Pyle (1997), Hale (1998) and Pudney *et al.* (2000). Historically, much of the interest has centred on the potential link between crime and unemployment. However, the current focus has shifted a little so that consumption is now also central to the discussion.

Dickinson (1993) examines the role of unemployment in a conceptually complex model in which he postulates an asymmetric relationship such that an increase in unemployment has a greater effect on criminal activity than does a corresponding decrease. Nevertheless, although he makes extensive use of graphs, his modelling is confined to simple linear regression using data expressed as percentage change series. He makes no attempt to test the asymmetry hypothesis in any formal manner. In concentrating on the crime/unemployment link, he also fails to consider the role of any other potential explanatory variables. Reilly and Witt (1992) use regional data for Scotland and develop a pooled time series/cross section model, but they are also restricted in terms of the explanatory variables used.

The analysis of Pyle and Deadman (1994) builds on an important and extensive Home Office study by Field (1990). Field considers twelve categories of crime together with a number of economic indicators, demographic and weather variables. He finds that consumers' expenditure performs better than other economic variables, including unemployment, in explaining crime. Further, it appears that while property crime has an inverse relationship to the business cycle (consumption growth having a negative effect on the growth in such crimes), personal crime responds in a pro-cyclical manner. Although taking Field's study as their starting point, Pyle and Deadman (1994) criticise him for conducting his analysis in terms of growth rates and, therefore, failing to model any long-run relationship between crime and economic variables. Although the next section argues that the analysis of Pyle and Deadman is flawed, it can be noted that the studies of Deadman and Pyle (1997), Hale (1998) and Pudney *et al.* (2000) also address these same shortcomings.

One important feature of the time series pattern of crime, which has been almost completely overlooked to date, is the nature of its seasonality. It is now recognised that seasonality is hugely important in terms of understanding the nature of month to month or quarter to quarter fluctuations in many macroeconomic variables (see, for example, Barsky and Miron, 1989; or Osborn, 1990) and corresponding issues arise in relation to understanding quarterly crime data. The nature of the seasonality in crime is a central issue in this chapter. Indeed, we model the patterns in quarterly crime data from both long-run and short-run perspectives. At the same time, the analysis here also formally examines the hypothesis put forward by Dickinson (1993) that increases and decreases in unemployment have distinct effects on crime.

The brief review above of recent UK work concentrates on empirical time series studies of how crime relates to the economy, and the present chapter constitutes another contribution in this sequence. Nevertheless, it needs to be emphasised that cross-section evidence is also available on this question. In this latter context, the most extensive UK data are those from the British Crime Surveys, which have been conducted since 1982. Extensive analysis of these has generally failed to find any evidence of a positive influence from local unemployment rates on property crime (Osborn *et al.*, 1992; Trickett *et al.*, 1995), although this relationship is revisited in Chapter Eight using data from the General Household Survey. That is not to say that economic conditions are found to be unimportant: indeed, Trickett *et al.* conclude that 'richer people in poor areas suffer property crime particularly heavily'.

The British Crime Surveys also throw some doubt on the accuracy of the police crime statistics used in time series studies (see, for example, Mayhew *et al.*, 1994). Nevertheless, in common with other studies of crime patterns over time, police statistics are used for the analysis conducted here. It is reassuring that Pudney *et al.* (2000) conclude that the biases from using police recorded crime data are not misleading in any serious way.

The outline of the chapter is as follows.[1] The next section considers the time series characteristics of recorded crime in England and Wales, including the nature of its seasonality and its long-run properties. The following section turns to modelling the long-run relationships between the major crime aggregates and macroeconomic variables. Subsequently, we turn to short-run relationships: in particular, we examine evidence for an asymmetric effect of movements in unemployment on crime. Conclusions complete the chapter.

Our most novel results are, perhaps, those concerned with personal crime. Seasonality is especially important in personal crime and, although no (linear) long-run relationship is established with economic variables, its short-run movements are inversely related with changes in unemployment. Further, the relationship is asymmetric, with decreases in unemployment having a much greater impact on personal crime than increases.

The Crime Data and their Characteristics

In this analysis we consider four categories of crime, namely burglary, theft and handling of stolen goods (referred to subsequently simply as theft), criminal damage and personal crime. The first three are types of property crime and the aggregate of the three is also considered. The fourth is formed as the sum of the number of recorded offences of violence against the person plus sexual offences. These latter two categories have been combined, as the numbers in each are relatively small while they have very similar seasonality and other characteristics.

Our crime data relate to the number of notifiable offences recorded by the police in England and Wales. The data are available quarterly from 1975; our sample period extends from 1975 to the end of 1993. The four categories we consider (mentioned above) constitute, on average, 95 percent of all recorded crimes. It may be noted that robbery, which cannot be comfortably categorised as purely a property or a personal crime, is excluded. As robbery accounts for less than one per cent of all crimes, its omission is relatively unimportant in terms of the aggregates used in this analysis. There have been some definitional changes over our period, but only one of these has a substantial effect. That change involves criminal damage, where all offences have been recorded since the beginning of 1977, whereas damage of value £20 or less had previously been excluded.

The crime data used in this study are shown in Figures 5.1 and 5.2. All three categories of property crime are shown in the first graph, while the upper two panels of Figure 5.2 separately show the aggregate property and personal crime series. The remaining two variables shown in this latter graph are used in the models of subsequent sections. As these series are later analysed in logarithmic form, (natural) logarithms have been taken for the graphs in Figure 5.2.

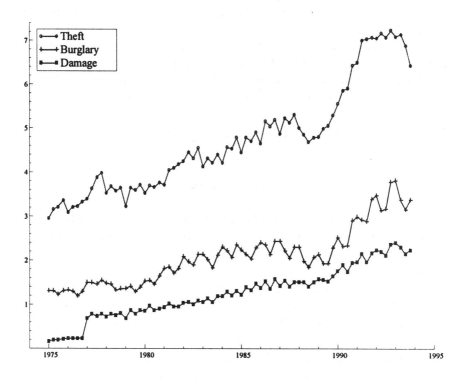

Note: The data relate to the number of notifiable offences (in multiples of 100,000) recorded by the police in each quarter.

Figure 5.1   The component series of property crime

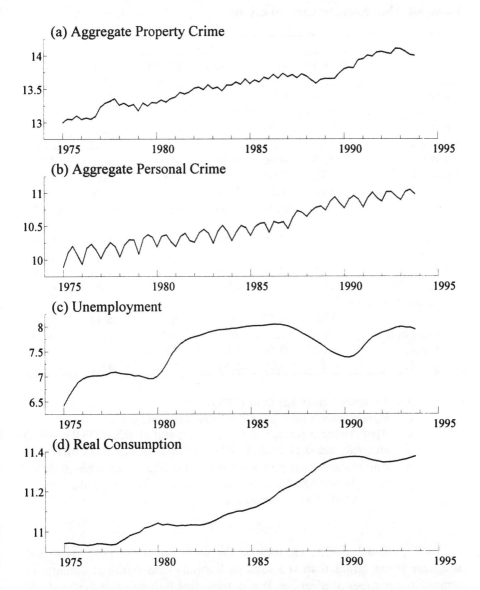

Notes: All variables are expressed as logarithms. Unemployment is seasonally adjusted total unemployment. Real consumption is the moving average of (seasonally unadjusted) total real consumers' expenditure in the current and three immediately preceding quarters.

Figure 5.2   Major series used in modelling

Table 5.1 The characteristics of crime

Statistic	Burglary	Theft	Crime Type Criminal Damage[a]	Aggregate Property[a]	Aggregate Personal	All Crime[a]
Average Growth[b]	1.30	0.97	1.72	1.11	1.29	1.10
Seasonal Patterns[b]: *Deviation from Overall Mean*						
Quarter 1	2.84	-4.92	-3.21	-2.70	-12.14	-3.24
Quarter 2	-5.91	4.53	5.60	1.89	14.42	2.35
Quarter 3	-6.79	-1.66	-8.54	-4.04	4.51	-3.42
Quarter 4	9.86	2.04	6.15	4.85	-6.80	4.30
SEE	4.91	3.54	5.19	3.68	4.18	3.51
R^2	0.674	0.518	0.603	0.500	0.864	0.500
Unit root tests[c]						
I(2) v I(1)	-7.47	-7.36	-3.53	-7.77	-8.41	-8.04
(augmentation)	(0)	(0)	(3)	(0)	(2)	(0)
I(1) v I(0)	-3.11	-3.43	-3.08	-3.72	-1.36	-3.63
(augmentation)	(4)	(4)	(5)	(4)	(3)	(4)
Seasonal unit root tests[d]						
H_0: $\Delta_1\Delta_4$	5.83	21.50	19.25	28.51	28.42	16.32
(augmentation)	(4)	(2)	(0)	(0)	(0)	(0)
H_a: Δ_4 only	-0.57	-0.56	-3.01	0.81	-3.58	0.69
H_a: Δ_1 only	-2.67	-4.82	-3.71	-5.28	-4.94	-5.22

Notes: a.   Computed using data from 1977Q1.
         b.   Figures (except for R^2) are expressed as percentages.
         c.   Approximate 5 per cent and 1 per cent critical values (Fuller, 1976)
              are: -2.89 and -3.51 for I(2) v I(1), -3.45 and -4.04 for I(1) v I(0).
         d.   Approximate 5 per cent and 1 per cent critical values (Osborn, 1990)
              are: 3.79 and 4.80 for overall test, -2.11 and -2.82 for Δ_4 alternative, -
              3.75 and -4.35 for Δ_1 alternative.

As Figure 5.1 illustrates, theft is the most important property crime category, being larger than the total of burglary and criminal damage in terms of the number of offences. It is notable that burglary and theft exhibit two periods of decrease, namely 1978/79 and 1988/89, with criminal damage also showing a slight decline in the latter period. The step increase evident for criminal damage at the beginning of 1977 is due to the definitional change mentioned above. Although not immediately evident from Figure 5.1, it should be noted that total crime is dominated by property ones, which constitute approximately 90 per cent of all recorded offences. Further, the characteristics of property and personal crimes are somewhat different. In contrast to the periods of decline noted for property crime, personal crime (except for seasonal effects) increases almost continuously throughout the period.

Table 5.1 provides a numerical summary of the important characteristics of crime in each of the categories considered, including all recorded crime. This, and all subsequent analysis, is carried out after taking (natural) logarithms. The first part of the table records the average percentage quarterly growth, while further statistics show the importance of seasonality. Finally, the table looks at the nature of the nonstationarity in this crime data; we return to this below.

The overall mean and the seasonal patterns shown in Table 5.1 are computed from the regression

$$\Delta Y_t = \alpha_0 + \alpha_1 (D_{1t} - D_{4t}) + \alpha_2 (D_{2t} - D_{4t}) + \alpha_3 (D_{3t} - D_{4t}) + u_t \qquad (5.1)$$

where ΔY_t is the first difference of the logarithm of the series, D_{it} is a dummy variable for quarter i ($i = 1,2,3,4$) and u_t is a disturbance. The reported overall growth rate is the estimate of α_0, while the seasonal patterns for the first three quarters are the estimates of α_i for $i = 1, 2$ and 3 respectively. The restriction $\Sigma \alpha_i = 0$ (summed over $i = 1,2,3,4$) yields the estimated seasonal pattern for quarter four. Note also that the coefficient estimates from equation (5.1) have been scaled by 100 to give the percentage values reported. Finally, SEE is the residual standard error (expressed as a percentage) and R^2 is the conventional coefficient of determination from equation (5.1). The form of (5.1) is identical to that in Osborn (1990) to enable seasonality in these crime variables to be compared with that of major UK macroeconomic aggregates.

All recorded crime has grown at about 1.1 percent per quarter over this period. Although the number of offences has increased in all categories examined here, the fastest growth (at about 1.7 per cent per quarter) has been in criminal damage. Burglary and personal crime also exceed the growth rate for the total. Theft, which constitutes about half of all recorded offences, has grown on average more slowly than total crime. It is also notable from the first part of Table 5.1 that, overall, personal crime has increased at a faster rate than property crime.

Quarter to quarter movements in the crime variables are dominated by seasonality in the sense that the R^2 value for each category is at least a half. The importance of seasonality in crime is, perhaps, surprising, but the extent is comparable to that for major real economic variables. The seasonal dummy variables in (5.1) 'explain' 86 per cent of the movements in personal crime; this figure is very similar to that for real consumption in the UK (Osborn, 1990, Table 3). It is, however, notable from Figure 5.2 that seasonality in personal crime does not appear to be constant over time: indeed, prior to the rapid increase experienced in the late 1980s, it seems that seasonality in personal crime was decreasing.

Economic theories of criminal behaviour, such as Becker (1968), usually view crime as deriving from utility maximisation. In this context it is notable that burglary, criminal damage and crime overall peak in the fourth quarter of the year, which is also the annual peak in many macroeconomic variables, but especially consumption (Barsky and Miron, 1989; Osborn, 1990). While it is not to deny that climatic seasonality, such as hours of daylight, may play a role, this Christmas peak and the reduced criminal activity in the first quarter suggest that criminals have seasonal utility functions similar to those of other consumers (Osborn, 1988). Theft and criminal damage are similar to each other in their seasonal patterns, with peaks in the second and fourth quarters. It is possible that a separation of vehicle from other thefts would clarify the pattern for that category, since seasonal patterns in thefts for material gain and thefts for enjoyment may exhibit different characteristics.

In contrast to the property crime seasonal patterns, personal crime peaks in the summer months. This may, to some extent, be directly associated with seasonal climatic changes, in particular temperature and hours of daylight, making activities outside the home more attractive. It is also worth noting that Field (1990) finds beer consumption to be the most influential contemporaneous variable in explaining annual data on violence. This explanation cannot extend to the quarterly pattern, however, because beer consumption peaks in the Christmas quarter.

The third aspect of Table 5.1 is the nature of nonstationarity in recorded crime. In their study of annual post-war crime data for England and Wales, Pyle and Deadman (1994) find that the crime series are integrated of order two, or I(2). It is, however, widely accepted that real macroeconomic variables are I(1). As a consequence, Pyle and Deadman conclude that the levels of crime and economic activity cannot be cointegrated (Banerjee *et al.*, 1993), so that the level of the economy cannot explain the long-run level of crime. Therefore, they model the *change* in crime as a function of the *level* of the relevant explanatory economic variable. The consequence is that crime would continue to grow indefinitely in the long-run even if the level of economic activity is static. If true, this has profound implications.

There are, however, some difficulties with Pyle and Deadman's implementation of the unit root tests. To test the null hypothesis of an I(2) process against an I(1) alternative, a constant needs to be included in the augmented Dickey-Fuller test regression so that the critical values are not sensitive to the 'starting value' of ΔY (Banerjee *et al.*, 1993, pp. 104-105). At least for their major categories of burglary and theft, acceptance of I(2) by Pyle and Deadman is not entirely convincing when their results with a constant are examined. In any case, their use of an order 1 for augmentation is entirely arbitrary. Further, their error-correction mechanisms (ECMs) indicate that the dependent variable may be overdifferenced since the estimates of the error-correction coefficients are always close to minus one, which can be interpreted as the model attempting to reduce the order of differencing for the relevant crime variable.[2] In any case, the ECMs appear to be subject to dynamic misspecification. The only diagnostic check they report is the Durbin-Watson statistic, which (although biased towards failing to indicate the presence of autocorrelation in such a context) suggests the presence of positive residual autocorrelation in the annual residuals.

Except for the marginal (at five per cent) test statistic for criminal damage, Table 5.1 gives no evidence that any of the crime series are I(2) over our sample period. Our test regression for testing the I(2) null hypothesis against I(1) includes an intercept and three seasonal dummy variables. Here, and in later analyses, the order of augmentation is chosen[3] to ensure satisfactory residual autocorrelation properties to order 4.

Continuing to 'test down', we also examine I(1) versus I(0), with this latter test regression including a trend to give invariance to the value of a nonzero drift (Banerjee *et al.*, 1993, pp. 104-105). With test statistics close to the five per cent critical values, these latter results indicate that the property crime categories and total crime may be more adequately described as trend rather than difference stationary. It is, however, also the case that Agiakloglou and Newbold (1992) find that a data-dependent augmentation order for the Dickey-Fuller test in the presence of a moving average component results in true significance values substantially exceeding the nominal ones. This, then, throws some doubt on results that are marginal in relation to the normal five per cent critical values and leaves the issue of difference versus trend stationarity unresolved for those categories. At least for the present, we proceed assuming difference stationarity for these property crime categories, but we will revisit this question briefly later for aggregate property crime. On the other hand, the I(1) hypothesis is clearly acceptable for personal crime in comparison to the I(0) alternative.

The discussion of Table 5.1 above noted the importance of seasonality in the crime series. Therefore, the final part of Table 5.1 examines seasonality in the context of unit roots using an identical approach to that adopted in Osborn (1990). The initial hypothesis is that first and annual differencing are required to induce stationarity, which can be viewed as a seasonal version of the I(2) null hypothesis. Using an F-type statistic in a regression including a constant and seasonal dummy variables, the I(2) hypothesis is once again very clearly rejected. When the two alternative possibilities of annual and conventional first differencing are compared using t-ratios in this regression, the results for theft, aggregate property crime and all crimes indicate that first differencing only is required (since the null hypothesis is rejected against this alternative hypothesis but not against the annual differencing alternative). On the other hand, this approach is unable to distinguish clearly whether first or annual differencing is required to render burglary, criminal damage and aggregate personal crime stationary. Therefore, these latter three variables may contain seasonal unit roots.

Crime and Economic Variables in the Long-Run

In addition to the major categories of property and personal crimes, Figure 5.2 shows two key macroeconomic variables, namely unemployment and total real consumers' expenditure. Although the crime data are analysed in seasonally unadjusted form, no consistent seasonally unadjusted data are available for unemployment over the period. Consequently, the series shown in Figure 5.2 is the total number unemployed on a seasonally adjusted basis. Consumers' expenditure is readily available unadjusted and it exhibits rich seasonal characteristics (Osborn, 1988). Nevertheless, for the analysis of this section we wish to emphasise the long-run movements, so that it is graphed in the form of a moving annual average of log real consumption, with the moving average taken over the current and immediately preceding three quarters.

As noted in the Introduction, the effect of unemployment on crime has been of considerable interest in the literature of criminology. However, Figure 5.2 indicates that a long-run *linear* relationship with unemployment cannot be used as an explanation of the rise in crime over this period. This is obvious in that roughly comparable levels of unemployment in 1986 and 1993 are associated with very different crime levels. Indeed, total crime is about a third higher at the later date whereas the peak of unemployment is actually lower. Further, as Field (1990) notes over his longer period, there is also a problem in relating periods of increasing crime with increasing unemployment, because the upturn in crime typically pre-dates that of unemployment.[4] Thus, we conclude that there cannot be linear cointegration between unemployment and crime.

Field stresses the role of real consumption in explaining short-run changes in crime. Since his models use differenced data, he does not explicitly address the issue of any long-run relationship. Nevertheless, there are plausible reasons why such a long-run relationship might exist. Crime, whether property or personal, yields utility to the offender. It is then reasonable to assume that offenders will aspire to similar levels of consumption as those attained by the population as a whole. This implies a long-run positive relationship. Any such relationship is, however, likely to be modified by many other factors, including the ease with which legal employment can be obtained.

The analysis here of crime and the economy is not to imply that only economic factors are considered to be important for crime in the long-run. It seems obvious that social and criminological influences will also be important. Nevertheless, these factors are not only complex, but they are also closely interrelated. Thus, for example, the factors that have resulted in decreasing social control on individual behaviour have been associated with a period of long-term post-war growth in the economy. Here we take the position that although it may be conceptually possible to separate different types of long-run influences on crime, many of these effects can be proxied by macroeconomic aggregates. As a single macroeconomic variable, we concentrate on real consumers' expenditure as capturing the long-run aspirations of criminals. As already noted, and as suggested by Figure 5.2, any long-run relationship of crime with consumption will be positive. However, the rapidly rising crime rate of the late 1980s and early 1990s then represents a substantial and prolonged deviation from the long-run, because consumption was essentially static at this time while the numbers of personal and property crimes grew substantially.

Long-run modelling is undertaken using cointegration, with Table 5.2 showing the first-stage results obtained using the Engle-Granger (1987) two-step method. The augmented Dickey-Fuller (ADF) test is applied to the residuals of the first-stage regression to test for cointegration. Given the relatively short time series available, this approach is preferred to the vector autoregressive one of Johansen (1988). Initially, crime is regressed separately on consumption and on real gross domestic product (GDP). All the cointegrating test regressions include a constant and three seasonal dummy variables. Note that, to allow for the discontinuity in the definition of criminal damage, a dummy variable taking the value one in each quarter of 1975 and 1976 is included where appropriate.

Table 5.2 Testing the long-run relationship of crime with economic variables

Statistic	Burglary		Theft		Criminal Damage[a]		Aggregate Property[a]		Aggregate Personal		All Crimes[a]	
	Cons.[b]	GDP	Cons.[b]	GDP	Cons.[b]	GDP	Cons.[b]	GDP	Cons.[c]	GDP	Cons.[b]	GDP
Cons./GDP	1.59	2.07	1.40	1.84	2.20	2.98	1.49	1.98	1.82	2.41	1.49	1.99
R^2	0.730	0.691	0.836	0.807	0.968	0.957	0.864	0.829	0.969	0.947	0.871	0.836
ADF[c]	-3.40	-3.17	-3.70	-2.78	-2.68	-2.91	-4.13	-3.88	-4.15	-1.39	-4.08	-3.76
(augmentation)	(4)	(4)	(4)	(2)	(4)	(4)	(4)	(4)	(0)	(2)	(4)	(4)
Unemployment added to regression												
Cons./GDP	1.11	1.39	1.17	1.52	1.92	2.57	1.27	1.68	1.76	2.33	1.29	1.70
Unemployment	0.320	0.333	0.152	0.157	0.277	0.302	0.210	0.230	0.039	0.042	0.196	0.215
R^2	0.875	0.845	0.885	0.859	0.986	0.980	0.916	0.892	0.972	0.949	0.918	0.894
ADF[c]	-2.48	-1.91	-2.91	-2.67	-2.17	-2.17	-2.93	-2.49	-4.04	-1.44	-2.44	-1.63
(augmentation)	(4)	(3)	(2)	(2)	(4)	(4)	(4)	(4)	(0)	(2)	(2)	(0)

Note: All regressions include an intercept and three seasonal dummy variables.

a.   These regressions also include a dummy variable for 1975 and 1976 to allow for definitional change in criminal damage.

b.   Consumption is expressed as an annual moving average.

c.   Approximate critical values (MacKinnon, 1991) are: -3.42 and -4.05 at five and one per cent respectively for one regressor, -3.86 and -4.49 for two regressors.

Consumption, as used in Table 5.2 and Figure 5.2 above, is expressed as the average of the annual moving sum. This annual moving sum removes the nonstationary seasonal unit roots exhibited by the unadjusted series (Osborn, 1990), leaving the non-seasonal long-run component of interest here (Hylleberg *et al.*, 1990). The cointegration analysis was also performed using untransformed quarterly consumption, but the annual average always performed better. The GDP series is seasonally adjusted, since no unadjusted series was available over our entire sample period.

For the aggregate property, personal and all crime series, the ADF statistics indicate that a long-run relationship may, indeed, be present between each of these variables and real consumption. The R^2 values confirm that consumption explains long-run crime better than does GDP. The cointegration results for personal crime are not, however, convincing when examined further. The quoted ADF test regression for this case only just passes the residual autocorrelation test at five per cent (the p-value is 0.078). With an augmentation of four lags the residual diagnostics are more satisfactory, but the ADF statistic becomes -2.11. There is, in any case, the possibility that personal crime contains seasonal unit roots. If the annual moving average of personal crime is used to remove such roots, the ADF test statistic (using four lags) is -1.08. This value suggests that that there is no cointegration relating to the nonseasonal (or zero frequency) component; see Hylleberg *et al.* (1990). Finally, cointegration of both property and personal crime with consumption would imply that the two crime aggregates were themselves cointegrated, but a direct test yielded no evidence of such cointegration. We conclude that personal crime is not cointegrated with either real consumption or GDP.

Although we noted that unemployment could not be cointegrated with crime in a linear bivariate context, this does not preclude the possibility that it plays some role in conjunction with a variable such as consumption. This is investigated in the second part of Table 5.2. It is striking, however, that the addition of unemployment results, in almost every case, in weaker evidence for cointegration. Therefore, we dismiss the role of unemployment in terms of cointegration with crime variables.

In the next section we move from the long-run to a complete specification of the dynamic relationship between crime and the economy. This modelling is pursued at the level of aggregate property and aggregate personal crimes. Because of the inherently different nature of these two types of crimes, it is preferable to keep them separate. The property crime sub-categories of burglary, theft and criminal damage are not considered further in order to concentrate on the major aggregates. For property crime, consumption is used as the sole long-run explanatory variable. The estimated elasticity greater than one (approximately 1.5 in Table 5.2) implies that, in the long-run, criminals aspire to more than match percentage aggregate increases in consumption. In the light of the above discussion for personal crime, we abandon long-run modelling of this variable and consider the extent to which short-run changes can be explained.[5]

Dynamic Models of Crime and the Economy

Prior to undertaking any short-run modelling, one adjustment was made to the property crime series to allow for the definitional change in criminal damage which occurred at the beginning of 1977. The adjustment used the dummy variable included for 1975 and 1976 in the cointegrating regression of property crime with consumption, and the value of the dummy variable coefficient was added to each of the (log) property crime values for this period.

To induce stationarity, first differences are applied to property crime, but annual differences are taken for personal crime. There is no question of taking annual differences for the former according to the seasonal unit root tests of Table 5.1, but these tests are inconclusive on whether first or annual differences are appropriate for personal crime. However, the use of annual differences resulted in more satisfactory models. The graph for personal crime in Figure 5.2 helps to explain this. We noted above that the seasonal movements in this variable declined until the steep increase in personal crimes of the late 1980s, after which seasonality is again marked. This points towards nonstationarity in these seasonal movements and hence to the variable containing seasonal unit roots. Although the earlier unit root tests were not decisive, this visual evidence, and the more satisfactory short-run models found, led to the adoption of the annual difference in personal crime.

The differenced variables employed in the dynamic models are graphed in Figure 5.3. Due to the use of logarithms, these differenced variables can be interpreted as growth rates. Whether used as the dependent variable or as an explanatory variable, first differences are always used for property crime and annual differences for personal crime. As to the macroeconomic explanatory variables, first differences are used for unemployment while annual ones are taken for consumption due to the seasonal unit roots in the latter series (Osborn, 1990).

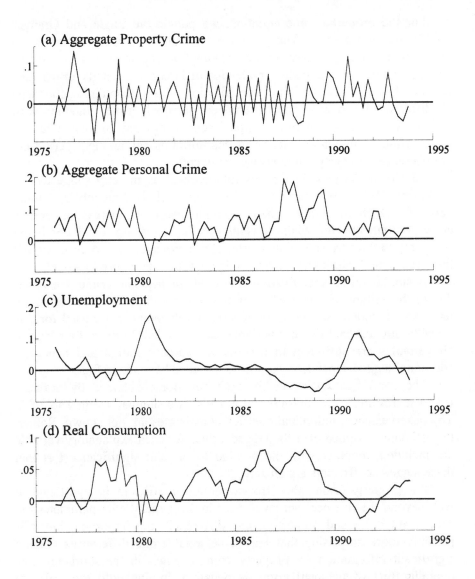

Note: First differences are taken for property crime and unemployment, annual differences are taken for personal crime and consumption.

Figure 5.3 Differenced variables used in dynamic models

For the property crime equation, we pursue the Engle and Granger (1987) two-step method. Thus, we now include the lagged residual from the cointegrated property crime/consumption equation as an error-correction term in a dynamic model for differenced property crime (see Chapter Two). A general initial specification is used, containing four lags of differenced property and differenced personal crime, together with differenced consumption and unemployment at lags zero to four inclusive. To alleviate some autocorrelation in this initial model, an eight period lag of differenced property crime is also included.

Due to our interest in the possible cyclical asymmetry suggested by Dickinson (1993), two further variables are included, namely a dummy variable which is unity when unemployment is increasing and a corresponding one for when consumption is increasing, the latter being compared to the corresponding quarter of the previous year. A constant and three seasonal dummies are also included in the property crime models.

A similar initial specification was used for personal crime. However, due to the failure to find a cointegrating relationship, no error-correction term was included. Secondly, since seasonal differences are used for this variable, no seasonal dummy variables are included. Further, four lags of all variables are sufficient to account for autocorrelation and hence no additional lagged dependent variable is included beyond lag four.

The coefficient estimates for both equations, obtained by ordinary least squares applied to these initial models,[6] are summarised in Table 5.3. To conserve space, individual coefficient estimates are not shown. Rather, the estimates summed over the lagged values for each explanatory variable are included, together with the p-value for a joint significance test that these lagged coefficients are all zero.

For property crime, the error-correction coefficient is significant at well beyond the five per cent level, even in this general over-parameterised specification. Lagged property crime differences are important, but it is possibly more surprising that lagged personal crime differences contain significant information for property crime changes in the short-run. The overall effect of personal crime is negative, in line with the different directions of short-run movement noted by Field (1990). In general, changes in consumption and unemployment appear to have little or no role in determining short-run property crime movements. An asymmetric effect for unemployment is, however, given credence by its significant positive coefficient when included as a simple sign dummy variable. On the other hand, increasing consumption seems to be unimportant as an explanation of property crime changes. The diagnostic tests do not throw up any problems with this equation. The results of the personal crime equation are discussed below.

Table 5.3   Initial models of short-run dynamics

Variable	Total Property[a]	Total Personal[b]	Total Personal[b]
Error-correction term	-0.214	-	-
Lag 1	(0.000)		
Property crime difference	0.868	-0.140	0.296
Lags 1,2,3,4[c]	(0.013)	(0.940)	(0.659)
Personal crime difference	-0.345	-0.032	-0.564
Lags 1,2,3,4	(0.008)	(0.371)	(0.362)
Consumption difference	-0.095	0.409	0.166
Lags 0,1,2,3,4	(0.938)	(0.588)	(0.479)
Unemployment difference	-0.248	-0.487	-2.332
Lags 0,1,2,3,4	(0.494)	(0.085)	(0.000)
Increasing unemployment dummy	0.0304	0.0038	0.0332
	(0.022)	(0.821)	(0.058)
Increasing consumption dummy	-0.0040	-0.0248	-0.0222
	(0.797)	(0.206)	(0.200)
Positive unemployment difference	-	-	1.883
Lags 0,1,2,3,4			(0.002)
R^2	0.804	0.507	0.680
SEE	0.029	0.039	0.034
Diagnostic tests: Significance levels			
Autocorrelation	0.283	0.521	0.209
Linearity	0.484	0.001	0.122
Normality	0.348	0.647	0.718
Heteroscedasticity	0.293	0.015	0.976

Note: The value shown is the sum of the individual coefficients, with the p-value for a (two-sided) joint test of zero coefficients given in parentheses.

   a.   The dependent variable in the property crime equation is the first difference.
   b.   The dependent variable in each personal crime equation is the annual difference.
   c.   Lag 8 is also included for the property crime equation.

Before leaving the property crime equation of Table 5.3, one further remark is in order. It will be recalled that Table 5.1 left the question of trend versus difference stationarity somewhat ambiguous for property crime. The issue was examined again in the context of the general model in Table 5.3 by comparing two specifications of the long-run, while maintaining the presence of short-run dynamics. In one the lagged cointegrating residual was replaced by a trend and the one-period lag of property crime itself, while in the other lagged average consumption and lagged property crime were used. The two sets of results were very similar, with R^2 values of 0.809 for the former and 0.808 for the latter. It remains true, therefore, that the data is unable to distinguish clearly between these two long-run specifications. On *a priori* grounds, we prefer the long-run explanation provided by consumption.

Beginning from the general property crime specification in Table 5.3, the model was refined. The strategy was to drop insignificant lagged (property and personal) crime terms and then insignificant consumption and unemployment terms. The failure to find any role for changes in consumption and unemployment was confirmed even when only one lag of each was included. Finally, the role of the two asymmetry dummy variables was investigated. Investigation revealed that the significance of the increasing unemployment dummy improved slightly when lagged by one quarter, with the lag 8 on the dependent variable then becoming insignificant. The consumption dummy was never close to a five per cent significance level for any specification. The final equation obtained by this process is shown in the first column of Table 5.4. Once again, results given include each estimated coefficient and its (two-sided) significance level.

In relation to the general specification of Table 5.3, the short-run dynamic equation for property crime in Table 5.4 holds no surprises. It is clear that recent past movements in personal crime retain a powerful role in explaining current property crime, with the negative coefficient indicating a possible substitution over time of property crime for personal crime. The annual lag for property crime itself suggests that the behaviour of criminals may include an element of seasonal habit-persistence, as does the action of other consumers (Osborn, 1988). The only short-run economic variable in this final specification is the lagged dummy indicating periods of increasing unemployment. As seen in Figure 5.2 or 5.3, swings in unemployment are smooth so this variable maintains a zero or one value for relatively long periods. This provides evidence to support Dickinson's (1993) asymmetry hypothesis, with crime increasing faster when unemployment grows than it declines in the opposite case.

Table 5.4   Dynamic models for property crime

Variable	Second-stage Equation 1975-1993	Single-stage Estimation 1975-1993	Single-stage Estimation 1975-1985	System Estimation 1975-1993
Error-correction Lag 1	-0.186 (0.000)	-	-	-
Consumption level Lag 1	-	0.344 (0.000)	0.388 (0.014)	0.337 (0.000)
Property crime level Lag 1	-	-0.203 (0.000)	-0.200 (0.010)	-0.201 (0.000)
Property crime diff.[a] Lag 4	0.452 (0.000)	0.412 (0.000)	0.307 (0.049)	0.432 (0.000)
Personal crime diff.[b] Lag 1	-0.322 (0.000)	-0.326 (0.000)	-0.354 (0.011)	-0.331 (0.000)
Personal crime diff.[b] Lag 2	0.204 (0.021)	0.173 (0.049)	0.168 (0.204)	0.187 (0.019)
Dummy variable ($\Delta_1 unemp_{t-1} > 0$)	0.029 (0.002)	0.035 (0.000)	0.027 (0.082)	0.034 (0.000)
Constant	-0.022 (0.045)	-1.101 (0.001)	-1.637 (0.104)	-1.052 (0.000)
Quarter 2	0.025 (0.025)	0.019 (0.076)	0.048 (0.015)	0.019 (0.049)
Quarter 3	-0.007 (0.448)	-0.009 (0.301)	-0.001 (0.947)	-0.008 (0.333)
Quarter 4	0.040 (0.002)	0.033 (0.011)	0.050 (0.013)	0.034 (0.003)
R^2	0.753	0.767	0.800	0.767
SEE	0.027	0.027	0.028	0.027
Diagnostic tests: Significance levels				
Autocorrelation	0.192	0.103	0.172	
Linearity	0.341	0.226	0.026	
Normality	0.193	0.312	0.686	
Heteroscedasticity	0.800	0.979	0.914	

Notes: The dependent variable is the first difference of aggregate property crime. Each value in parenthesis is the (two-sided) p-value for the significance test that the corresponding coefficient is zero.

The model was checked in a number of ways. To investigate whether asymmetry was pervasive, all the coefficients of the model were allowed to take different values when lagged unemployment changes were positive and when they were negative. No role could be found, however, beyond that of the simple switch dummy (the p-value for the test of constant slopes was 0.747). The second column of Table 5.4 shows the results when the two-stage estimation is collapsed into a single equation by explicitly including levels of lagged property crime and lagged average consumption in this dynamic specification. The effects are relatively slight, although the implied long-run elasticity of property crime with respect to consumption rises from 1.5 in Table 5.2 to 1.7 here. Further, results are shown in Table 5.4 for this latter equation estimated to the end of 1985. Although there is then some evidence of nonlinearity, the coefficient estimates themselves are quite robust. When the final 32 observations (1986-1993) are used to check structural stability, the Chow test is comfortably passed (p-value 0.701). This may be seen as a tough test since the date of the 'break' was chosen to pre-date the latest increase in unemployment.

The final column of Table 5.4 records the results of a joint estimation of the property and personal crime equations. We will return to that after considering the investigations of personal crime in a single equation context.

Returning to Table 5.3, the diagnostics for the personal crime model in the second column indicate that the model is unsatisfactory. The linearity and heteroscedasticity checks are not independent, but the problem seems to be that changes in personal crime are not a linear function of the variables employed here. Further investigation was undertaken and the key appeared to be an interaction of the dummy variable for increasing unemployment with unemployment itself. This led to the addition of a separate variable for unemployment increases; this variable is defined by multiplying the first difference of unemployment by the dummy variable for increasing unemployment. The new variable is included with the same lags (0 to 4 inclusive) as unemployment differences and hence has the effect of allowing each slope coefficient for unemployment to differ over quarters of increasing and decreasing unemployment. Both unemployment difference variables are highly significant, as seen in the final column of Table 5.3. Indeed, these results indicate that *only* unemployment changes are important in the explanation of personal crime movements. The success of this specification does, however, indicate that asymmetric responses to unemployment are far more pervasive for personal than for property crime.

Starting from this new general specification, an analogous approach to that for property crime was taken in order to specify a more parsimonious personal crime equation. In line with the results of Table 5.3, no role could be found for consumption differences or for lagged property crime differences. However, various forms of unemployment (both as a simple increasing unemployment dummy variable and through the unemployment differences) remained important and the annual lag of the dependent variable was also required. Indeed, when checking for slope asymmetry, the coefficient for the annual lag of personal crime differences was found to interact with the sign of the change in unemployment. This led to the dynamic specification for the personal crime equation shown in the first column of Table 5.5. Note, however, that the specification used for lagged unemployment differs slightly[7] from that in the final column of Table 5.3. In particular, Table 5.5 classifies two 'regimes', namely one when quarterly unemployment is currently rising and the second when it is falling.

Before looking at Table 5.5, it is worth examining further the relationship between changes in personal crime and changes in unemployment as revealed by Figure 5.3. The inverse relationship between the two variables appears obvious, but it is particularly marked in times of decreasing unemployment. Especially notable is the latter part of the 1980s when decreasing unemployment seems to be related to large positive changes in personal crime. It is, however, less clear that moderate increases in unemployment have any relationship at all with patterns in these crimes.

That message from Figure 5.3 lies behind the results of Table 5.5. Comparing the coefficient estimates of the first column over the two 'regimes', unemployment has much less effect on personal crime when unemployment is rising. Further, lagged personal crime itself plays a lesser role in this case. Despite the individual lack of significance of the three variables (other than the constant) in the increasing unemployment regime relationship, these variables are jointly highly significant (significance level 0.006). To put a numerical measure on these differences, the total multiplier can be used. For the case of increasing unemployment, the total multiplier for the effect of unemployment on personal crime is estimated to be -0.34, while in the decreasing unemployment case it is more than four times as great, at -1.53. Thus, an unfortunate side-effect of a long-term steady decline in unemployment is an increase in personal crime.

Table 5.5   Dynamic models for personal crime

Variable	Single Equation Estimation 1975-1993	Single Equation Estimation 1975-1985	System Estimation 1975-1993
Increasing unemployment regime			
Personal crime difference	-0.164	-0.097	-0.152
Lag 4	(0.201)	(0.583)	(0.193)
Unemployment difference	-0.196	-0.163	-0.158
Current	(0.375)	(0.583)	(0.436)
Unemployment difference	-0.201	-0.287	-0.200
Lag 1	(0.339)	(0.309)	(0.301)
Constant	0.060	0.056	0.058
	(0.000)	(0.000)	(0.000)
Decreasing unemployment regime			
Personal crime difference	-0.522	-0.143	-0.490
Lag 4	(0.000)	(0.736)	(0.001)
Unemployment difference	-1.479	-2.000	-1.528
Current	(0.002)	(0.166)	(0.000)
Unemployment difference	-0.855	-0.670	-0.777
Lag 1	(0.024)	(0.581)	(0.023)
Constant	0.0378	0.022	0.036
	(0.004)	(0.638)	(0.002)
R^2	0.598	0.370	0.596
SEE	0.032	0.035	0.032
Diagnostic tests: Significance levels			
Autocorrelation	0.989	0.957	
Linearity	0.175	0.635	
Normality	0.800	0.988	
Heteroscedasticity	0.942	0.541	

Notes: The dependent variable is the annual difference of aggregate personal crime.

Each value in parenthesis is the (two-sided) p-value for the significance test that the corresponding coefficient is zero.

As with property crime, other diagnostic checks were carried out on the estimated equation. Not surprisingly, a test that the three explanatory variables (lagged personal crime, current and lagged unemployment) have equal slopes across increasing and decreasing unemployment regimes clearly rejected equality (p-value 0.000). Further, when the equation was estimated to the end of 1985, the structural stability test was comfortably passed (p-value 0.517). This is quite remarkable, since it implies that the equation estimated using data to 1985 is compatible with the steep increase in personal crime experienced in the late 1980s; see Figure 5.3. Indeed, it is worth noting that the coefficients in the first and second columns of Table 5.5, representing estimates over the whole period and to 1985, are similar. The only exception is that of lagged personal crime, where its significance in periods of decreasing unemployment seems to derive principally from 1986 onwards.

The final econometric investigation undertaken here is a system estimation of the two equations for property and personal crime. This exploits the fact that the equations form a seemingly unrelated system and, if there is correlation in the disturbances across the two equations, then estimation exploiting this will yield increased efficiency. In practice, although a correlation of 0.21 was found between the residuals from the estimated equations, the coefficient estimates differ little from those obtained using ordinary least squares. Nevertheless, the results are shown in the final columns of Tables 5.4 and 5.5. A chi-squared test for vector residual autocorrelation to lag 4 in this dynamic system yields a satisfactory p-value of 0.38.

Conclusions

This chapter set out to examine the relationship between crime and UK macroeconomic aggregates in the context of quarterly crime data. One important relationship examined is that between consumption and crime. This was first emphasised by Field (1990) in the context of the annual growth in crime, but here the effect of consumption appears to be even more important. The effect is, however, restricted to property crime. Although not pursued, our seasonality analysis suggests that quarterly patterns in property crime may be linked to the same type of seasonal utility function as that which underlies consumers' expenditure. Indeed, our empirical models of the long-run indicate consumption provides an explanation of the secular increase in property crime. Short-run movements in such crimes are, however, modelled using the dynamics of crime and a dummy variable for periods of increasing unemployment. This last variable provides some evidence supporting Dickinson's (1993) argument that an increase in unemployment has a 'greater upward impact on criminal activity than does a decrease'.

The relationship between personal crime and the economy has not been as extensively studied to date as has the property crime case. Perhaps this is because recent empirical studies of crime have tended to focus on consumption and the rationale for a link of personal crime to consumption is less obvious than for property crime. Our failure to find an empirical link of personal crime to consumption is then, perhaps, not surprising. Indeed, at least within a linear framework, we do not find any economic explanation for the increase in personal crime observed over the last 20 years. Nevertheless we do find that short-run changes in personal crime react to the economy, with unemployment providing the link and with asymmetric responses of personal crime to increases and decreases in unemployment. This asymmetry appears to be more pervasive than that for property crime and it explains the failure to find a linear long-run relationship. If personal crime increases steeply when unemployment decreases, but responds little when unemployment rises, then a 'ratchet' effect will result which cannot be captured by a linear long-run specification. If correct, this ratchet implies that it will be very difficult to reverse the increases in personal crime observed in recent years.

Another interesting aspect of the results is that past changes in personal crime contain explanatory information for property crime, but the reverse does not apply. The negative effect appears to imply substitution over time from personal to property crime.

There remain a number of issues which this study has not been able to address. One is why the seasonal pattern in personal crime appears to be changing over time. Another is whether there is any time series relationship between crime and economic inequality. Evidence of a strong role for inequality has been found in cross-section analyses of British Crime Survey victimisation data (including Trickett *et al.,* 1995), while Chiu and Madden (1998) provide an economic theory of burglary based on inequality. It is known that inequality in the UK rose rapidly in the late 1980s (see, for example, Jenkins, 1996), but it remains to be established whether this played any role in the rise in crime over this period. Unfortunately, inequality data is not readily available in the same way as variables like consumption and unemployment, so this remains an area that is yet to be explored in a time series context.

Notes

1. The results contained in this chapter have been previously circulated under the title 'Crime and the UK Economy' as Working Paper 95/15 of the Robert Schuman Centre, European University Institute, Florence.
2. Written in terms of a single explanatory variable for simplicity, their ECM is of the form $\Delta^2 Y_t = \beta_1 \Delta X_t + \beta_2 (\Delta Y_t - \gamma_0 - \gamma_1 X_t) + \varepsilon_t$. With $\beta_2 = -1$ and $\gamma_1 = 0$, this becomes a model for ΔY in terms of ΔX.
3. All regressions commenced with four lagged values of the dependent variable added. This order of augmentation was decreased or increased as indicated by the significance of estimated coefficients and the F-test version of the autocorrelation test. Recent research concerned with seasonal unit roots does, however, throw doubt on the validity of this procedure. As shown by Ghysels, Lee and Noh (1994), the Dickey-Fuller test remains valid in the presence of seasonal unit roots, but at least three lags of the dependent variable have to be included in the quarterly case for this validity to hold. Rodrigues and Osborn (1999) show empirically that it is inappropriate to apply conventional tests to these initial lags and that doing so (as here) can result in a Dickey-Fuller test statistic which is substantially over-sized.
4. Dickinson (1993) argues that youth, not total, unemployment is the relevant measure for explaining crime and that youth unemployment has different turning points. The measure he uses is not, however, available quarterly.
5. Further investigation of a long-run relationship for personal crime and consumption was undertaken in the context of a single stage estimation of a short/long run model, but no satisfactory results were obtained.
6. The diagnostic tests reported are conventional. The significance levels are obtained using the F-test variants of a test for autocorrelation to order four, the addition of the squared fitted value (linearity) and a regression of the squared residual on the squared fitted value (heteroscedasticity). The normality test is a chi-squared test of skewness and kurtosis.
7. In Table 5.3 the sign of the appropriate lagged unemployment variable was used in defining the positive change in unemployment variable, whereas Table 5.5 is a switching model where the switch is defined in terms of the sign of current unemployment changes. These differ only when the sign changes between the lagged and current value.

References

Agiakloglou, C. and Newbold, P. (1992), 'Empirical Evidence on Dickey-Fuller Tests', *Journal of Time Series Analysis*, vol. 13, pp. 471-83.

Banerjee, A., Dolado, J. Galbraith, J.W. and Hendry, D.F. (1993), *Co-Integration, Error-Correction, and the Analysis of Non-Stationary Data*, Oxford University Press, Oxford.

Barsky, R.B. and Miron, J.A. (1989), 'The Seasonal Cycle and the Business Cycle', *Journal of Political Economy*, vol. 97, pp. 503-34.

Becker, G.S. (1968), 'Crime and Punishment: An Economic Approach', *Journal of Political Economy*, vol. 76, pp. 169-217.

Chiu, W.H. and Madden, P. (1998), 'Burglary and Income Inequality', *Journal of Public Economics*, vol. 69, pp. 123-41.

Deadman, D.F. and Pyle, D.J. (1997), 'Forecasting Recorded Property Crime Using a Time-Series Econometric Model', *British Journal of Criminology*, vol. 37, pp. 437-31.

Dickinson, D. (1993), *Crime and Unemployment*, Unpublished Paper, Department of Applied Economics, University of Cambridge.

Engle, R.F. and Granger, C.W.J. (1987), 'Cointegration and Error Correction: Representation, Estimation and Testing', *Econometrica*, vol. 55, pp. 251-76.

Field, S. (1990), *Trends in Crime and Their Interpretation. A Study of Recorded Crime in Post-War England and Wales*, Home Office Research Study no. 119, Home Office, London.

Fuller, W.A. (1976), *Introduction to Statistical Time Series*, Wiley, New York.

Ghysels, E., Lee, H.S. and Noh, J. (1994), 'Testing for Unit Roots in Seasonal Time Series: Some Theoretical Extensions and a Monte Carlo Investigation', *Journal of Econometrics*, vol. 62, pp. 415-42.

Hale, C. (1998), 'Crime and the Business Cycle in Post-War Britain Revisited', *British Journal of Criminology*, vol. 38, pp. 678-98.

Hylleberg, S., Engle, R.F., Granger, C.W.J. and Yoo, B.S. (1990), 'Seasonal Integration and Cointegration', *Journal of Econometrics*, vol. 44, pp. 215-38.

Jenkins, S.P. (1996), 'Recent Trends in the UK Income Distribution: What Happened and Why?', *Oxford Review of Economic Policy*, vol. 12, pp. 29-46.

Johansen, S. (1988), 'Statistical Analysis of Cointegration Vectors', *Journal of Economic Dynamics and Control*, vol. 12, pp. 231-54.

MacKinnon, J. (1991), 'Critical Values for Cointegration Tests', in R.F. Engle and C.W.J. Granger (eds), *Long-Run Economic Relationships*, Oxford University Press, Oxford.

Mayhew, P., Mirrlees-Black, C. and Maung, N.A. (1994), *Trends in Crime: Findings from the 1994 British Crime Survey*, Home Office Research and Statistics Department, Research Findings No. 14, Home Office, London.

Osborn, D.R. (1988), 'Seasonality and Habit Persistence in a Life Cycle Model of Consumption', *Journal of Applied Econometrics*, vol. 3, pp. 255-66.

Osborn, D.R. (1990), 'A Survey of Seasonality in UK Macroeconomic Variables', *International Journal of Forecasting*, vol. 6, pp. 327-36.

Osborn, D. R., Trickett, A. and Elder, R. (1992), 'Area Characteristics and Regional Variates as Determinants of Area Property Crime Levels', *Journal of Quantitative Criminology*, vol. 8, pp. 265-85.

Pudney, S., Deadman, D.F. and Pyle, D.J. (2000), 'The Relationship Between Crime, Punishment and Economic Conditions: Is Reliable Inference Possible When Crimes are Under-Recorded?', *Journal of the Royal Statistical Society Series A (Statistics in Society)*, vol. 163, pp. 81-97.

Pyle, D.J. and Deadman, D.F. (1994), 'Crime and the Business Cycle in Post-War Britain', *British Journal of Criminology*, vol. 34, pp. 339-57.

Reilly, B. and Witt, R. (1992), 'Crime and Unemployment in Scotland: An Econometric Analysis using Regional Data', *Scottish Journal of Political Economy*, vol. 39, pp. 213-28.

Rodrigues, P.M.M. and Osborn, D.R. (1999), 'Performance of Seasonal Unit Root Tests for Monthly Data', *Journal of Applied Statistics*, vol. 26, pp. 985-1004.

Trickett, A., Osborn, D.R. and Ellingworth, D. (1995), 'Property Crime Victimisation: The Roles of Individual and Area Influences', *International Review of Victimology*, vol. 3, pp. 273-95.

6. The Relationship Between Economic Conditions and Property Crime: Evidence for the United States

AMOR DIEZ-TICIO

Introduction

In recent years there has been an extensive discussion in the Social Science literature concerning the empirical relationship between economic conditions and crime. Although discussion of the link between these phenomena is not new, developments in economics of crime and improvements in econometric methods have stimulated such an investigation.

Until the mid 1980s, empirical papers used correlation analysis, single equation regressions or simultaneous equation systems to study the link (see Tarling, 1982; Freeman, 1983; Chiricos, 1987 or Pyle and Deadman, 1994a for a review of the literature). In some cases, the purpose was to show the influence of a unique magnitude related with the economic conditions on the level of crime. In others, mainly in the simultaneous equation systems, the economic variables were accompanied by other demographic, deterrence or social factors that could have an influence on criminal activity. Most of the studies used cross section data.[1]

However, as Field (1990) and Pyle and Deadman (1994b) pointed out, it is difficult to discover a causal relationship between crime and economic conditions in cross section studies. Crime spillovers across areas and the influence of third factors which may simultaneously affect both economic variables and crime may distort the relationship.

Since the mid 1980s, several studies have followed different data oriented approaches. Some researchers (Reilly and Witt, 1992; Cornwell and Trumbull, 1993; Marselli and Vaninni, 1997 and Levitt, 1998) have used panel data to control the unobservable characteristics of the units of observation that can be correlated with certain explanatory variables of the model. Other papers have used time series techniques to examine the relationship between the economy and recorded crime statistics. Initial studies using time series data usually transformed the variables of the model in an attempt to solve some statistical problems, so only provided evidence of the determinants of crime in the short run (Cook and Zarkin, 1985; Cantor and Land, 1985; Field, 1990). However, recent literature based on cointegration analysis does not make it necessary to transform the variables and, at the same time, tells us about the short and long run influence of different variables on crime (Viren, 1994; Pyle and Deadman, 1994a; Osborn, 1995 and Hale, 1998).

Surprisingly, the literature applying cointegration techniques to the study of the relationship between economic conditions and crime has been rarely used outside the UK (although see Corman *et al.*, 1987; Scorcu and Cellini, 1998 and Koskela and Viren, 1993). This fact plus the contradictory conclusions found in different studies of this relationship do not allow us to draw general conclusions about the influence of the economic conditions upon crime. Nevertheless, ultimately, whether or not there is a relationship between economic conditions and crime is an empirical issue.

The purpose of this chapter is to provide new evidence on this subject using annual data from the United States during the period 1950-1996. We make use of the cointegration tools provided by Johansen (1988) and Sims *et al.* (1990) to approach the question of modelling this issue and derive both the long and short term effects of economic variables on crime. In common with other studies, the model includes other explanatory variables in order to control for the impact of deterrence and demographic factors on criminal behaviour. In particular, we include the probability of being caught as representative of the deterrence factors and the proportion of young people in the population because they are considered to be a group that is more prone to act illegally.

The plan of the chapter is as follows. In the next section we describe the theories that relate crime to economic conditions, and report the main results given in recent papers. We then explore our data and the trends in criminal activity in both the United States and England and Wales. Finally we present our empirical analysis, which is used to derive the long and short-run relationship, and discuss our results.

The Relationship between Economic Conditions and Crime

One of the fundamental dilemmas confronting studies interested in establishing the determinants of crime is the role which economic conditions play in explaining variations in criminal activity. The association between these magnitudes is far from being a simple one, especially when we consider the conflicting effects indicated on both theoretical and empirical grounds.

In general terms, and following Field (1990), the relationship between economic conditions and crime can be explained in three different ways, namely motivation, opportunity and lifestyle effects. The first two approaches are closely related with the economic model of crime in which it is assumed that the individuals examine both legal and illegal options and choose the mixture of activities with the highest expected returns. The main difference between them lies in the emphasis that they give to either the benefits or the costs of crime. The motivational theory assumes that the condition of the economy determines the expected returns from legitimate activities. Hence, whilst economic prosperity enhances the possibility of acting legally, economic deprivation makes it more difficult to find a legal job with a legal income. Some researchers like Ehrlich (1973) and more recently Sala-i-Martin (1997) defend this perspective but have gone more deeply into it pointing out that this influence depends upon the social context of the economic changes. For example, if economic growth reduces the gap between the rich and the poor it could deter criminal inclination, otherwise, it could be associated with an increase on criminal activity.

Opportunity theory emphasises the benefits of illegal action instead of the returns of legal activities. From this point of view, it is argued that changes in economic conditions alter the number of suitable crime targets. In periods of economic growth more goods are available and the expected benefits from crime will be higher than in periods of bad economic conditions, providing favourable circumstances to criminal activity.

In addition to these two approaches, there is another explanation that focuses upon the victims of crime instead of the potential offender. This is known as the lifestyle or the guardianship effect and is more closely associated with sociologically oriented disciplines. The lifestyle effect relates economic conditions to changes in the pattern of routine activities. Economic growth contributes to drawing more people into the job market or allows more families to leave home for recreation and leisure activities and these factors increase the probability of being a victim of crime.

Although these three perspectives share the idea that the state of the economy plays an important role in explaining variations in crime, there is no consensus about the direction of the relationship. Whilst the second and the third effects predict a positive relationship between economic growth and crime, the first suggests an inverse association, at least, if there is an improvement in social conditions.

From a theoretical point of view, there are no strong grounds for preferring one argument to another. They all seem to be relevant in the explanation of the influences of economic conditions on crime and, perhaps, each perspective may be applicable in some situations though not in others. In particular, while some theories could be relevant in explaining criminal behaviour in the long run, others might well be appropriate in the short term. This makes it especially important to undertake empirical studies, which will shed light on both short and long run causal relationships between crime and economic indicators.

This kind of research was only recently developed in Europe, firstly by Pyle and Deadman (1994a) for England and Wales, using the modern tools supplied by cointegration methods and error correction models.[2] This pioneering work builds on a study by Field (1990) who analysed the short run impact of several variables on twelve different categories of offences. Pyle and Deadman improve this work by analysing the long-run relationship between crime and economic conditions. They also react to one of Field's main conclusions that suggests that consumption is the principal economic driver of crime rates. Their results indicate that consumption is only as important as other economic variables (GDP or unemployment) in explaining criminal statistics.

Since then, a small but increasing number of studies has appeared, based on the same methodology. Most of these works have used data from England and Wales either to re-examine some Pyle and Deadman's conclusions (Osborn, 1995; Hale, 1998); or to investigate some additional issues related to criminal activity (Pudney *et al.*, 2000 or Deadman and Pyle, 1997). Alternatively, several researches have applied the same approach to analyse other countries (Viren, 1994; Scorcu and Cellini, 1998; Beki *et al.*, 1999) in order to provide additional evidence of the influence of economic conditions on crime in different contexts.

In a general sense and leaving on one side the discrepancies in the results, this still scarce literature confirms that the economic situation is important in explaining either the trends in crime, the short run movements or both. The findings also show differences in the direction of the relationship between these two temporal scopes. Hence, the results of this incipient applied work acknowledge the importance of distinguishing between the long and short run determinants of crime in the study of the effects of economic conditions. Moreover, they support the view that several conflicting theories are compatible and provide some explanation in different situations. These ideas are taken as a point of departure for this chapter, which examines such a relationship using United States data. In the following sections we build an empirical model based on cointegration methods that allows us to analyse both the long and short run influence of economic conditions on crime rates.

Data

To specify our model, we have used annual data on aggregated crime rates, clear up rates, and variables representing the economic conditions of the United States from 1950 to 1996. Full details of the definitions of the variables and sources of data are given in Appendix A of this chapter.

The aim of this chapter is to determine the influence of several factors, mainly economic conditions, on criminal activity. However, our analysis does not take into account all criminal offences. We consider robberies (ROB), burglaries (BUR) and motor vehicle thefts (AUT) only. There are two reasons for doing this. First, other papers have examined similar crime categories (for example, Pyle and Deadman, 1994a; Osborn, 1995 and Hale, 1998). Concentrating on the same offences will allow us to compare our results with theirs.[3]

Second, although some studies have found that sex and violent crimes are related to economic conditions (Field, 1990; Scorcu and Cellini, 1998), property crimes seem more suitable cases for study in that they might be expected to respond directly to economic motivations.

The main sources of statistical information on crime in the United States are the Uniform Crime Report (UCR) and the National Crime Survey (NCS). The former presents estimates of the main categories of offence known and recorded by the police. The latter provides victimisation information of different types of offences from 1972. In order to obtain a longer time series, an important requirement in applying econometric methods, we make use of the information provided by the UCR. However, one of the most widely recognised disadvantages of these official criminal statistics is that there is a reporting and recording bias which can produce, if it is systematic, a spurious correlation among several variables, particularly deterrence factors. Although this chapter does not deal with the problem of underreporting of official crime statistics, some recent studies (Levitt, 1998; Pudney, *et al.*, 2000; MacDonald, 2000 and Chapter Three of this volume) show that measurement error may not be an important problem. We accept the results of these papers and assume that criminal statistics are a suitable source of data with which to undertake our analysis.

Information on robbery, burglary and motor vehicle theft rates in the United States from 1950-1996 are presented in Figure 6.1. As the plot shows, crime rates grew sharply in the 1960s. This upward trend is especially important in burglaries after the middle of the decade. In the 1970s, the crime rates fluctuate, whilst at the beginning of the 1980s crime rates fell. This pattern continued in burglary rates until the end of the period, while rates for robbery and motor vehicle thefts fluctuated. However, since the beginning of the 1990s these two latter crimes have turned downward. An interesting point is to compare these trends with those of other countries. In Appendix B, Figures B1, B2 and B3 show robbery, burglary and motor vehicle theft rates for both the United States and England and Wales. Similar patterns of burglary rates are found in both countries up to the early 1980s. From then on burglary rates in England and Wales are larger than in United States and the trend turns in the opposite direction. The robbery series indicates that this offence is much more important in United States than in England and Wales and the growth rates have been lower in the latter than in the United States.[4] In the case of motor vehicle theft, the existence in the English series of a break at the end of the 1960s prevents us from making comparisons, but since the 1970s the series have fluctuated in a similar pattern.

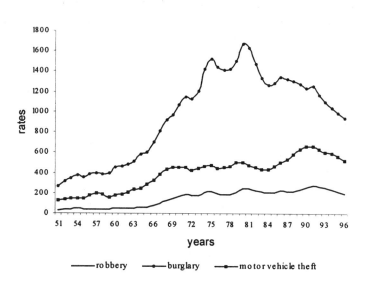

Figure 6.1 Crime rates in the United States

To explain the crime statistics, a range of economic, deterrence and demographic factors are included in the model. As pointed out above, there is no consensus as to what is the best variable to represent economic conditions. Given the importance of choosing the appropriate indicator, our investigation is conducted using three different specifications: a) in the first, we include personal consumption per capita (CONS); b) in the second, we include the unemployment rate (UNEM) and c) in the third, both variables are incorporated.[5] Whatever the chosen indicator(s), *a priori*, we do not know the influence of these variables on crime. As we have seen, opportunity and lifestyle theories predict a different relationship between crime and economic circumstances than do motivational theories.

The measurement of economic conditions through any one of the indicators mentioned above may fail to take account of the social consequences of economic change. For this reason, we include a measure of income inequality (INC). Two alternative measures are available for the whole period. The first is the standard index of income concentration (the gini index). The second measure is the share of aggregate income going to the poorest paid 20 per cent of income earners compared with that going to the highest paid 20 per cent. In the results reported below we have used the latter indicator only. The expected effect of this measure on crime is positive; as the inequality of income increases, so should criminal activity.

The model is completed with other variables related to illegal activity: the clear up rates for the different crime categories studied (CROB, CBUR, CAUT) and the proportion of the population aged between 15-24 years (YO). The former indicates the impact of the Criminal Justice System on the crime while the latter is set to show whether crime rates are affected by the age structure of the population. Finally, in conformity with common practice in this area, all variables are in natural logarithms.

Methodology

Once the relevant factors for explaining criminal behaviour have been chosen, we seek to select and estimate an econometric model that allows us to determine their impact in the United States' case. Earlier studies (Field, 1990; Deadman and Pyle, 1994a, Osborn, 1995; Hale, 1998) have shown that the effects of economic conditions could be different between the long and the short term. Hence, in what follows, we estimate an error correction model (ECM), as this is one of the most common approaches to incorporating both the long run relationship between the variables and short run behaviour (see Charemza and Deadman (1997) for a description of this method).

This section is organised in conformity with the three steps that should make up any study of time series data. Firstly, we study the time-series properties of the data we are dealing with. That is we attempt to determine the orders of integration of the variables in the study. Secondly, we test for existence of cointegrating relationships among the variables we are interested in. And finally, we estimate the model.

Orders of Integration

Before any estimation work can begin, we need to establish the properties of the series we are dealing with. The regression analysis will yield efficient estimates provided that the variables are stationary. However, the time series may not be stationary and so conventional regressions could lead to spurious relationships among variables.

Taking into account previous papers, it is assumed that economic and demographic variables are integrated of order one. There is, however, some ambiguity regarding the order of integration of the crime variables. While Pyle and Deadman (1994a) argued that these series were integrated of order two, Hale (1998), Osborn (1995), Scorcu and Cellini (1998) and Beki *et al.* (1999) found evidence to support the hypothesis of stationarity in first differences. Recently, Pudney *et al.* (2000), after adjusting the burglary series in England and Wales for the effect of a structural break caused by the Theft Act in 1968, conclude that the burglary rates are integrated of order one.

In this chapter, we use the Augmented Dickey-Fuller unit root test to analyse the stationarity of the crime series and the clear up rates for the offences under consideration. The level of augmentation has been chosen taking into account the Akaike Information, Schwarz Bayesian and Hannan-Quinn criteria. The results of the test (without trend) are reproduced in Table 6.1. They provide evidence that both the crime and clear up rate series for the United States are integrated of order one.

In 1957 the procedures used in the Uniform Crimes Reports to calculate the crime index changed. This fact could cause an alteration of the trend of the criminal statistics. As is well known, in such cases the Dickey-Fuller tests are biased towards non-rejection of the non-stationarity null hypothesis. For this reason the Perron type test that tests for unit roots in presence of a structural break is applied. The results, which are omitted in order to save space, do not reject the null of unit roots in levels. In other words, the conclusion about the stationarity of the variables does not change when this test is applied.

Since we have found evidence to show that the order of integration of the variables is one, the next issue to investigate whether there is a cointegrating relationship between them.

Table 6.1   Augmented Dickey-Fuller unit root test applied to crime variables

Variable	I(0)	I(1)
ROB	-1.3885 * (2.9303)	-3.6536 (2.9320)
BUR	-1.8096 * (2.9303)	-3.5586 (2.9320)
AUT	-1.4838 * (2.9303)	-3.0966 (2.9320)
CROB	-1.0070 (2.9303)	-3.2848 * (2.9320)
CBUR	-0.6272* (2.9303)	-4.7294 (2.9320)
CAUT	-2.8952 (2.9303)	-7.3479 (2.9320)

Note: The variables are as defined in the text. The critical value for Augmented Dickey-Fuller test is in parentheses. Results presented in this table are a test of stationarity around a non-zero constant. We also test for stationarity of the level of the variables around a linear trend and none of the variables are found to be stationary in levels. The results are confirmed by the Phillips and Perron (1988) test. The asterisk indicates one level of augmentation.

Testing for Cointegration Relationships

The aim of this section is try to find a cointegrating relationship between the variables that allows us to specify a long run relationship and an error correction model that shows the deviations from the long run path.

It is well known that there are different ways to test for the existence of cointegrating relationships between any set of variables. In this chapter, we use the maximum likelihood method introduced by Johansen (1988). One advantage of this methodology, which is based upon vector autoregressive modelling, is that the long run relationship can be analysed within a system of variables without having prejudged the endogenous-exogenous division between them. The possible simultaneity between some variables of an economics of crime model (see Chapter Two) makes this method especially fruitful. In the early literature, the most likely feedback was thought to be between crime rates and clear up rates. In other words, whilst criminal activity may respond to the performance of the criminal justice system, the success of these institutions in solving offences could depend on the level of crime.[6]

To avoid any simultaneity bias between the crime and deterrence variables included in the model, both crime and clear up rates are treated as endogenous. The rest of the variables of the model (those representative of the economic conditions, income inequality and young population) are considered to be exogenous.

In order to determine the number of cointegrating relationships (cointegration rank) we have carried out the long-run structural modelling approach described by Pesaran and Pesaran (1997) and have estimated an unrestricted vector autoregressive model (VAR) for each offence as follows.[7]

$$\Delta y_t = a_{0y} + a_{1y}t - \Pi_y z_{t-1} + \sum_{i=1}^{p-1} \Gamma_{iy} \Delta z_{t-1} + \psi w_t + u_t \qquad (6.1)$$

where $z_t = (y_t', x_t')$ with y_t being a column vector of jointly determined variables (both crime and clear up rates) and x_t a column vector of exogenous variables integrated of order one (unemployment, youth population and inequality index); w_t is a column vector of exogenous I(0) variables (a dummy variable to allow for the change in recording practice in 1957); α_0 is an intercept, t is a trend; p the order of the augmented VAR model and μ_t is a vector of serially uncorrelated shocks.

The lag order and the inclusion of trends and intercepts in the implicit VAR are required in order to obtain accurate conclusions. The lag order was chosen as $p = 1$ for robbery and burglary and $p = 2$ for motor vehicle theft which is the value preferred by both Akaike's information criterion (AIC) and Schwarz Bayesian criterion among $p = 1,...4$. With respect to the treatment of the intercept and trend, following a general criterion, we have incorporated an unrestricted intercept and trend.[8] The maximum likelihood approach provides two likelihood ratio tests for the number of cointegrating vectors that may exist as well as empirical estimates for each of the cointegrated relationships. We consider both of them in testing for cointegration, but if there is no agreement between these procedures we consider the test based on the maximal eigenvalue instead of the test based on the trace of stochastic matrix because, as Johansen and Juselious (1990) pointed out, the former is more powerful than the latter.

Model Estimates

Results of the test for the number of cointegrating relations in the robbery, burglary and motor vehicle theft models are presented in Table 6.2.

Table 6.2   Testing for cointegration: maximal eigenvalue test

	Null	Alternative	Test Statistic	95% critical value
ROB 1.	$r=0$	$r=1$	66.57**	29.74
	$r\leq1$	$r=2$	21.20	22.35
ROB 2.	$r=0$	$r=1$	65.47**	26.95
	$r\leq1$	$r=2$	17.92	19.62
ROB 3.	$r=0$	$r=1$	49.67**	26.95
	$r\leq1$	$r=2$	15.44	19.62
BUR 1.	$r=0$	$r=1$	53.12**	29.74
	$r\leq1$	$r=2$	14.84	22.35
BUR 2.	$r=0$	$r=1$	49.73**	26.95
	$r\leq1$	$r=2$	14.78	19.62
BUR 3.	$r=0$	$r=1$	41.13**	26.95
	$r\leq1$	$r=2$	12.43	19.62
AUT 1.	$r=0$	$r=1$	32.78**	29.74
	$r\leq1$	$r=2$	7.14	22.35
AUT 2.	$r=0$	$r=1$	24.34	26.95
	$r\leq1$	$r=2$	7.49	19.62
AUT 3.	$r=0$	$r=1$	33.38**	26.95
	$r\leq1$	$r=2$	4.76	19.62

Notes: Model 1. Includes unemployment and consumption.
            Model 2. Includes unemployment.
            Model 3. Includes consumption.
            All regressions include INC variable.
            ** denotes rejection of the null hypothesis.

According to the maximal eigenvalue, the hypothesis of no cointegrating vectors is clearly rejected in all the specifications with the exception of motor vehicle theft when the economic variable included in the model is the unemployment rate. In the other cases, the null hypothesis $r = 1$ against the alternative $r = 2$ cannot be rejected at the 95 per cent significant level. As a consequence, it would seem that there is only one cointegrating vector for the crimes analysed. Moreover, almost always one finds a cointegrating relation when unemployment and consumption are used either singly or in combination. This result is in accordance with those of Pyle and Deadman (1994) and Scorcu and Cellini (1998) who analyse three different variables individually and Pudney *et al.* (2000) who considered the role of unemployment and consumption jointly. By contrast, Hale (1998) and Osborn (1995) find only a cointegrating relation when the economic variable considered is consumption, a result that they use to argue that this magnitude is the best indicator of the economic conditions for explaining criminal activity. Finally, Beki *et al.* (1999) cannot obtain a cointegrating relationship between the 13 categories of Dutch theft rates analysed and each of the economic variables considered. This forces them to restrict their analysis to estimating the regressions in first differences.[9]

The cointegrating vector estimates of the economic conditions after being normalised on the crime rate variables are presented in Table 6.3. The results show a similar pattern in all the models estimated. In the long run, economic conditions, whether unemployment or personal consumption (either independently or jointly), have a strong influence on robbery, burglary and motor vehicle theft rates in the USA. Economic growth, associated with an increase in personal consumption and a reduction in unemployment, lead to an increase in the United States crime rates. These findings suggest that, in the long run, the relationship between the economic conditions and crime can be explained in terms of opportunity theories which associate improved economic conditions with an increase in criminal targets. This analysis, however, finds no evidence for the effect of inequality of income upon crime.

Table 6.3 **Estimated coefficients of the economic variables in the cointegrating vector**

Model	UNEM	CONS	INC
ROB 1.	-0.7113	1.2270	0.5930
	(0.2368)	(1.0982)	(0.6981)
ROB 2.	-0.8763	-	0.5403
	(0.2288)		(0.7564)
ROB 3.	-	3.4050	-0.0390
		(0.9167)	(0.6157)
BUR 1.	-0.3932	1.4379	0.2096
	(0.1576)	(0.7298)	(0.5163)
BUR 2.	-0.5647	-	0.1924
	(0.1910)		(0.6054)
BUR 3.	-	2.1794	0.4162
		(0.6188)	(0.3833)
AUT 1.	-0.8782	0.6738	1.9456
	(0.42)	(2.4743)	(1.6679)
AUT 3.	-	0.8245	1.8020
		(0.2916)	(1.4014)

Notes: See notes to Table 6.2 for a description of the models.
Standard errors are in parentheses.

The results relating to the influence of consumption on crime are in accordance to those of Hale (1998) and Osborn (1995).[10] However, our findings on the effect of unemployment on robbery, burglary and motor vehicle theft are in marked contrast with those of the previous literature. Hale and Osborn find no long run relationship when the economic conditions are represented by the unemployment rate. Pudney *et al.* (2000) obtain a cointegrating relation, but the coefficients appear not to be significant. By contrast, our results yield a significant, negative effect, which is consistent with the existence of an opportunity or lifestyle effect.

Error Correction Models

Having found a cointegrating vector between the variables of interest, it is possible to derive an error correction model (ECM) that incorporates both short run and long run relationships between the variables. The error correction mechanism describes how the system adjusts in each time period towards its long-run equilibrium state. In the short-run, deviation from the long-run equilibrium will feed back on the changes in the dependent variables in order to force its movements towards the long-run equilibrium state.

There are several ways to estimate error correction models such as Engle and Granger (1987) procedure, the Sims, Stock and Watson short-run dynamic model and those based on a vector autoregressive models. Whichever is chosen depends, to some extent, on the characteristics of the underlying theoretical model. If there is no clear division between the exogenous and endogenous variables it is best to estimate an error correction model based on a vector autoregressive approach. If there is only one endogenous variable, either the Sims, Stock and Watson specification or Engle and Granger procedure are also suitable.

The ECM estimates derived from the analysis developed previously (including consumption and unemployment in all crime categories) are presented in Table 6.4. The coefficients associated with the error correction term in the equations of robbery, burglary and motor vehicle theft in first differences (i.e. Δ ROB, Δ BUR, Δ AUT) are all significant and negative. It indicates the role of the variables in correcting for any deviation from the long run. The error correction terms for burglary and robbery are similar and much larger than that for motor vehicle theft, which suggests a faster adjustment for the former types of offence.

The error correction terms are in accordance with those that appear in other studies. For example, the error correction terms that Hale (1998) obtains are -0.223 for burglary and -0.208 for theft. Osborn (1995) estimates -0.63 for property crimes while Scorcu and Cellini's (1998) results range from -0.63 in the case of homicide to -0.19 for robbery.

Sims, Stock and Watson models

The estimation process developed in the previous section shows a significant long run effect of economic conditions on crime rates. However, the influence of these factors could be different in the short term. For this reason, it is interesting to investigate the impact of the economic factors on crime in both the long run and the short run.

One way to analyse the short run influence of different variables on the crime rates is to estimate a Sims, Stock and Watson (1990) type model. This approach is a derivation of the Engle and Granger (1987) procedure involved in estimating the long and the short run parameters of the model in a single step. Once it is demonstrated that there is a cointegrating relationship between the variables, the dynamic model is written in the form:

$$\Delta y_t = \alpha + \vartheta_1 \Delta x_t + \vartheta_2 y_{t-1} - \vartheta_2 \beta_0 - \vartheta_2 \beta_1 x_{t-1} + \varepsilon_t \qquad (6.2)$$

in which the long run regression is given by:

$$y_t = \beta_0 + \beta_1 x_t + \mu_t \qquad (6.3)$$

where y is the variable to be explained and x represents the explanatory variables.

Table 6.4   Error correction specification for the models

	Δ ROB	Δ BUR	Δ AUT
ECM	-0.3131	-0.3530	-0.1573
	(-7.8236)	(-8.6452)	(-1.7999)
TREND	-0.0068	0.0046	0.0033
	(-7.2449)	(4.3014)	(-1.1967)
INTER	1.7117	-3.4151	-0.1758
	(8.0593)	(-8.4375)	(-1.7399)
$\overline{R}^2$	0.63	0.75	0.53
	0.1517	1.9908	3.2937
SC	(0.697)	(0.158)	(0.070)
	0.0023	0.1058	0.0335
FF	(0.959)	(0.745)	(0.855)
	1.2109	0.9289	0.6926
N	(0.546)	(0.628)	(0.707)
	0.5156	0.1215	0.7922
H	(0.473)	(0.727)	(0.373)

Note: t-statistics are given in parentheses. The diagnostic tests are chi-squared statistics for serial correlation (SC), functional form (FF), normality (N) and heteroscedasticity (H).

As shown in equations (6.2) and (6.3), one of the requirements for applying this model is to ensure that there is only one dependent variable and, in consequence, all of the variables on the right- hand side are exogenous. If this is not the case, the estimated coefficients will show a simultaneous equation bias and the model will be miss-specified. Therefore, if we wish to apply this method in our analysis we need to determine whether the explanatory variables are actually exogenous or, if there is feedback between them, which advises against using this procedure.

The number of cointegrating vectors found in the Johansen procedure and the analysis of the error correction terms developed in the previous section are used to examine causality between the crime and the clear up rates (see for this issue Charemza and Deadman, 1997). If there is only one cointegrating vector and the ECM is only significant in the equation representative of the crime rates, there are no reasons to support simultaneity between crime rates and clear up rates.[11] Our previous analysis found only one cointegrating vector for all crime categories analysed (see Table 6.2) and at the same time, the error correction mechanism is insignificant in the robbery, burglary and motor vehicle theft clear up rate regressions.[12]

For these reasons, we assume exogeneity between the crime rates and the clear up rates. These results are in accordance with those of Corman *et al.* (1987), who used a vector autoregressive regression to examine the simultaneity between the arrest rates and the crime rates in New York City (see also Chapter Two of this volume). Given that causality is going in only one direction, we can use the Sims, Stock and Watson model to estimate the offence equations.

As a first step, the regressions are estimated by adding two lags to the economic variables in first differences to allow for the possibility of lagged effects. Following the general-to-specific approach we drop those variables in differences with a t-value of less than one.

The results of the final models are presented in Tables 6.5-6.7. They all pass the main tests of mis-specification and have high coefficients of determination, indicating that they are well-specified with a suitable goodness of fit. Further, the signs of the long run estimated coefficients are similar to those calculated in the previous section, although in the regressions based on the Sims, Stock and Watson model the influence of unemployment appears to be stronger than the influence of consumption. In addition to that, the indicator of income inequality has a strong positive effect on robbery rates, indicating that when income inequality increases, rates of robbery are higher. Clear up rates are significant with the expected sign in all offences analysed, which corroborates the deterrent effect of the Criminal Justice System.

Table 6.5 The Sims, Stock and Watson model for robbery

	Coefficient	t value
INTER	-0.9581	-0.5444
ROB(-1)	-0.3352	-2.8064
CROB(-1)	-0.5340	-2.2456
UNEM(-1)	-0.3205	-5.0401
CONS(-1)	0.0569	0.2802
INC(-1)	0.7698	2.7058
YO(-1)	1.1157	3.3855
D57	0.1441	3.5641
Δ CROB	-0.9914	-6.3523
Δ CONS	-1.1635	-1.993
Δ CONS(-2)	0.6823	1.61
Δ UNEM	-0.0794	-1.1055
Δ UNEM(-1)	0.1226	1.7480
Δ UNEM(-2)	0.0687	1.1584
Δ INC	0.7064	2.7640
Δ D57	0.1635	2.6011

Note: Δ indicates that the variables are in first differences.
Diagnostic tests: $R^2 = 0.84$
Test for serial correlation $\chi^2 (1) = 1.987$ ($p = 1.159$)
Functional form $\chi^2 (1) = 1.492$ ($p = 0.222$)
Normality $\chi^2 (2) = 1.586$ ($p = 0.452$)
Heteroscedasticity $\chi^2 (1) = 0.125$ ($p = 0.724$).

The coefficients of the first difference regressors indicate the short run influences of the explanatory variables on each category of crime. Again, economic conditions play an important role, as the estimated coefficients of both consumption and unemployment are often significant. In the short term changes in consumption per capita appear to be significant in all regressions (the current value in both robbery and burglary regressions and two lagged value in motor vehicle theft). The negative effect is opposite to that found in the long run. It provides support to the motivational theory and indicates that an improvement of the economic conditions reduces the criminal activity in the short run. These results are in accordance to those of Pyle and Deadman (1994a), Pudney *et al.* (2000) Hale (1998) and Beki *et al.* (1999).[13]

By contrast, Osborn (1995) fails to find any short run relationship between the economic variable and crime rates.

Table 6.6 The Sims, Stock and Watson model for burglary

	Coefficient	t value
INTER	-1.2856	-0.8149
BUR(-1)	-0.3844	-4.0845
CBUR(-1)	-0.0625	-0.2986
UNEM(-1)	-0.1192	-3.2548
CONS(-1)	0.3419	1.3129
INC(-1)	0.1123	0.5509
YO(-1)	1.0202	4.1654
D57	0.0640	2.4806
Δ CBUR	-0.4228	-2.1350
Δ CONS	-1.1823	-3.4011
Δ CONS(-2)	0.7151	1.4506
Δ UNEM(-2)	0.05314	1.3183
Δ INC	0.2950	1.5497

Note: Δ indicates that the variables are in first ifferences.
Diagnostic tests: $R^2 = 0.79$
Test for serial correlation $\chi^2 (1) = 1.329$ ($p = 0.249$)
Functional form $\chi^2 (1) = 1.411$ ($p = 0.235$)
Normality $\chi^2 (2) = 7.329$ ($p = 0.260$)
Heteroscedasticity $\chi^2 (1) = 0.152$ ($p = 0.6964$).

The short-term effect of the unemployment rate is less straightforward. In its 'current' form it is only found to be significant in the motor vehicle theft equation (Table 6.7). The signs of the lagged values in the robbery and burglary equations are positive, although the level of significance is not high. This indicates that changes in current unemployment have a negative effect on crime while the lagged values seem to work in the opposite direction. These results are in marked contrast with those of Pyle and Deadman (1994a), Pudney *et al.* (2000) and Hale (1998) who all find a clear positive relation. However, they are in accordance with some earlier work using United States data (Cantor and Land, 1985; Allen, 1996).

Table 6.7   **The Sims, Stock and Watson model for motor vehicle theft**

	Coefficient	t value
INTER	-0.1538	-0.2356
AUT(-1)	-0.1093	-1.3397
CAUT(-1)	-0.2850	-1.2406
UNEM(-1)	-0.1278	-3.0739
CONS(-1)	0.0574	0.3514
INC(-1)	0.0495	0.2862
YO(-1)	0.1540	0.8944
D57	0.1399	3.6546
Δ CAUT	-0.1077	-1.998
Δ CONS(-2)	-0.901	-2.2022
Δ UNEM	-0.1299	-3.4172
Δ YO	1.0509	1.5212

Note: Δ indicates that the variables are in first differences.
Diagnostic tests: $R^2 = 0.62$
Test for serial correlation $\chi^2 (1) = 2.573$ ($p = 0.109$)
Functional form $\chi^2 (1) = 0.527$ ($p = 0.468$)
Normality $\chi^2 (2) = 1.368$ ($p = 0.505$)
Heteroscedasticity $\chi^2 (1) = 0.400$ ($p = 0.527$).

Conclusion

This chapter has estimated the effect of the economic conditions on robbery, burglary and motor vehicle theft rates in the United States in the post-war period. There is a good deal of theoretical and empirical literature that supports the assertion that variation in the level of economic well-being is associated with changes in the rate of crimes. But there are few studies that apply cointegration tools to discover both the short and the long run effects of economic conditions upon crime. Following the approach of Pyle and Deadman (1994a), we have developed an error correction model to study these issues trying to discover whether the role of economic conditions is the same in both the long and the short run.

Our findings are consistent with those of recent studies, in the sense that economic conditions appear to play an important role in explaining criminal behaviour. Moreover, the influence of economic conditions seems to be different in the short and the long run. While in the latter there is clear evidence of an opportunity effect, the motivational effect seems to dominate in the short run. The one major difference we find is the consistently negative long run effect of unemployment upon all rates of crime.

In summary, our results confirm the usefulness of error correction models for dealing with these issues. This approach captures both short run dynamics and long run relationships. However, little empirical work has been done up to now. It would be valuable to examine whether the results can be replicated with other data. It is hoped that, in the future, new research using this methodology will be applied to data sets for other countries and time periods.

Notes

1. There was also some work using time series data in this period. See, for example, Wolpin (1978), Phillips *et al.* (1972) and Danzinger and Wheeler (1975).
2. Koskela and Viren (1993) report an error correction model which was used to study motor vehicle thefts in Finland. However, they mainly investigated the impact of deterrence variables rather than those related to economic conditions.
3. In fact, the studies mentioned above consider different kinds of offence categorised as theft instead of the single category of motor vehicle thefts. In the United States, larcenies have been the subject of definitional changes during the period under consideration. To avoid inconsistencies in the data we examine motor vehicle theft only.
4. However, recall that we use crime series based on offences recorded by the police. Langan and Farrington (1998) point out that the trends are different if crime rates are measured by crime surveys. In particular, in their study of Crime and Justice in the United States and England and Wales over the period 1981-96, they show that whilst the U.S. robbery rate as measured in victim surveys was nearly double England's in 1981, by 1995 the rate in England was 1.4 times the rate in the USA.
5. Some papers include additional indicators of economic conditions. For example, Pyle and Deadman (1994a), Osborn (1995), Hale (1998) investigate the importance of gross domestic product (GDP) as an explanatory variable. The consensus seems to be that consumption and/or unemployment are preferred to GDP.
6. The argument that crime rates are a determinant of the clear up rates is usually founded on production theory grounds. It is argued that the level of criminal activity determines the workload of the police. So, the more criminal activity there is, the lower the clear up rate.
7. This is a generalised version of Johansen's (1991,1995) maximum likelihood approach to the problem of estimation in the context of vector autoregressive error correction models.
8. We also calculated the cointegrating vector with restricted intercept and no trend and the results were quite similar.
9. Pyle and Deadman (1994a), Osborn (1995) and Hale (1998) consider three different specifications with three alternative economic indicators: gross domestic product, personal consumption and unemployment. The same procedure is followed in Scorcu and Cellini (1998) but, in this case, gross domestic product is substituted by nonhuman

wealth. Beki *et al.* (1999) choose five alternative variables: real personal consumption per capita, number of unemployed people, basic social security benefits, number of cars and new cars and the number of births.

10. Although Scorcu and Cellini (1998) obtain significant findings between economic conditions and crime in the long run, it is difficult to compare our results with theirs. They investigate whether the series are cointegrated in the presence of a structural break. As a result, the long run regression includes the economic variables both before and after the break. The instability of the coefficients in this situation prevents them from reaching a general conclusion about the influence of economic conditions on crime.

11. This second condition is based on the concept of short run causality provided by Engle and Granger (1987). A variable can be regarded as weakly exogenous if the error correction mechanism is not significant in the regression representing the short-run dynamics of this variable.

12. The ECM coefficients for robbery, burglary and motor vehicle theft clear up rates equations are 0.020, -0.165 and -0.157 with t-values of 0.558, -0.533, and -0.936 respectively.

13. Hale (1998) and Beki *et al.* (1999) also include current and lagged values of the economic variables. In general, their results support the existence of a current motivational effect and a lagged opportunity effect.

References

Allen, R.C. (1996), 'Socioeconomic Conditions and Property Crime: A Comprehensive Review and Test of the Professional Literature', *American Journal of Economics and Sociology*, vol. 55, pp. 293-307.

Beki, C., Zeelenberg, K. and Monfort, K. (1999), 'An Analysis of Crime in the Netherlands 1950-93', *British Journal of Criminology*, vol. 39, pp. 401-15.

Cantor, D. and Land, K.C. (1985), 'Unemployment and Crime Rates in Post World War II United States: a Theoretical and Empirical Analysis', *American Sociological Review*, vol. 50, pp. 317-32.

Charemza, W.W. and Deadman, D.F. (1997), *New Directions in Econometric Practice*, Edward Elgar, Cheltenham.

Chiricos, T.G. (1987), 'Rates of Crime and Unemployment: an Analysis of Aggregate Research Evidence', *Social Problems*, vol. 34, pp. 187-212.

Cook, P.J. and Zarkin, G.A. (1985), 'Crime and the Business Cycle', *Journal of Legal Studies*, vol. 14, pp. 115-28.

Corman, H., Joyce, T. and Lovitch, N. (1987), 'Crime, Deterrence and the Business Cycle in New York City: a VAR Approach', *The Review of Economics and Statistics*, vol. 69, pp.695-700.

Cornwell, C. and Trumbull, W.N. (1993), 'Estimating the Economic Model of Crime with Panel Data', *The Review of Economics and Statistics*, vol.75, pp. 360-66.

Danzinger, S. and Wheeler, D. (1975), 'The Economics of Crime: Punishment or Income Redistribution?', *Review of Social Economy*, vol. 33, pp. 113-31.

Deadman, D.F. and Pyle, D.J. (1997), 'Forecasting Recorded Property Crime using a Time-Series Econometric Model', *British Journal of Criminology*, vol. 37, pp. 437-45.

Ehrlich, I. (1973), 'Participation in Illegitimate Activities: A Theoretical and Empirical Analysis', *Journal of Political Economy*, vol. 81, 521-64.

Engle, R.F. and Granger, C.W.J. (1987), 'Co-integration and Error Correction: Representation, Estimation and Testing', *Econometrica*, vol. 55, pp. 251-76.

Field, S. (1990), *Trends in Crime and Their Interpretation. A Study of Recorded Crime in Post-War England and Wales*, Home Office Research Study no. 119, Home Office, London.

Freeman, R.B. (1983), 'Crime and Unemployment', in J.Q. Wilson (ed), *Crime and Public Policy*, Institute of Contemporary Studies Press, London, pp. 89-106.

Hale, C. (1998), 'Crime and the Business Cycle in the Post-war Britain Revisited', *British Journal of Criminology*, vol. 38, pp. 681-98.

Johansen, S. (1988), 'Statistical Analysis of Cointegration Vectors', *Journal of Economic Dynamics and Control*, vol.12, pp. 231-54.

Johansen, S. (1991), 'Estimation and Hypothesis Testing of Cointegrating Vectors in Gaussian Vector Autoregressive Models', *Econometrica*, vol. 59, pp. 1551-80.

Johansen, S. (1995), *Likelihood-based Inference in Cointegrating Vector Autoregressive Models*, Oxford University Press, Oxford.

Johansen, S. and Juselius, K. (1990), 'Maximum Likelihood Estimation and Inference on Cointegration-with Applications to the Demand for Money', *Oxford Bulletin of Economics and Statistics*, vol. 52, pp. 169-210.

Koskela, E. and Viren, M. (1993), 'An Economic Model of Auto-Theft in Finland', *International Review of Law and Economics*, vol. 13, pp.179-91.

Langan, P.A. and Farrington, D.P. (1998), *Crime and Justice in the United States and England and Wales, 1981-96*, U. S. Department of Justice, Bureau of Justice Statistics, NCJ 169284.

Levitt, S.D. (1998), 'Why do Increased Arrest Rates Appear to Reduce Crime: Deterrence, Incapacitation or Measurement Error?', *Economic Inquiry*, vol. 36, pp. 353-72.

MacDonald, Z. (2000), 'Revisiting the Dark Figure: A Microeconomic Analysis of Underreporting of Property Crime and its Implications', *British Journal of Criminology*, forthcoming.

Marselli, R. and Vannini, M. (1997), 'Estimating a Crime Equation Model in Presence of Organised Crime: Evidence from Italy', *International Review of Law and Economics*, vol. 17, pp. 89-113.

Osborn, D.R. (1995), *Crime and the UK Economy*, Robert Schuman Centre, Working Paper, no. 95/15, European University Institute.

Perron, P (1989), 'The Great Crash, the Oil Price Shock and the Unit Roots Hypothesis', *Econometrica*, vol.57, pp. 1361-1401.

Pesaran, M.H. and Pesaran, B. (1997), *Working with Microfit 4.0*, Oxford University Press, Oxford.

Phillips, L., Votey, H.L. and Maxwell, D. (1972), 'Crime, Youth and the Labor Market', *Journal of Political Economy*, vol. 80, pp. 491-504.

Phillips, P.C.B. and Perron, P. (1998), 'Testing for a Unit Root in Time Series Regression', *Biometrika*, vol. 75, pp. 335-46.

Pudney, S., Deadman, D.F. and Pyle, D.J. (2000), 'The Relationship Between Crime, Punishment and Economic Conditions: Is Reliable Inference Possible When Crimes are Under-Recorded?', *Journal of the Royal Statistical Society Series A (Statistics in Society)*, vol. 163, pp. 81-97.

Pyle, D.J. (1983), *The Economics of Crime and Law Enforcement*, Macmillan, London.

Pyle, D.J. (1995), 'The Economic Approach to Crime and Punishment', *Journal of Interdisciplinary Economics*, vol.6, pp. 1-22.

Pyle, D.J. and Deadman, D.F. (1994a), 'Property Crime and the Business Cycle in Post-War Britain', *British Journal of Criminology*, vol. 34, pp. 339-57.

Pyle, D.J. and Deadman, D.F. (1994b), 'Crime and Unemployment in Scotland: Some Further Results', *Scottish Journal of Political Economy*, vol. 41, 314-24.

Reilly, B. and Witt, R. (1992), 'Crime and Unemployment in Scotland', *Scottish Journal of Political Economy*, vol. 39, pp. 213-28.

Sala-i-Martin, X. (1997), 'Transfers, Social Safety Nets, and Economic Growth', *International Monetary Fund Staff Papers*, vol.44, pp. 81-102.

Scorcu, A.E. and Cellini, R. (1998), 'Economic Activity and Crime in the Long Run: An Empirical Investigation on Aggregated Data from Italy, 1951-1994', *International Review of Law and Economics*, vol.18, pp. 279-92.

Sims, C.A., Stock, J.H. and Watson, M.W. (1990), 'Inference in Linear Time Series Models with Some Unit Roots', *Econometrica*, vol. 58, pp. 113-44.

Tarling, R. (1982), *Crime and Unemployment*, Home Office Research and Planning Bulletin, 12, Home Office, London.

Viren, M. (1994), 'A Test of an Economics of Crime Model', *International Review of Law and Economics*, vol. 14, pp. 363-70.

Wolpin, K.I. (1978), 'An Economic Analysis of Crime and Punishment in England and Wales, 1894-1967', *Journal of Political Economy*, vol. 86, pp. 815-40.

APPENDIX 6.1

Definitions of variables and data sources

All variables used are in logarithmic form.

ROB:

Number of robberies known to the police per 100,000 inhabitants.

Source: Uniform Crime Reports and Crime in United States. Federal Bureau of Investigation.

BUR:

Number of burglaries known to the police per 100,000 inhabitants.

Source: Uniform Crime Reports and Crime in United States. Federal Bureau of Investigation.

AUT:

Number of motor vehicle thefts known to the police per 100,000 inhabitants.

Source: Uniform Crime Reports and Crime in United States. Federal Bureau of Investigation.

CROB, CBUR and CAUT:

Percentage of robberies, burglaries and motor vehicle thefts cleared by arrest, respectively.

Source: Uniform Crime Reports.

UNEM:

United States unemployment rate.

Source: Bureau of Labour statistics.

CONS:

Personal consumption expenditures per capita, 1992 prices.

Source: Survey of Current Business.

YO:

Number of people between 15-24 years as a proportion of U.S. population.

Source: Historical Statistics of the United States and The Digest of Education Statistics (Table 14).

INC:

Share of aggregate income received by the lowest fifth compared with the highest fifth.

Source: March Current Population Survey.

APPENDIX 6.2

Crime rates in England and Wales and the United States.

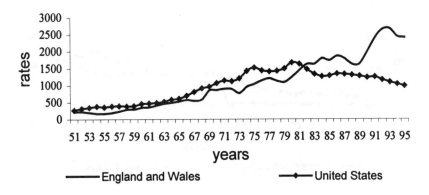

Figure 6.A.1 Robbery rates

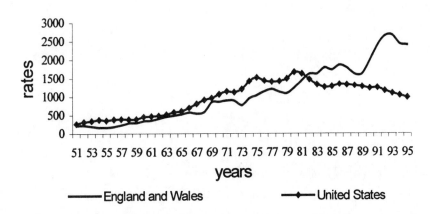

Figure 6.A.2 Burglary rates

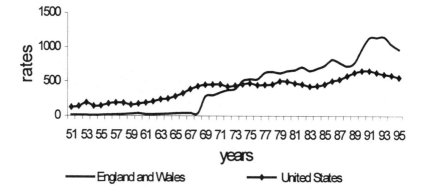

Figure 6.A.3   Motor vehicle theft rates

7. Imprisonment versus Fines: A Theoretical Perspective

INGOLF DITTMANN*

Introduction

The economic literature on crime and punishment, pioneered by Becker (1968) and Polinsky and Shavell (1979, 1984), applies the economic approach of decision making under uncertainty to criminal behaviour, assuming that the behaviour of criminals does not differ in principle from the behaviour of other economic agents. This chapter reviews and develops this literature by considering the question of which type of punishment, imprisonment or fine, is optimal under various circumstances. Note that, in these models, the sole purpose of any form of punishment is to deter individuals from committing crimes.

Apart from deterrence, two further rational justifications for punishing criminals have been given: rehabilitation, which aims at reducing individual recidivism through training and other incentives; and incapacitation (i.e., restraining the offender so that he is unable to repeat his offence), which is usually achieved by lengthy imprisonment. Using a market model of crime and punishment, Ehrlich (1981) shows that rehabilitation and incapacitation have only limited influence on the overall crime rate compared to the deterrent effect of punishment. Ehrlich argues that other individuals will replace most of the convicted and successfully removed offenders, in order to exploit the prevailing opportunities for illegitimate rewards. Moreover, Ehrlich demonstrates that successful rehabilitation increases the incentives to commit a crime in the first place. Hence, from a theoretical point of view, deterrence is more effective than incapacitation or rehabilitation, if criminals do not differ substantially from other individuals.

Furthermore, empirical studies have failed to demonstrate that rehabilitation could be achieved in any systematic way. In an extensive review of rehabilitation evaluation studies, Lipton et al. (1975) draw the overall conclusion that most programs did not show consistent evidence of effectiveness. Therefore, rehabilitation does not seem to be a convincing economic justification for punishing criminals.

Empirical evidence for incapacitation, on the other hand, is difficult to obtain, because it is often impossible to separate incapacitation and deterrence effects on the rate of crime. An increase in the expected length of imprisonment can reduce the crime rate either because criminals are deterred by the higher punishment or because more criminals are imprisoned and hence incapable of committing further crimes. Taking advantage of differences in arrest rates over time and between major U.S. cities, Levitt (1998a) presents empirical evidence that deterrence is generally more important than incapacitation (significant incapacitation effects could only be found for robbery and rape). The result that imprisonment has a strong deterrent effect is confirmed in further empirical studies by Levitt (1998b) and Kessler and Levitt (1999). Therefore, this chapter (and most of the economic literature on crime and punishment) focuses on the deterrent effect of punishments.

An important and straightforward result of the literature on crime and punishment is that fines are more efficient than imprisonment, in the sense that – if the same deterrent effect can be achieved by a fine and by a prison term – it is preferable to use the fine. The obvious reason is that fines are a much cheaper way to punish an individual than imprisonment, since imprisonment wastes numerous economic resources, including the criminal's time, the prison buildings and the security personnel. A fine, on the other hand, is a simple monetary transfer which hurts the criminal but can be used elsewhere, e.g., to compensate victims or to pay the police. As a consequence, fines should be the predominant form of punishment that should be supplemented by imprisonment only if the offender cannot fully pay the fine.[1]

This simple result is clearly at odds with reality. In England and Wales, for instance, imprisonment is not regarded as a supplement to a maximum fine but rather as the appropriate alternative in the case of serious crimes. As in many other European countries, criminals are typically punished with either jail or fine but seldomly with both types of punishment. As an illustration, Table 7.1 displays the proportions of different punishments chosen by British magistrates' courts and the Crown Court for indictable offences in 1997. It shows that more severe crimes, which are heard by the Crown Court, are punished in 61 per cent of all cases with imprisonment compared to only ten per cent of the less severe crimes, heard by the magistrates' courts. On the other hand, magistrates' courts use fines in 35 per cent of all cases, whereas the Crown Court uses them in only four per cent of all cases. Table 7.1 thus demonstrates that serious crimes are usually punished only with imprisonment and not with a fine or with a fine *and* imprisonment, as the above mentioned theory predicts.[2] Interestingly enough, the use of fines has declined in Britain over the last 20 years: In 1975, 63 per cent of all offenders aged 21 and older were fined, but by 1996 this had fallen to 36 per cent (Flood-Page and Mackie, 1998).

Table 7.1   Sentencing of British Courts in 1997*

Type of Punishment	Magistrates' Courts	Crown Court
Prison (immediate custody)	10%	61%
Fine	35%	4%
Community sentence	29%	28%
Conditional or absolute discharge	23%	3%
Other	3%	5%

* *Source*: Adapted from Home Office (1999).

Recently, papers by Chu and Jiang (1993), Levitt (1997) and Dittmann (1999) have advanced independent models, which can explain the existence of imprisonment even if the offender could be fined instead. The purpose of this chapter is to review and compare these three approaches and to assess to what extent current economic theory can explain the continued reliance upon imprisonment found in practice. To this end, we first present the basic model of punishment and provide a brief review of the most important contributions in the literature. After that, we introduce and discuss the three most recent papers in detail. The chapter finishes with a short comparison of the three approaches and draws conclusions.

The Basic Model of Punishment

This section introduces the basic micro-economic model of punishment, which was first proposed by Polinsky and Shavell (1979,1984). This model has two prominent implications.[3] Firstly, it is optimal to use fines whenever possible and to resort to imprisonment only if the offender's wealth is exhausted. Secondly, it is optimal to fix the fine as high as possible (i.e. complete expropriation) whilst spending only little money on police. Both implications are clearly at odds with what we see in reality. Fines are typically less than the offender's wealth and offenders are often sent to jail even though they could pay a fine instead. As a consequence, these two results have triggered a sizeable literature, which extends the basic model in order to find conditions under which the two results do not hold. After introducing and discussing the basic model, we will survey the larger part of this literature, which is about the maximum punishment result. Papers that analyse the optimality of fines and imprisonment will be discussed in detail in later sections.

The standard model considers only one specific crime that can be committed by any of an infinite number of individuals. All individuals are risk-neutral and have the initial wealth w. By committing the crime, individual i gains extra utility (A_i) and another randomly chosen individual j suffers the harm (H). Alternatively, the harm H, which does not depend on i, can be regarded as damage to public property (i.e. as a public 'bad'). The utility from crime, A_i, is individual i's private knowledge, whereas the distribution of the A_i's is public knowledge. Let $g(A)$ denote the corresponding density function with support [0, 1], i.e., the highest utility from crime is normalised to 1. Individuals only differ in the utility A_i they can derive from committing the considered crime. In all other respects, they are identical.

An individual who has committed the crime is convicted with probability r. If convicted, he or she must pay a fine $f \le w$ and go to prison for a period t. Let $p(t)$ be the monetary equivalent which the individual attaches to a prison term of length t, with $p'(t) > 0$ and $p(0) = 0$. Accordingly, individual i chooses to commit the crime if:

$$A_i > r[f + p(t)] \tag{7.1}$$

Hence, the proportion of criminals, q, is given by:

$$q = q(r, f, t) = \int_{r(f+p(t))}^{\infty} g(A) dA \tag{7.2}$$

Imprisonment of length t causes costs of $k(t)$ to the public, while the detection probability r causes costs of $c(r)$. The latter can be interpreted as expenditure on the police. We further assume $k'(t) > 0$ and $c'(r) > 0$. Consider the following utilitarian welfare function (normalised for one individual):

$$W = \int_{r(f+p(t))}^{\infty} Ag(A)dA - qH - c(r) - qr\left[k(t) + p(t)\right] \qquad (7.3)$$

where the first term is the gain from criminal activity, $-qH$ is the overall loss from crime, $c(r)$ is the cost of policing and $qr[k(t) + p(t)]$ are the total costs of imprisonment, including the public costs $qrk(t)$ and the individual cost $qrp(t)$. Note that the fine f does not directly affect social welfare, because the loss to the offenders who must pay the fine is exactly offset by the gain of the public who can spend that money, e.g. to pay the police. In contrast, imprisonment costs clearly reduce social welfare.

Note that the social welfare function (7.3) includes the gains from criminal activity, which is a reasonable assumption if we consider minor offences (e.g. parking offences). It is a problematic assumption, however, if we consider serious crimes such as robbery, rape or murder. Comparing the gains and losses for this type of crime is generally considered as unethical, because it would potentially lead to 'efficient' criminal acts if the criminal's gain exceeds the victim's loss. Moreover, the inclusion of gains from criminal activity raises interesting social questions for some less serious crimes like drug abuse and tax evasion. Under the assumption that a drug addict attaches an extremely high utility to his present drug consumption and that the social loss caused by this single consumption is limited (but see Chapter Eleven), the use of a utilitarian utility function would necessarily lead to the conclusion that the drug consumption of addicts is efficient and should therefore not be prosecuted and punished. For tax evasion or fraud, the welfare function (7.3) yields another interesting implication. As the criminal gain from evading taxes is roughly equal to the public's loss, tax evasion does not affect social welfare (see Chapter Twelve). The same is true for fraud, where the criminal gain exactly offsets the victim's loss. Hence, using a utilitarian welfare function which sums up only direct gains and losses will lead to the implication that tax evasion and fraud should not be prosecuted and punished. Nevertheless, most papers in the crime and punishment literature use a welfare function that contains the gains from criminal activity. Note, however, that the relevant results discussed in this chapter do not depend on the inclusion of the gain from crime in the social welfare function. Results that depend on this assumption will be clearly marked.

The issue can then be described as a multi-stage 'game'. In the first stage, a social planner maximises the function (7.3) subject to (7.2) by choosing the detection probability r, the size of the fine f and the length of the prison term t. In the second stage, each individual decides whether or not to commit the crime. Finally, criminals are prosecuted and punished as announced. Now, we can easily formulate and prove the two main results concerning the type and the size of the optimal punishment.

Result One: Fines are more efficient than imprisonment and should be used whenever possible. Only if the fine cannot be raised further, can it be optimal to supplement it with a prison term.

This result follows directly from the social welfare function (7.3). In order to prove it formally, suppose the contrary, i.e., that there is imprisonment, $t > 0$, while the fine could still be raised, $f < w$. Now lower t slightly and increase f, so that the total expected sanction $r[f + p(t)]$ remains constant. Then the proportion of criminals, q, as given in (7.2) does not change and neither do the first three terms in the social welfare function (7.3). However, the private and public cost of imprisonment $qr[k(t) + p(t)]$ decreases, so that the original t and f cannot be optimal. Thus, the optimal fine cannot be less than the individual's wealth if imprisonment is used in addition.

Result Two: The optimal fine is always equal to the offender's wealth.

Result One already states that the optimal fine is maximal if fines and imprisonment are both used. So it remains to show that the fine is maximal if there is no imprisonment, i.e., if $t = 0$. The argument is similar to the proof of Result One. Consider the opposite, i.e., $f < w$. Now slightly raise the fine f and reduce the detection probability r such that the expected punishment rf remains constant. Then, the proportion of criminals, q in (7.2), and the first two terms in (7.3) do not change, but the cost of policing $c(r)$ decreases, so that social welfare increases.

If we further assume that individual and public costs of imprisonment, $p(t)$ and $k(t)$, are linear in t, we obtain the same result for imprisonment, i.e., that a maximum prison term is optimal (on top of a maximum fine). In this case, complete expropriation and life-long imprisonment would be optimal. Generally, however, it might not be optimal to use a maximum prison term, because personal and public costs of imprisonment might outweigh the corresponding reduction in the cost of policing.

The Optimality of Less-Than-Maximum Fines

The aim of a large part of the theoretical literature on crime and punishment is to overturn Result Two. These papers introduce more realistic assumptions and identify conditions under which a maximum fine is not optimal.

Risk Aversion

Polinsky and Shavell (1979) and Kaplow (1992) assume that individuals are risk averse. There are two sources of risk; first, that an individual may become a victim and second, that an offender may be caught and punished. Both papers assume that individuals can buy insurance for the first type of risk, so that qH becomes the insurance premium, whereas the second type of risk is not insurable. Hence, the social welfare function has the following form (we consider only fines and no imprisonment at this point):

$$ W = \int_{r[f+p(t)]}^{\infty} U(A - rf)g(A)dA - qH + qrf - c(r), \qquad (7.4) $$

where $U(\cdot)$ is the utility function of the individuals which is positive, increasing and concave. In contrast to (7.3), the fine f directly affects social welfare in (7.4). Due to the individuals' risk aversion, the individual's utility loss is not offset by the public gain. Polinsky and Shavell (1979) and Kaplow (1992) show that it is optimal to choose a fine that is smaller than each individual's wealth if the costs $c(r)$ are not too high.[4] Note that this result crucially depends on the inclusion of the gains from criminal activity in the social welfare function. If the social planner does not take the criminal's utility into account, risk aversion alone does not change Result Two.

Wealth Differences

Polinsky and Shavell (1991) (see also Garoupa, 1998) assume that wealth w differs among individuals. They establish that the optimal fine is smaller than most individuals' wealth. The reason is that the detection probability must be chosen high enough to deter poor individuals (who still pay a fine equal to their wealth). If rich individuals, who face the same detection probability, have to pay a very high fine, socially desirable offences (if $A_i > H$) would be deterred, so the optimal fine for rich individuals is smaller than their wealth. Note that this argument crucially depends on the inclusion of the offender's utility in the social welfare function.

General Enforcement

Shavell (1991) considers a model in which the harm H differs from individual to individual, whereas all individuals have the same wealth. Each individual knows their own H_i and the fine can depend on the offender's H_i. The detection probability r, on the other hand, cannot depend on the harm H_i, i.e., enforcement is general. Shavell (1991) shows that only those individuals with the highest harm should pay the maximum fine (i.e. their wealth) if they commit the crime and are caught. Individuals who cause less harm should pay a fine that is smaller than their wealth. The intuition again is that otherwise socially desirable crimes, which cause a private benefit that is larger than the public harm, would be deterred. This argument also depends on the inclusion of the gain from criminal activity being an argument in the social welfare function.

Marginal Deterrence

Formalising an idea introduced by Stigler (1970), Shavell (1992) and Mookherjee and Png (1994) present models of marginal deterrence (see also Friedman and Sjostrom, 1993). In these models, each individual can choose among various crimes which differ in harm and benefit.[5] Mookherjee and Png (1994) assume that a crime which causes a greater harm also provides more private benefits to the offender. Under this assumption, they show that Result Two does not hold. Instead, only the most harmful crime should be punished with the maximum penalty, whereas less severe crimes should receive smaller punishments. The intuition is that this policy provides incentives for individuals who cannot be fully deterred to commit less harmful crimes. Consider, for instance, the distinction between the punishments for robbery and armed robbery, an example used by Friedman and Sjostrom (1993). Traditionally, armed robbery is punished more severely than ordinary robbery. If we increased the penalty for ordinary robbery to that of armed robbery, the number of robberies would decrease, but the probability of being robbed by somebody carrying a gun would increase. The reason is that a formerly unarmed robber, who is not deterred by the higher punishment, has no reason not to carry a gun anymore; he is not marginally deterred from the more severe crime. Therefore, it might be optimal to punish less harmful crimes less severely.

Police Corruption

Bowles and Garoupa (1997) extend the standard model by introducing a police officer, who might (depending on his personal 'costs') be willing to take a bribe in order not to report the detected crime. In addition, there is a probability R that such collusive behaviour is detected, in which case the police officer must pay a fine F and the criminal must pay the fine f. Bowles and Garoupa (1997) show that an increase in the fine f leads to more corruption. If corruption is valued as socially harmful by itself, a less-than-maximum fine f might be optimal.

Risk Aversion and Possible Errors

In a quite different framework, Andreoni (1991) considers the decision of a jury that is risk averse, makes wrong decisions with a positive probability, and attaches a high negative utility to a false conviction. He argues that an increase in the penalty increases the jury's negative utility attached to a false conviction, so that the jury becomes more reluctant to impose such a penalty. As a consequence, the probability r that a criminal is convicted decreases as the fine f increases, so that a less-than-maximum fine can be optimal. Here, the probability r and the fine f cannot be set independently as assumed in the standard model.

We argued above that the standard model with risk-averse individuals can explain less-than-maximum fines only if the utility from criminal activity is included in the social welfare function. If we additionally introduce the possibility of errors, i.e., that a non-criminal is convicted and punished with a positive probability, then Result Two might not hold even if the criminals' utility is not taken into account. The reason is that an increase in the fine f has a clear negative effect on social welfare now, because it increases the risk borne by non-criminals.

The Case for Imprisonment I: Marginal Deterrence and Wealth Differences

The papers reviewed so far present extensions of the standard model in which the maximum punishment result (Result Two) does not hold. The volume of this literature indicates that Result Two is not very robust to model alterations. In contrast, Result One, which states that fines are more efficient than imprisonment, turns out to be robust, since it is confirmed by all of the papers reviewed above. This and the following two sections introduce and discuss three models which establish conditions under which imprisonment is preferable to a fine. Due to the robustness of Result One, these models are somewhat more involved.

Chu and Jiang (1993) combine a number of additional assumptions, some of which have been separately discussed above, in order to show that imprisonment and a fine, which is smaller than the offender's wealth, can be optimal. The basic idea of this paper is that different groups of individuals have different valuations of the two types of punishment, so that the social planner can effectively discriminate between different groups by using both types of punishment simultaneously. We first introduce the main assumptions maintained by Chu and Jiang (1993) and then demonstrate that discrimination between different wealth groups is desirable. After that, it is easy to see why a combination of imprisonment and fine can be optimal.

Additional Assumptions

1) Criminals can choose the intensity, A, of their criminal activity, $A \in [0,1]$. As in the standard model, A denotes the utility derived from the criminal act. The harm caused to the public H is a linear function of A: $H = h \cdot A$ with $h > 0$. Note that this is the 'marginal deterrence' setting, as individuals can choose between different crimes with different harms.

2) Individuals are risk-averse. This assumption is needed to generate an interior solution for the choice of A. If individuals are risk-neutral, they would choose either $A = 0$ or $A = 1$, so that marginal deterrence could not be an issue.[6]

3) Individuals differ in wealth. We consider two different groups: rich individuals with wealth w_1 and poor individuals with wealth w_2.[7]

4) A crucial assumption of Chu and Jiang's argument is that rich individuals are more prison averse than poor individuals. This assumption is justified by the higher opportunity costs of time for rich individuals (see, e.g., Lott, 1987).[8]

5) The detection probability r is exogenous. This assumption greatly reduces the model's complexity, because the costs $c(r)$ are constant and can be dropped.

6) The fine f depends linearly on the utility (and thereby on the harm) of the crime: $f = \varphi A$, i.e., a convicted criminal must pay the actual fine $\min\{w, \varphi A\}$. The amercement rate φ is the social planner's main decision variable. Note that this assumption implies that the fine f cannot depend on the offender's wealth, which is another driving assumption of Chu and Jiang's argument. It is not possible, for instance, to set the fine equal to half of the offender's wealth.[9]

The Individual's Choice of Criminal Activity

For the time being, we assume that no imprisonment is possible. Then the individuals' decision problem in the second stage of the model is

$$\max_{A \in [0,1]} (1-r)U(w+A) + rU(w - \min\{w, \varphi A\}). \qquad (7.5)$$

Chu and Jiang establish that rich individuals with $w = w_1$ always lower their criminal activity A_1^* if the amercement rate φ increases. If φ becomes large enough, rich individuals choose $A_1^* = 0$, i.e., they are deterred from any criminal activity. Poor individuals with $w = w_2$, on the other hand, reduce their optimal criminal activity A_2^* with increasing φ only until φ reaches a certain threshold $\overline{\varphi}$. If φ is larger, poor individuals always commit the most harmful crime, i.e., $A_2^* = 1$. Figure 7.1 illustrates these findings by plotting the optimal decisions of the two groups, A_1^* and A_2^*, against the amercement rate φ for an example.

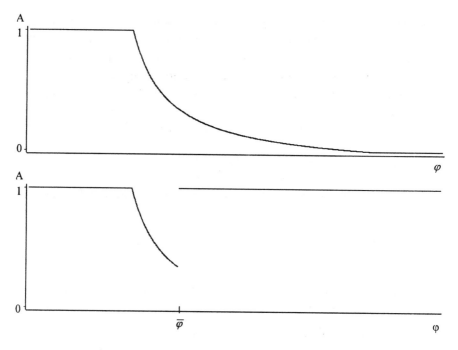

Figure 7.1 **Optimal criminal activity A for rich individuals (top) and for poor individuals (bottom) dependent on the amercement rate φ**

The Social Planner's Problem

In view of Figure 7.1, the social planner would like to discriminate between rich and poor individuals and choose a very high amercement rate φ for rich individuals while choosing $\varphi = \overline{\varphi}$ for poor individuals. Due to assumption 6, however, this is not possible. Since rich individuals are more prison-averse than poor individuals (assumption 4), the social planner can nevertheless punish rich offenders more severely than poor offenders by using a combination of fine and imprisonment. Thereby, poor individuals can be deterred from the most severe crimes while rich individuals are further deterred – ideally from all crimes. Chu and Jiang (1993) show formally that this intuition is right: A combination of fine and imprisonment increases social welfare if the proportion of poor individuals is large enough and if imprisonment is not too expensive. The bottom line of this argument is that a combination of penalties can be optimal if the deterrence effects of different types of punishment vary across different groups of individuals. This reasoning can be extended easily to more than two penalties, e.g., to house arrest and community service. In general, a combination of all available penalties will be optimal. Note that this argument can only explain a combination of a fine and imprisonment; it cannot explain imprisonment without a fine.

The Case for Imprisonment II: Unobservable Wealth

Another explanation for the optimality of imprisonment if fines are not maximal is given by Levitt (1997). He assumes that individuals can hide their wealth, so that they cannot be forced to pay a fine. In order to still collect a fine, the enforcement agency can offer the convict the choice between a prison term (which can be enforced) and a fine. If the fine is smaller than the disutility attached to the prison term, the individual will pay the fine. The problem is that the enforcement agency cannot observe the offender's disutility of jail. As criminals typically are poor and hence have a low disutility of jail, the fine which can be enforced under threat of a given prison term is quite small. Yet, a small fine would make the crime more attractive for rich individuals. Therefore, it might be optimal not to use fines but only imprisonment in many situations.

In order to fully understand this argument, consider Levitt's additional assumptions on our standard model. First, he assumes that the individual's disutility of prison, $p(t)$, and the public costs of imprisonment, $k(t)$, are linear in t, while the costs of policing, $c(r)$, are convex. As argued in a note after Result 2 above, these additional assumptions result in the optimality of a maximum prison term. Further, Levitt assumes that there are two groups of individuals $i \in \{R, P\}$, which differ in their utility from crime, A_i, and their disutility of jail, $p_i(t) = \theta_i t$, with $\theta_R > \theta_P$. The group with the higher disutility of prison is referred to as 'rich individuals' (R) while the other group is called 'poor individuals' (P). Finally, Levitt supposes that individuals cannot be forced to pay a fine (although he implicitly assumes that all individuals can pay the fine if they want to). Possible reasons underlying this assumption are that individuals can hide their wealth or that their wealth mainly consists of human capital.

As fines alone cannot be optimal (nobody would pay them), the obvious benchmark case is imprisonment only. Due to the linearity of private and public costs of imprisonment, the social planner will always choose a maximum prison term $\bar{t}$. Given this benchmark, we now consider whether the alternative of paying a fine can increase social welfare. Since there are only two groups of individuals, we need to distinguish four cases.

1) Individuals of both groups do not commit the crime. In this case, there is no social loss from crime or imprisonment, so fines cannot improve the situation.

2) All individuals commit the considered crime. In this case, the optimal detection probability, r, is zero, and again there is no scope for alternative fines.

3) Only rich individuals commit the crime. Now, the optimal fine is $f^* = \theta_R \bar{t}$, because it makes rich individuals indifferent between paying the fine f^* and serving the prison term $\bar{t}$, so that we can assume that they pay the fine.

4) Only poor individuals commit the crime. Analogously to 3), one could set the fine to $\hat{f} = \theta_p \bar{t}$, so that poor individuals are indifferent between paying the fine $\hat{f}$ and serving the prison term $\bar{t}$. However, doing so will decrease deterrence for rich individuals, because $\hat{f} = \theta_p \bar{t} < \theta_R \bar{t}$. For rich individuals, the punishment $\hat{f}$ is smaller than the disutility they attach to the prison term $\bar{t}$, so that they might also commit the crime, if the alternative fine $\hat{f}$ is introduced. Therefore, it might be optimal not to offer a fine at all.

Levitt's main result is that fines accompanied by the threat of imprisonment are optimal for crimes which are committed only by rich individuals (Case 3), like tax evasion. On the other hand, he shows that it might be optimal to use imprisonment only (without an alternative fine) for crimes that are committed by poor individuals (Case 4).

An important assumption in this argument is that the enforcement agency cannot observe the offender's type and, in particular, his prison-aversion. In practice, the court is likely to have at least some information about an individual's disutility of jail. Therefore, Levitt argues that the judge should be allowed to use this information in order to tailor punishments to the situation of individual criminals. Consequently, he argues against mandatory sentencing guidelines, which restrict the judge's discretion.

The Case for Imprisonment III: Restricting the Government's Power

Dittmann (1999) presents a very different approach, which in contrast to Levitt (1997) and Chu and Jiang (1993), can also explain mandatory imprisonment. The basic idea is that citizens might vote for mandatory imprisonment in order to limit the government's power to maximise revenues from fines. The reason is that maximising revenues from fines can induce the government to choose a lower detection probability and to spend less money on police compared to the situation when only prison sentences and no fines are available.

A Positive Model of Crime and Punishment

In contrast to all of the papers reviewed so far, which are concerned with normative issues, the approach in Dittmann (1999) is positive. Starting out from the basic model as described above, I replace the social planner with a government that is in charge of criminal prosecution in practice. An important difference between the government and a social planner is that the government typically cannot choose all variables of the criminal justice system. While it can determine the expenditure on police and thereby the detection probability for a specific crime, it usually cannot change the type and the size of the punishment – at least not during one parliamentary term. Typically, the type and the size of the punishment are laid down as a law by the parliament (which in turn is elected by the people) so that these two variables are less flexible than the detection probability.

In order to model this complicated decision process, I consider a three-stage game. In the first stage, all individuals decide in a referendum whether the considered crime should be punished by a prison term, by a fine or not at all. In the second stage, the government chooses the detection probability r by determining the police budget $c(r)$. In the third stage, each individual decides whether or not to commit the crime. Finally, criminals are prosecuted and punished as announced. The referendum in the first stage of the game can be regarded as a convenient approximation to the complex decision process in reality.

This model focuses on the detection probability and the *type* of punishment, whereas the *size* of punishment is treated as an exogenous variable. Consider an exogenously fixed prison term t. Since all individuals are equally prison averse, they all attach the same disutility $P = p(t)$ to this punishment, so that all individuals are indifferent between spending the period t in prison and paying the amount P. The model assumes that P is exogenously fixed, so that, in the first stage of the model, the individuals can only choose between a fine of P and a prison term of length $t = p^{-1}(P)$. As outlined above (see subsections entitled 'general enforcement' and 'marginal deterrence'), there are already satisfactory results concerning the optimal size of punishment, which link the size of punishment to the amount of harm caused by the crime. Moreover, I assume that the utility gains from criminal activity A_i are uniformly distributed, i.e. $g(A) = 1$ if $A \in [0,1]$ and $g(A) = 0$ otherwise, and, that there are no public costs of imprisonment, i.e., $k(t) = 0 \ \forall t$. Note that the last two assumptions are made to keep the model solvable and to arrive at clear-cut results; they do not influence the main qualitative results.

The government maximises social welfare, given by (7.3), without taking the utility of criminals into account:

$$U_G(r) = \begin{cases} -qH + qrP - c(r), & \text{if the punishment is a fine} \\ -qH - c(r), & \text{if the punishment is a prison term} \end{cases} \qquad (7.6)$$

The individuals' utility function is given by

$$U_i(r) = \max\{A_i - rP, 0\} - qH . \qquad (7.7)$$

Note that the costs $c(r)$ of the police system and potential revenues from fines paid by other individuals do not appear in the individuals' utility function (7.7) even though these costs or revenues might affect the individual's future income via a tax increase or decrease. In this sense, I assume that individuals are myopic. They judge the law enforcement system only by their personal expected harm and gain but not by the social costs and gains. Note that this is the main assumption which drives the model's results, as it establishes conflicting interests between government and individuals.

The Government's Choice of the Detection Probability

In order to understand the individuals' voting behaviour in the first stage of the model, we first consider the government's choice of the detection probability, given the type of punishment, in the second stage of the model. Figure 7.2 summarises the government's behaviour using an example; it shows the detection probability r dependent on the size of the punishment P for the cases where the punishment is a prison term (solid line) and a fine (broken line).

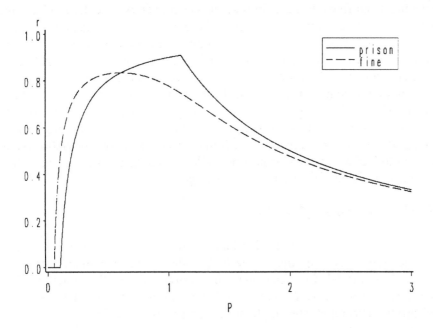

Figure 7.2   The government's choice of the detection probability r

First consider the solid line, i.e., the case that the individuals have voted for mandatory imprisonment in the first stage of the model. If the punishment is very small, a given level of deterrence $r \cdot P$ is very expensive to achieve so that the government does not prosecute criminals. If the punishment P is larger than some small threshold, the government chooses a positive r, which rapidly increases with increasing size of the penalty. It increases until $r = 1/P$. At this point the expected punishment $r \cdot P$ is equal to the highest private utility A_i from crime, so that all individuals are deterred from committing the crime. Obviously, it is not optimal to increase the detection probability r any further, so that the government chooses $r = 1/P$ from now on.

Now consider the broken line in Figure 7.2, which displays the government's behaviour if individuals have voted for a fine, and compare it with the solid line. If the size of the punishment is small, the government chooses a higher detection probability r if the punishment is a fine than if it is a prison term. This is due to the fact that the number of criminals is quite large if the punishment is small. Therefore, increasing the detection probability increases the number of convictions and thereby the expected revenues from fines. Hence, fines serve as a monetary incentive to improve policing if the punishment is small. If the punishment is large, on the other hand, the government chooses a higher detection probability if the punishment is a prison term than if it is a fine, a result that might seem counter-intuitive at first glance. The reason is that only a few individuals – or even none – commit the crime if the punishment is a large prison term. If the punishment is a large fine instead, the government has an incentive to choose a *lower* detection probability in order to *increase* the number of criminals. A larger number of criminals lead to more convictions and thereby to higher revenues from fines. Consequently, fines are an incentive to *reduce* policing if the punishment is large.

The Outcome of the Referendum

In view of the government's behaviour as illustrated in Figure 7.2, it is easy to understand why individuals vote for mandatory imprisonment in the first stage of the model. Consider again the individuals' utility function (7.7) and note that $q = 1 - rP$, due to (7.2) and the assumption that the A_i are uniformly distributed. Hence, the utility of a non-criminal is

$$U_i^N(r) = -(1 - rP)H,\qquad(7.8)$$

whereas the utility of a criminal is

$$U_i^C(r) = A_i - rP - (1 - rP)H = A_i + (H - 1)rP - H.\qquad(7.9)$$

As a consequence, the utility of *all* individuals increases with increasing detection probability r if $H > 1$. In other words, if the harm is larger than the largest private utility from crime, all individuals prefer a higher detection probability. Taking the government's behaviour in the second stage of the game into account, individuals will vote unanimously for a fine if the punishment is small and unanimously for mandatory imprisonment if the punishment is large. For $H < 1$, individuals are no longer unanimous and the derivation of the referendum's outcome becomes more complicated.

Figure 7.3 depicts the outcome of the referendum dependent on the size of punishment P and the amount of harm H. It shows that – given a small punishment P – individuals vote for a fine if $H > 1$ and for no prosecution if $H < 1$. For large punishments fines are never chosen. Instead, individuals vote for imprisonment if the harm is large and for no prosecution if the harm is small. In particular, the majority of individuals vote for no prosecution if $H < \frac{1}{2}$.

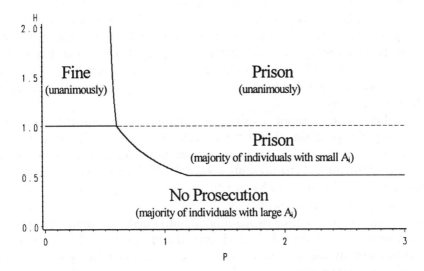

Figure 7.3   The result of the referendum on the type of punishment

If, in addition, we take into account the idea that more harmful crimes should be (and typically are) punished with larger penalties (due to marginal deterrence and general enforcement), this model can explain why, in practice, serious crimes are punished with prison terms whereas less serious crimes are punished by fines.

Conclusions

The traditional model of crime and punishment leads to the conclusion that fines should be used whenever possible and only be supplemented with an additional prison term if the offender's wealth is exhausted. This result, which is clearly at odds with the use of fines and imprisonment in practice, turned out to be remarkably robust.

The discussion of three relatively new contributions to the economic theory of punishment has shown that this discrepancy between theory and practice can be overcome. Chu and Jiang (1993), Levitt (1997) and Dittmann (1999) present three independent models in which imprisonment is used without a maximum fine. Chu and Jiang (1993) and Levitt (1997) use the standard model of Polinsky and Shavell (1984) and introduce a set of reasonable additional assumptions. Levitt (1997) assumes that the court cannot enforce a fine, because individuals are able to hide their wealth. Hence, individuals only pay fines if threatened with imprisonment. Chu and Jiang (1993) assume that individuals differ in their wealth and that they have a choice between crimes of different severity. Their bottom line is that the social planner will choose a mixture of all available penalties in order to discriminate between different groups of criminals, so that each group is optimally deterred.

Neither paper cannot explain *mandatory* imprisonment, i.e., the commonly observed situation that the judge has no discretion to impose a fine instead of the prison term, no matter how rich the offender is. In contrast, Dittmann (1999) presents a model which can explain mandatory imprisonment. This model changes the structure of the standard model of crime and punishment by separating the decision on the type of punishment from the decision on police expenditures. Individuals determine the type of punishment in a referendum and are shown to vote for mandatory imprisonment in many situations in order to restrict the government's power to generate revenues from fines by prosecuting criminals.

To sum up, current economic theory can explain the use of imprisonment without maximum fines, even under the assumption that the only purpose of punishing criminals is to deter individuals from committing crimes. If incapacitation arguments are additionally taken into account, the current judicial practice, which heavily relies on imprisonment for serious crimes, can be explained convincingly.

Notes

*   I would like to thank Sabine Bockem of the University of Dortmund for helpful comments upon an earlier version of this paper.
1.   If offenders differ in their wealth, the size of the fine should be properly adjusted, so that the utility loss is the same for all criminals.
2.   Compensation orders, which are officially not counted as fines, occasionally accompany a prison sentence and could be regarded as a kind of fine. However, the proportion of compensation orders is small and has decreased in recent years. In 1996, the Crown Court awarded compensation to victims of violent crimes in 12 per cent of the cases, compared with 20 per cent in 1990. Moreover, the maximum compensation currently is £5,000 (£2,000 before 1991), which can hardly be regarded as the maximum possible fine for the majority of individuals (source: Flood-Page and Mackie, 1998).
3.   Both implications were derived by Becker (1968), although he uses a macro-economic approach and does not model individual behaviour explicitly.

4. Polinsky and Shavell (1979) show this result for $H < 1$, i.e., for a harm which is smaller than the largest utility from crime. Kaplow (1992) establishes eventually the same result for the case $H = 1$, in which there are no socially desirable offences.

5. Notice the difference between marginal deterrence and general enforcement. Under general enforcement, individuals cannot choose between different crimes.

6. Due to the linearity of the fine f (see assumption 6), the maximisation problem (7.5) would be linear if individuals were not risk averse. Note that risk-aversion is not needed if the fine f can be a convex function of the criminal activity level A (see Mookherjee and Png, 1994).

7. Note that the argument does not hold for any wealth levels w_1 and w_2. Chu and Jiang (1993) derive thresholds w' and w'' ($w' < w''$), so that individuals with wealth larger than w'' are 'rich' and individuals with wealth between w' and w'' are 'poor'. Hence, $w_1 > w''$ and $w_2 \in (w', w'')$. 'Very poor' individuals with wealth smaller than w' cannot be deterred from the most harmful crime $A = 1$ by any punishment.

8. This assumption is questionable. First, rich individuals might use their time in prison more productively than poor individuals, e.g., by writing a bestseller, and have fewer problems in finding an appropriate employment after being released. Second, there is an additional, 'personal' disutility of imprisonment, which varies across individual. If rich individuals have characteristics (e.g., intelligence, self-confidence, drive) which make life in prison easier and less depressing, poor individuals might possibly have a higher disutility of imprisonment than rich individuals.

9. Note that, contrary to assumption 6, fines typically depend upon the wealth of the offender in England and Germany (cf. Flood-Page and Mackie, 1998, and Friedman, 1983).

References

Andreoni, J. (1991), 'Reasonable Doubt and the Optimal Magnitude of Fines: Should the Penalty Fit the Crime?', *RAND Journal of Economics*, vol. 22, pp. 385-95.

Becker, G.S. (1968), 'Crime and Punishment: An Economic Approach', *Journal of Political Economy*, vol. 76, pp. 169-217.

Bowles, R. and Garoupa, N. (1997), 'Casual Police Corruption and the Economics of Crime', *International Review of Law and Economics*, vol. 17, pp. 75-87.

Chu, C.Y.C. and Jiang, N. (1993), 'Are Fines More Efficient Than Imprisonment?', *Journal of Public Economics*, vol. 51, pp. 391-413.

Dittmann, I. (1999), 'Crime and Punishment: On the Optimality of Imprisonment Although Fines are Feasible', mimeo.

Ehrlich, I. (1981), 'On the Usefulness of Controlling Individuals: An Economic Analysis of Rehabilitation, Incapacitation, and Deterrence', *American Economic Review*, vol. 71, pp. 307-22.

Flood-Page, C. and Mackie, A. (1998), *Sentencing Practice: An Examination of Decisions in Magistrates' Courts and the Crown Court in the mid-1990s*, Home Office Research Study 180, Home Office, London.

Friedman, D. and Sjostrom, W. (1993), 'Hanged for a Sheep-The Economics of Marginal Deterrence', *Journal of Legal Studies*, vol. 22, pp. 345-66.

Friedman, G.M. (1983), 'The West German Day-Fine System: A Possibility for the United States?', *The University of Chicago Law Review*, vol. 50, pp. 281-304.

Garoupa, N. (1998), 'Optimal Law Enforcement and Imperfect Information When Wealth Varies Among Individuals', *Economica*, vol. 65, pp. 479-90.

Home Office (1999), *Digest 4: Information on the Criminal Justice System in England and Wales*, Home Office, London.

Kaplow, L. (1992), 'The Optimal Probability and Magnitude of Fines for Acts That Definitely are Undesirable', *International Review of Law and Economics*, vol. 12, pp. 3-11.

Kessler, D. and Levitt, S.D. (1999), 'Using Sentence Enhancements to Distinguish Between Deterrence and Incapacitation', *Journal of Law and Economics*, vol. 42, pp. 343-63.

Levitt, S.D. (1997), 'Incentive Compatibility Constraints as an Explanation for the Use of Prison Sentences Instead of Fines', *International Review of Law and Economics*, vol. 17, pp. 179-92.

Levitt, S.D. (1998a), 'Why do Increased Arrest Rates Appear to Reduce Crime: Deterrence, Incapacitation, or Measurement Error?', *Economic Inquiry*, vol. 36, pp. 353-72.

Levitt, S.D. (1998b), 'Juvenile Crime and Punishment', *Journal of Political Economy* vol. 106, pp. 1156-85.

Lipton, D., Martinson, R. and Wilks, J. (1975), *The Effectiveness of Correctional Treatment: A Survey of Treatment Evaluation Studies*, Praeger, New York.

Lott, J.R. Jr. (1987), 'Should the Wealthy be Able to 'Buy Justice'?', *Journal of Political Economy*, vol. 95, pp. 1307-16.

Mookherjee, D. and Png, I.P.L. (1994), 'Marginal Deterrence in Enforcement of Law', *Journal of Political Economy*, vol. 102, pp. 1039-66.

Polinsky, A.M. and Shavell, S. (1979), 'The Optimal Trade-off Between the Probability and Magnitude of Fines', *American Economic Review*, vol. 69, pp. 880-91.

Polinsky, A.M. and Shavell, S. (1984), 'The Optimal Use of Fines and Imprisonment', *Journal of Public Economics*, vol. 24, pp. 89-99.

Polinsky, A.M. and Shavell, S. (1991), 'A Note on Optimal Fines When Wealth Varies Among Individuals', *American Economic Review*, vol. 81, pp. 618-21.

Shavell, S. (1991), 'Specific Versus General Enforcement of Law', *Journal of Political Economy*, vol. 99, pp. 1088-1108.

Shavell, S. (1992), 'A Note on Marginal Deterrence', *International Review of Law and Economics*, vol. 12, pp. 345-55.

Stigler, G.J. (1970), 'The Optimum Enforcement of Laws', *Journal of Political Economy*, vol. 78, pp. 526-36.

8. The Victims of Property Crime

ZIGGY MACDONALD AND STEPHEN PUDNEY

Introduction

The social consequences of criminal activity are a serious concern for public policy makers, as is the public's anxiety about crime, particularly that involving attacks on property and the person. Evidence from the 1996 International Crime Victims Survey revealed England and Wales to have the highest burglary rate of the countries sampled (Austria, Canada, England and Wales, Finland, France, Netherlands, Northern Ireland, Scotland, Sweden, Switzerland and USA.), this being almost twice the average observed (Mayhew and van Dijk, 1997). This survey also showed that England and Wales had the second highest rate of perceived risk of burglary, the highest being in France. At the individual level, two thirds of adults questioned for the 1996 British Crime Survey were very or fairly worried about burglary, with 20 per cent of the sample regarding themselves as very or fairly likely to be the victims of burglary (Mirrlees-Black et al., 1996). Although the figures for fear of crime are beginning to fall, evidence from the 1998 British Crime Survey suggests that individuals still tend to over-estimate the problem (Mirrlees-Black and Allen, 1998; Kemshall 1997).

Study of the actual rather than perceived incidence of property crime is now well established. Research in this area has tended to emphasise the role of area characteristics (seen as indicators of social deprivation) upon property crime victimisation (for example see Osborn et al., 1992; Trickett et al., 1993, 1995). Individual or household characteristics have usually been found to be of less importance in 'explaining' the incidence of property crime, although Osborn et al. (1992) suggest that repeat victimisation is associated with key characteristics at the micro level. A common finding in these studies is that less affluent areas are most likely to be targeted by burglars, although it may be wealthier people in these areas that become victims.

Freeman et al. (1996) suggest that such behaviour is at odds with economic rationality. After all, if it is the area that is the primary influence upon target selection, then one might expect property crime to be concentrated in affluent neighbourhoods where the pickings are rich and plentiful. An alternative perspective is presented by Fishman *et al.* (1998), who focus on the impact of the immediate locality and deterrence factors on the probability of a house being burgled. Using data from a survey of 22,000 households in Greenwich, Connecticut (US), they found that houses that are situated in a dead-end street or those that are difficult to access or retreat from are less likely to be burgled (although the single most effective deterrent was the use of a burglar alarm), whereas corner properties and those adjacent to wooded areas were more prone to burglary.

The focus of this chapter differs from that of the existing literature in that we approach property crime victimisation from the viewpoint of distributional analysis. The distress caused by being a victim of burglary is viewed as a negative element of household welfare, and we are interested specifically in the distributional pattern of this welfare loss, just as we might be interested in the distribution of income or of tax payments. Seen from this viewpoint, crime victimisation must be analysed ultimately in terms of household rather than neighbourhood characteristics, since it is the household that we are interested in.[1] This chapter is organised as follows. In the next section the source of UK property crime data is discussed. A description and examination of the current data set follows. The incidence of burglary victimisation is then modelled using a probit model. As it may be the case that once burgled a household is likely to be burgled again in the same year, burglary occurrence is estimated in the following section using the negative binomial regression technique. We conclude our analysis by considering the financial losses from burglary and the distributional impact of these combined outcomes. The implications of the results are then discussed in the final section.

Victimisation Data

Previous empirical analysis of property crime victimisation has tended to focus on a single year of the British Crime Survey (BCS) with area characteristics taken from matched Census data. For example, Osborn *et al.* (1992) and Trickett *et al.* (1995) use the 1984 BCS and 1981 UK Census to estimate a model of burglary incidence that relates individual and area characteristics to victimisation via a simple logit model. In this chapter we use several sweeps of the General Household Survey[2] (GHS) to provide information on crime victimisation and individual and household characteristics. Since our motivation is the distributional impact of burglary on economic welfare, the use of GHS rather than BCS data allows us to exploit the much better GHS information on household income.

The General Household Survey

The GHS provides a particularly rich data set with which to analyse the burglary experience of households. Questions on burglary were introduced to the General Household Survey in 1972, and there have since been a further seven survey years including burglary questions. For the purpose of this analysis household and burglary details are taken from the Main Household Questionnaires of the 1985, 1986, 1991-2 and 1993-4 General Household Surveys. Earlier years are excluded from this analysis due to inconsistencies across survey years. For example, up to 1984 the sampling framework for the GHS was taken from the Electoral Register, but, due to concerns about the coverage biases inherent in electoral registers, from 1984 onwards the Postcode Address File (the Post Office's list of addresses) was used. The same change in sampling framework has occurred with the BCS (between 1988 and 1992) and Lynn (1997) suggests that the change can have a significant effect on estimation of victimisation rates. As such we only use the relevant GHS sweeps from 1985 onwards. Pooling the data for the four survey years under consideration yields a sample size of 45,411 households, which, after exclusion for incomplete records, provides a final sample size of 30,692 households.

The 1985 survey is the first since the change of sampling framework to include burglary questions. The primary burglary question simply asks whether 'during the past 12 months has anyone got into this (house/flat/room) without your permission and stolen or attempted to steal something?'. This is followed up by questions concerning the number of incidents in the previous year at the current address, the method of entry, whether goods were stolen and if they were insured, and finally, whether the incident was reported to the police.

Victimisation Rates

In the current data set, 1040 (3.39 per cent) households have been burgled at least once during the year preceding the survey. The burglary figures are presented by survey year in Table 8.1. The incidence of burglary covers a 12-month reference period prior to the survey year and includes households where the head of household has been resident at the current address for less than 12 months. As the burglary question relates to the current address, recent movers will have had a shorter period of exposure to the risk of burglary. In the analysis presented later in this chapter, recent relocation is controlled for. However, all cases are included in Table 8.1. Foster *et al.* (1995) report on research suggesting that recent movers have a higher risk of burglary than households with a longer residence. In our data set, of the 3019 households for whom the head has not been resident at the current address for 12 months, 94 (3.11 per cent) have been victims of burglary, which is slightly less than for those with a longer residence. Since the average tenure at the current address for recent movers is approximately six months, this implies a roughly doubled burglary risk, confirming the conclusion of Foster *et al.*

Table 8.1   Percentage of households burgled*

Survey year	Burgled	Repeat burglaries
1985	2.77	14.93
	(0.19)	(2.52)
1986	2.75	10.84
	(0.19)	(2.19)
1991/2	3.34	14.52
	(0.21)	(2.24)
1993/4	4.50	11.34
	(0.22)	(1.61)

* standard errors in parenthesis.

Table 8.1 also includes information about the prevalence of repeat burglary (i.e. the percentage of the burgled households that have experienced more than one burglary during the reference year). In terms of the overall distribution of repeat burglaries, 908 (87.31 per cent) of the 1040 burgled households experienced only one burglary during the reference year, whereas 110 (10.58 per cent) were the victims of two incidents, 17 (1.63 per cent) experienced three burglaries, four (0.38 per cent) experienced four burglaries and one household was the victim of five burglaries during the reference year.

Socio-Economic Differences

There are important socio-economic differences between victims of burglary. Minority ethnic groups are generally more likely to regard burglary as a serious problem in their neighbourhoods than are whites (Budd, 1999; Fitzgerald and Hale, 1996). In the GHS data set only four per cent of heads of households are non-White. Of these, 7.28 per cent have been victims of burglary compared to a rate of 3.23 per cent for households with a White head. The experience of different ethnic groups is summarised in Table 8.2.

Table 8.2 Burglary rates by income and ethnic group*

	% Burgled	% Repeat burglaries
Current net weekly household income		
Less than £50	4.18	15.57
	(0.37)	(3.30)
£50 - £99	3.64	15.38
	(0.23)	(2.30)
£100 - £149	3.28	15.06
	(0.25)	(2.78)
£150 -£199	2.68	8.04
	(0.25)	(2.58)
£200 - £249	3.25	8.49
	(0.31)	(2.72)
£250 - £299	2.79	12.12
	(0.34)	(4.05)
£300 - £349	2.88	12.00
	(0.40)	(4.64)
£350 - £449	2.96	11.11
	(0.37)	(3.99)
greater than £450	4.80	10.19
	(0.45)	(2.92)
Ethnic Origin of Head of Household		
White	3.23	12.41
	(0.10)	(1.07)
Black	9.17	19.35
	(1.57)	(7.21)
Asian	6.83	19.35
	(1.19)	(7.21)
Other	6.27	7.41
	(1.17)	(5.14)

* standard errors in parenthesis.

Also shown in Table 8.2 are the burglary rates for different income groups. A common finding is that income, or a proxy for household income, is strongly associated with the risk of being burgled. For instance, Hough (1995) finds that lower income is associated with high degrees of anxiety about crime. The GHS provides a number of measures of household income, although not all are consistent across surveys. For this analysis we have chosen current net weekly household income, deflated to a base year price level to provide real income. In the analysis that follows in later sections we have used an equivalence scale to construct a standard of living indicator, which allows us to compare the incomes of households with different demographic structures. However, in Table 8.2 we have simply used unequivalised real net weekly household income for the purpose of comparison. Table 8.2 suggests that households in the middle-income range experience proportionately fewer burglaries than those at the lower and upper ends of the income distribution. A possible explanation for this could be related to location. Those on lowest income, who tend to live in densely populated areas, are likely to be victims of opportunistic crime whereas those on the highest income might be targeted specifically.

The Financial Loss from Burglary

Like the BCS, the GHS burglary files provide information about the value of any goods stolen, whether the loss was insured and if the incident was reported to the police. A casual analysis of the data suggests that the frequency of burglaries involving loss and the reporting rates are relatively constant across income groups, although the size of the loss tends to increase with household income. However, the interesting feature of the data is that the level of insurance increases considerably with income. Looking at the extremes, about a quarter of the burglaries experienced by low-income households and which involve some positively valued loss, are insured. On the other hand, almost 95 per cent of loss-incurring burglaries experienced by the highest income group are insured. This finding is consistent with BCS and Family Expenditure Survey data (Lewis, 1989). This problem with under-insurance by lower income households is considered in greater detail later. In the following section we take a closer look at the influence of household characteristics on property crime victimisation.

Incidence of Burglary

Probit Estimates

The probability of the discrete event of burglary is most naturally modelled as a logit or probit relation. We use a probit model, which expresses the conditional probability of a household being burgled, given its characteristics, as:

$$\Pr(b=1 \mid x) = \Phi(x\beta) \tag{8.1}$$

where b is a binary indicator of the occurrence of at least one burglary in the past 12 months, $\Phi(.)$ is the distribution function of the standard normal distribution, x is a row vector of covariates describing the household and β the corresponding coefficient vector. Estimation proceeds by maximum likelihood.

This model of burglary incidence is specified very simply, and contains a basic set of covariates describing the current demographic nature of the household. For a description of all the variables used in this analysis see Appendix Table 8.A.1. The results of the probit model are presented in Table 8.3. Many of the explanatory variables are qualitative and captured by of sets of dummy variables. These are specified so that the baseline characteristics are: a white head of household, occupying detached housing, and located in London.

The coefficient estimates are broadly consistent with previous studies. In particular, the risk of being burgled increases if the head of household is unemployed or a non-participant, lives in rented accommodation, or resides in a detached house. On the other hand, burglary risk appears to decline where households are headed by someone who is over retirement age (without children in the house), married, or who has recently moved (as the variable does not take into account the proportion of the reference year at the current address). The results also support the previous suggestion that non-white ethnic groups are significantly more likely to be victims of burglary. Interestingly, the results in Table 8.3 suggest a significant positive association between household income and victimisation.[3] We will explore this aspect of victimisation later in this chapter. Finally, as with previous studies, living in London or Northern metropolitan areas appears to increase the likelihood of victimisation.

Table 8.3   The probability of being burgled: probit estimates*

Covariates	Coefficient	|t| value
Head of Household Characteristics		
Age/10	-0.253	4.864
$(Age/10)^2$	0.019	3.503
Black	0.287	2.892
Asian	0.265	2.821
Other ethnic origin	0.187	1.845
Age > 60, no children	-0.150	2.015
Married	-0.179	4.872
Non-participant	0.111	2.423
Unemployed	0.221	4.017
Household Characteristics		
Equivalised household income	0.062	2.939
Lone parent household	0.046	0.736
Children in household	-0.020	0.493
All pensioner household	-0.082	1.148
Rented accommodation	0.118	3.176
Moved within last year	-0.251	4.646
Semi-detached house	-0.152	3.342
Terraced house	-0.096	2.070
Flat or maisonette	-0.152	2.699
Other accommodation	0.076	0.633
Regions		
North England - metropolitan	0.095	1.903
North England - non-metropolitan	-0.103	1.851
South of England	-0.196	3.809
East of England	-0.196	3.098
Wales	-0.277	3.194
North Scotland	-0.177	2.152
South Scotland	-0.211	2.597
Constant	-0.809	5.124
Log likelihood	-4347	
Observations	30692	

* Also included (but not reported) are five year dummies.

Modelling the Number of Occurrences

In Table 8.1 above we observed that a number of households suffered repeat victimisation. There are a number of factors that might increase a household's probability of repeat victimisation. For example, one household may present the burglar with particularly rich pickings or relatively simple entry. Alternatively, households in some areas (those with a high burglary rate) may be the victims of different burglars covering the same 'patch'. We now proceed to develop a model to predict the number of burglaries that a household suffers in the reference year, conditional on at least one occurrence.

We started our analysis with a simple Poisson regression model, estimated from the sub-sample of data on households burgled at least once. However, a more flexible alternative to the Poisson model is the negative binomial model, which can be generated by a stochastic mixture of Poisson processes, using a gamma mixing distribution. Thus:

$$\Pr(n \mid x, n \geq 1) = \frac{\Gamma(\alpha^{-1} + n - 1)}{\Gamma(n)\Gamma(\alpha^{-1})} \left(1 + \alpha e^{xy}\right)^{-(\alpha^{-1}+n-1)} \left(\alpha e^{xy}\right)^{n-1} \quad (8.2)$$

where n is the number of burglaries recorded. Note that model (8.2) is the negative binomial model as usually defined, applied to the number of additional burglaries, $n-1$, rather than n. The parameter α is the variance of the gamma mixing distribution, and the model (8.2) becomes the Poisson model as $\alpha \rightarrow 0$. We present the results for only the negative binomial model in Table 8.4, as there is very little difference between the two models in terms of the estimated coefficients γ. However, the restriction $\alpha = 0$ can be rejected at any reasonable significance level ($\ln \alpha = 1.57$, $t = 2.69$).

The results are given in Table 8.4. Very few of the estimated coefficients are statistically significant but there is a strong positive association between the head of household being unemployed and the risk of repeat victimisation. There are marginally significant negative estimated coefficients for dummy variables indicating a married head of household and recent removal. The latter result is predicable as those who have not been resident at the current address for the full reference period have a shorter period of exposure to risk.

Table 8.4   The probability of burglary occurrence

Covariates	Coefficient	|t| value
Head of Household Characteristics		
Age/10	-0.386	1.133
$(\text{Age}/10)^2$	0.027	0.692
Black	0.154	0.264
Asian	0.541	1.042
Other ethnic origin	-0.761	0.983
Age > 60, no children	-0.020	0.037
Married	-0.427	1.695
Non-participant	0.507	1.608
Unemployed	0.906	2.902
Household Characteristics		
Equivalised household income	0.136	0.972
Lone parent household	-0.185	0.533
Children in household	-0.155	0.552
All pensioner household	-0.946	1.590
Rented accommodation	0.193	0.685
Moved within last year	-0.754	1.895
Semi-detached house	0.277	0.711
Terraced house	0.443	1.204
Flat or maisonette	0.148	0.327
Other accommodation	-0.346	0.316
Regions		
North England - metropolitan	0.159	0.514
North England - non-metropolitan	0.328	0.931
South of England	0.128	0.389
East of England	0.472	1.210
Wales	-0.248	0.392
North Scotland	0.054	0.087
South Scotland	-0.147	0.232
Constant	0.074	0.063
Ln α	1.570	2.694
Log likelihood	-438	
Observations	1040	

* Also included (but not reported) are five year dummies.

Financial Losses from Burglary

Value of Goods Stolen

The value of goods stolen varies widely across burglary incidents, with many burglaries involving no financial loss at all in terms of the value of items stolen, but many others leading to the loss of goods that are expensive to replace. Moreover, there is a significant distributional pattern in this variation. We analyse this variation in two stages, using a double-hurdle model.

Firstly, we consider the probability that something is reported by the respondent to have been stolen and then, given that this is the case, we investigate the financial size of the loss itself. Note that this financial loss may be zero, because it is possible that items of zero value were taken. Thus, for a positive financial loss to be recorded, two hurdles must be cleared: something must have been taken, and what was taken must have been of positive value. Unusually for double-hurdle models, we are able to observe both hurdles separately. In our model, the first stage is represented by a probit relationship, while the second is specified as a censored linear regression model with the financial loss as dependent variable. Both are estimated from the full set of recorded burglary incidents. There is a further complication stemming from the fact that losses are recorded only within bands, and not as a precise figure, and we take account of this in estimating the censored regression. Consequently, our complete model for loss from burglary is:

$$\Pr(\text{loss} \mid z_i) = \Phi(z_i \delta) \tag{8.3}$$

$$\Pr(l_i = 0 \mid z_i, \text{loss}) = 1 - \Phi\left(\frac{z_i \lambda}{\sigma}\right) \tag{8.4}$$

$$\Pr(c < l_i \leq d \mid z_i, \text{loss}) = \Phi\left(\frac{d - z_i \lambda}{\sigma}\right) - \Phi\left(\frac{c - z_i \lambda}{\sigma}\right) \tag{8.5}$$

where l_i is the assessed value of the stolen property and $i = 1 \dots n$ indexes burglary incidents. The limits of the band in which the value of the loss for incident i is observed to lie are (c, d); these bands vary slightly across GHS sample years. The row vector z_i contains explanatory variables, δ and λ are the corresponding coefficient vectors and σ is the residual variance.

The results for our analysis of the financial loss from burglary are presented in Table 8.5. The first column of results relates to the probit model (8.3) and the second column of results relate to the grouped censored regression (8.4)-(8.5).

Considering first the estimated coefficients from the probit, we observe that the probability of having property stolen in a burglary is positively associated with unemployment and with living outside the South, Wales or Northern Scotland. The probability tends to be lower if there are children in the household, if the accommodation is not a house or is rented, and if the head of household is Asian. In the censored regression for the value of stolen goods, married status, lone-parenthood and high income are associated with increased loss, while minority ethnicity, children, rented accommodation and residence outside London all reduce the expected loss.

Incidence of Forced Entry

Not all burglaries involve a break-in. Entry may be effected by deception, or through unlocked doors and windows, and in such cases damage to property will be avoided. Since the cost of damage is an important element of the cost of property crime, we need some way of modelling its incidence. The cost of damage is not directly recorded in the GHS, but we do observe whether or not forced entry occurred. Our strategy is to model the binary variable recording forced entry, and then use the British Crime Survey figure of £203 in 1996 for the average cost of damage caused by break-in. The probability of forced entry for any burglary incident was modelled through a probit relationship. However we found few significant influences on the incidence of forced entry and the probit estimates are not reproduced here. The estimates are used to perform the simulations reported in the next section.

Table 8.5   The value of stolen goods*

Covariates (N = 1200)	Probit	|t| value	Censored regression	|t| value
Head of Household Characteristics				
Age/10	40.47	0.455	-0.073	0.531
$(Age/10)^2$	-5.157	0.522	-0.006	0.381
Black	-199.7	1.272	0.058	0.220
Asian	-106.1	1.019	0.445	1.719
Other ethnic origin	-241.7	2.113	-0.296	1.149
Age > 60, no children	-191.0	1.531	-0.074	0.360
Married	172.9	3.270	-0.055	0.526
Non-participant	-13.07	0.184	0.161	1.296
Unemployed	62.42	0.834	0.458	3.100
Household Characteristics				
Equivalised household income	168.1	6.285	0.050	0.725
Lone parent household	287.8	3.273	-0.093	0.586
Children in household	-124.2	2.241	-0.328	2.883
All pensioner household	162.6	1.321	0.011	0.054
Rented accommodation	-190.3	3.303	-0.204	2.006
Moved within last year	-60.09	0.742	-0.058	0.372
Semi-detached house	-18.64	0.306	-0.084	0.633
Terraced house	-114.3	1.746	-0.178	1.377
Flat or maisonette	-69.48	0.853	-0.337	2.188
Other accommodation	104.5	0.619	-0.544	1.867
Regions				
North England - metropolitan	-140.5	2.144	0.111	0.812
North England - non-metropolitan	-194.0	2.428	-0.097	0.636
South of England	-192.7	2.637	-0.311	2.198
East of England	-150.4	1.765	-0.212	1.200
Wales	-123.4	0.779	-0.650	2.623
North Scotland	-271.1	2.027	-0.620	2.774
South Scotland	48.92	0.357	-0.120	0.498
Incident number	-77.24	1.518	0.053	0.539
Constant	363.7	1.457	1.141	2.588
σ	626.9	40.71		
Log likelihood	-2731		-718	
Observations	1200		1200	

* Also included (but not reported) are five year dummies.

Distributional Impact

We can use the estimates presented in the previous sections to explore the distributional impact of burglary using simple simulation methods. The objective of the study is to give a picture of the distribution of the impact of burglary in money terms. In doing this, we capture the impact of burglary by means of an estimate of the expected annual rate of loss for each household. It is this expected rate of loss that is the true long-term cost of burglary, rather than the actual loss that happens to occur during an arbitrarily chosen 12-month period. The expected loss can be interpreted as the 'fair' annual insurance premium that would be charged by a costless risk-neutral insurer in a perfect insurance market, and it therefore measures the impact of burglary in quite natural expenditure-equivalent terms.

The non-uniform take-up of property insurance complicates the interpretation of this welfare measure. Elementary microeconomic theory holds that insurance will be taken out if the quoted premium is less than the expected loss plus a factor for risk aversion. The drawback of our expected loss measure is that it omits this latter element. If insurance premia are set with a roughly constant mark-up over expected loss, then this implies that our underestimation of the welfare loss is greater for wealthy households (which tend to be the ones that take out insurance and therefore must have a greater average risk aversion factor) than for poor ones. Different insurance pricing structures may vary this conclusion, but in any case it seems unlikely that our neglect of risk aversion will distort the distributional pattern of welfare loss in a major way.

The algorithm we use for constructing the expected loss variable for each household h is as follows.

Step 1 Generate the predicted probability of at least one burglary incident as $P_h = \Phi(x_h\beta)$.

Step 2 Calculate the predicted probabilities of all possible numbers of incidents, $Q_h(1)$, $Q_h(2)$, ..., using the fitted negative binomial distribution (8.2).

Step 3 Calculate the predicted probabilities of items being stolen, for each possible incident, $R_h(1)$, $R_h(2)$, ..., using the probit model (8.3).

Step 4 Predict the expected financial loss from each possible incident, $E_h(1)$, $E_h(2)$, ..., where $E_h = z_{hi}\lambda\ \Phi(z_{hi}\lambda) + \sigma\ \phi(z_{hi}\lambda)$

is the mean of the relevant censored normal distribution. Note that, as in step 3, we use the sequence number of the incident as an explanatory variable, so the vector z varies with i.

Step 5   Calculate the predicted probabilities of entry being forced, for each possible incident, $B_h(1)$, $B_h(2)$, ..., using the probit model (8.6).

Step 6   Construct the expected loss for household h as:

$$L_h = P_h\left(\sum_{n=1}^{\infty} Q_h(n)\sum_{i=1}^{n} R_h(i)\big[E_h(i) + B_h(i)C\big]\right) \tag{8.6}$$

where $C = £203$ is the assumed expected cost of damage caused by a break-in, based on the average figure from the British Crime Survey.

After constructing the expected loss in this way, our aim is to summarise its distributional character, and we use a non-parametric regression technique to achieve this (see Härdle (1990) and Pudney (1993) for a survey and economic examples of its use). Let y_h be the dependent variable (in practice either the simulated expected loss or its ratio to income), and let x_h be a single covariate (typically equivalised real income). Our aim is to summarise the 'average' relationship between y_h and x_h. We do this by estimating the conditional expectation function $E(y_h \mid x_h)$ nonparametrically, in other words without imposing any particular mathematical shape on the relationship *a priori*.

Nonparametric regression can be thought of heuristically as a form of local averaging. The simplest type of nonparametric regression is the bar chart. To illustrate the relationship between y_h and x_h in a bar chart, we divide the range of x into a set of intervals or 'bins', and calculate the average value of y_h for the set of households whose x–value falls within each bin. Thus, if one of the bins is defined as the interval $A = (x^*-b/2, x^*+b/2)$, where x^* is the centre of the bin and b is its width, then the height of the bar to be plotted for that bin is:

$$\hat{\mu}(x^*) = \frac{\sum\limits_{h:x_h \in A} y_h}{H_A} \tag{8.7}$$

where H_A is the number of observations in the bin A. Expression (8.7) can be written:

$$\hat{\mu}(x^*) = \frac{\sum_{h=1}^{H} k\left(\frac{x_h - x^*}{b}\right) y_h}{\sum_{h=1}^{H} k\left(\frac{x_h - x^*}{b}\right)} \tag{8.8}$$

where $k((x - x^*)/b)$ is a kernel function equal to 1 if $|x - x^*|/b < 1$, and 0 otherwise. The non-continuous kernel function imposes an undesirably ragged appearance on the estimated regression function $\hat{\mu}(x^*)$, and this approach also gives no natural way of choosing the bin-width, b. The Nadaraya-Watson kernel estimator improves upon the simple bar chart by using a kernel function that tails off smoothly as $|x - x^*|$ increases, rather than switching abruptly to zero. It also offers an asymptotic analysis of the sampling properties of the estimate, allowing an approximately optimal choice of b (now called the bandwidth). We use an adaptive variant (due to Breiman *et al.*, 1977) of the Nadaraya-Watson estimator, using the Gaussian kernel $k(\varepsilon)=(2\pi)^{-1/2}\exp(-\varepsilon^2/2)$. In this approach, the bandwidth parameter b is varied to take account of the local density of observations in different parts of the range of x.

The results of the simulated distributional impact of burglary are represented in Figures 8.1 to 8.4. Before discussing these results, we begin by defining our measure of equivalised real income. As the basis of our income figure we use the GHS variable for current net weekly household income, which is consistently defined across survey years. To take account of household composition we then use a weighting system similar to an OECD equivalence scale that attaches weights of one to the first adult in the household, 0.7 to all other adults, and 0.5 to each child. After deflating household income to 1985 prices, we then divide the deflated income figure by the equivalence index. The outcome of this is an equivalised real income figure for each household that takes account of the composition of that household.

Turning to the results of the simulation, our first observation concerns the distribution of expected annual loss from burglary by income group, as depicted in Figure 8.1. Here we see that expected loss is at its highest for those with the lowest household income, after which expected losses begin to decline until approximately the 25th income percentile. In general terms, the simulated results mirror the figures given in Table 8.2, where we observed that those in the middle income groups tended to be less likely to be burgled that those in the lower and higher groups. However, the rise in expected loss from the 30th percentile onwards is modest. Figure 8.2 shows expected loss as a proportion of income plotted against the income percentile. Expressed thus, in relation to income, burglary losses decline more or less monotonically, and burglary is therefore a 'regressive' distributional process.

In Figures 8.3 and 8.4 we take the analysis further by considering the distribution of loss by demographic group. Consider first the loss-income profiles for different ethnic groups. Although we observe the same U-shaped distribution of expected annual loss for each ethnic group, the expected loss is considerably lower for Whites than for minority ethnic groups. In particular, it is White, middle-income households who suffer the lowest rate of burglary loss. Figure 8.4 shows the relationship of expected annual loss to age of victim. Expected loss declines strongly with the age of the household head.

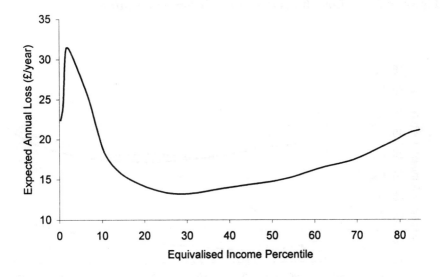

Figure 8.1   Expected annual loss by income percentile

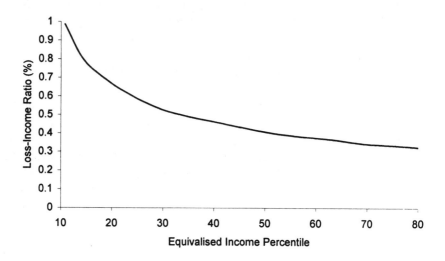

Figure 8.2   Loss-Income ratio by income percentile

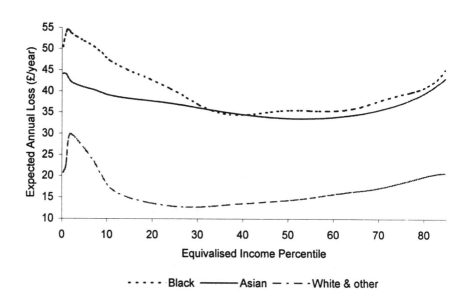

Figure 8.3   Expected annual loss by income percentile and ethnic origin

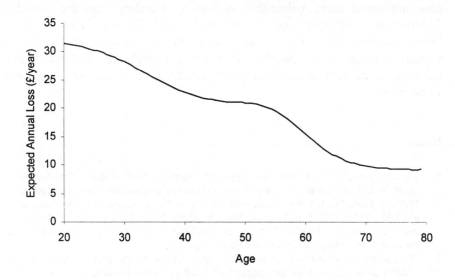

Figure 8.4   Expected annual loss by age of victim

Conclusions

We began by considering the possible influences on the probability of a household being burgled. Using data from the General Household Survey we estimated a simple probit model, the results of which suggested that households with the greatest risk of burglary are those with an ethnic minority head, who is unemployed, young, single and living in rented accommodation. However, the risk of burglary also has a positive association with household income and detached accommodation. These results reflect the general distribution of burglaries revealed earlier in Table 8.2 in which those households at the bottom and top of the income distribution had a much higher rate of victimisation than those in the middle of the income distribution. To a lesser extent, this pattern was also observed when we considered the probability of repeat victimisation by estimating a negative binomial model for burglary occurrence.

Having considered the likelihood of a household being burgled, we then turned our attention to the consequences of victimisation in terms of the losses incurred by victims. We focused on financial loss, including the costs associated with the damage that might occur during a break-in, but took no account of intangible losses such as the emotional cost of being a victim. We found that, both in absolute terms and relative to income, the poor are much more vulnerable to loss by burglary than the wealthy. Contrary to popular opinion, our results suggest that it is White, middle-income households that have the lowest risk of burglary and the lowest expected annual loss. On the other hand, households with an ethnic minority head and a relatively low standard of living are the most vulnerable.

Notes

1. The analysis of Budd (1999), who used data from the 1998 British Crime Survey to study the risk of burglary, was also based on household rather than area characteristics.
2. Material from the General Household Survey is Crown Copyright; has been made available by the Office for National Statistics through The Data Archive and has been used by permission. Neither the ONS nor The Data Archive bear any responsibility for the analysis or interpretation of the data reported here.
3. We also experimented with an alternative specification for the probit, which included additional factors such as the number of durables in the household. None of these additional factors were significantly associated with the probability of being burgled. This is an important result, as recent Home Office estimates using time-series data for England and Wales suggest a positive association between the aggregate stock of goods in the economy and the property crime rate (Dhiri *et al.*, 1999).

References

Breiman, L., Meisel, W. and Purcell, E. (1977), 'Variable Kernel Estimates of Multivariate Densities', *Technometrics*, vol. 19, pp. 135-44.

Budd, T. (1999), *Burglary of Domestic Dwellings: Findings from the British Crime Survey*, Home Office Statistical Bulletin, 4/99, Home Office, London.

Dhiri, S., Brand, S., Harries, R. and Price, R. (1999), *Modelling and Predicting Property Crime Trends in England and Wales*, Home Office Research Study 198, Home Office, London.

Fishman, G., Hakim, S. and Shachmurove, Y. (1998), 'The Use of Household Survey Data – The Probability of Property Crime Victimisation', *Journal of Economic and Social Measurement*, vol. 24, pp. 1-13.

Fitzgerald, M. and Hale, C. (1996), *Ethnic Minorities, Victimisation and Racial Harassment*, Home Office Research Findings No. 39, Home Office, London.

Foster, K., Jackson, B., Thomas, M. and Bennet, N. (1995), *General Household Survey 1993*, HMSO, London.

Freeman, S., Grogger, J. and Sonstelie, J. (1996), 'The Spatial Concentration of Crime', *Journal of Urban Economics*, vol. 40, pp. 216-31.

Härdle, W. (1990), *Applied Nonparametric Regression*, Cambridge University Press, Cambridge.

Hough, M. (1995), *Anxiety about Crime: Findings from the 1994 British Crime Survey*, Home Office Research Study No. 147, Home Office, London.

Kemshall, H. (1997), 'Sleep Safely: Crime Risks May Be Smaller Than You Think', *Social Policy and Administration*, vol. 31, pp. 247-59.

Lewis, H. (1989), *Insuring Against Burglary Losses*, Home Office Research and Planning Unit Paper 52, Home Office, London.

Lynn, P. (1997), 'Sampling Frame Effects on the British Crime Survey', *Journal of the Royal Statistical Society – Series A*, vol. 160, pp. 253-69.

Mayhew, P., and van Dijk, J. (1997), *Criminal Victimisation in Eleven Industrialised Countries*, Research and Policy No. 162, Ministry of Justice (WODC), The Hague.

Mirrlees-Black, C. and Allen, J. (1998), *Concern About Crime: Findings from the 1998 British Crime Survey*, Home office Research Findings No.83, Home Office, London.

Mirrlees-Black, C., Mayhew, P. and Percy, A. (1996), *The 1996 British Crime Survey - England and Wales*, Home Office Statistical Bulletin No. 19/96, Home Office, London.

Osborn, D.R., Trickett, A. and Elder, R. (1992), 'Area Characteristics and Regional Variates as Determinants of Area Property Crime Levels', *Journal of Quantitative Criminology*, vol. 8, pp. 265-85.

Pudney, S. E. (1993), 'Income and Wealth Inequality and the Life Cycle: A Nonparametric Analysis for China', *Journal of Applied Econometrics*, vol. 8, pp. 249-76.

Trickett, A., Osborn, D.R. and Ellingworth D. (1993), *Simple and Repeat Victimisation: The Influences of Individual and Area Characteristics*, Discussion Paper ES239, Department of Econometrics and Statistics, University of Manchester.

Trickett, A., Osborn, D.R. and Ellingworth, D. (1995), 'Property Crime Victimisation: The Roles of Individual and Area Influences', *International Review of Victimology*, vol. 3, pp. 273-95.

APPENDIX 8.1

Table 8.A.1 Descriptive statistics

Covariates (N = 30692)	Mean	Std. Dev.
Head of Household Characteristics		
Age	5.102	1.820
Ethnicity (base = White)	0.960	0.196
Black	0.011	0.104
Asian	0.015	0.121
Other ethnic origin	0.014	0.118
Age > 60, no children	0.343	0.475
Married	0.628	0.483
Employment status (based = employed)	0.548	0.498
Non-participant	0.391	0.488
Unemployed	0.061	0.239
Household Characteristics		
Equivalised household Income (£)	85.263	64.999
Lone parent household	0.051	0.219
Children in household	0.274	0.446
All pensioner household	0.270	0.444
Rented accommodation	0.382	0.486
Moved within last year	0.098	0.298
House type (base = detached)	0.175	0.380
Semi-detached house	0.312	0.463
Terraced house	0.297	0.457
Flat or maisonette	0.204	0.403
Other accommodation	0.013	0.115
Region (base = London)	0.113	0.317
North England – metropolitan	0.203	0.402
North England - non-metropolitan	0.155	0.362
South of England	0.275	0.446
East of England	0.112	0.315
Wales	0.049	0.216
North Scotland	0.045	0.208
South Scotland	0.049	0.215

9. The Under-Reporting of Property Crime

ZIGGY MACDONALD

Introduction

In recent years there has been considerable attention paid to the relationship between criminal activity and the incentives generated by the economy and the criminal justice system. Since the pioneering work of Field (1990), there have been many contributions to this literature, examples of which include Pyle and Deadman (1994), Hale (1998), and Witt *et al.* (1999). Comprehensive reviews of the literature can be found in Ehrlich (1996), Allen (1996) and Pyle (1998). Although the connection between crime and the economy is well considered in the literature of 19th century criminology and social science (Taylor, 1997), much of this recent work takes its motivation from Becker (1968) and subsequently Ehrlich (1973), who argued that the relationship between economic incentives and criminal activity is a consequence of rational behaviour. Put simply, some individuals will participate in criminal activity if the expected returns exceed those from legal activity (taking into account the probability of apprehension and conviction, etc.).

Although it is intuitively appealing, the literature concerned with the relationship between economic and criminal activity is not without controversy. For example, there is considerable debate about the incentives generated by unemployment (Pyle, 1998), and the results given in the literature are far from unequivocal (Young, 1993). This debate concerns two conflicting theories about the relationship: opportunity theories and motivational theories (Cantor and Land, 1985). Those advocating motivational theories (perhaps the majority view) tend to argue that unemployment or economic hardship, by generating relative poverty, stimulate criminal activity (see for example Phillips *et al.*, 1972; Sjoquist, 1973; Myers, 1983). This view has tended to receive the greatest support in the empirical literature (e.g. Witt *et al.*, 1999; Raphael and Winter-Ebmer, 1998; Elliot and Ellingworth, 1998). The opposing view, driven by opportunity theories, suggests that the crime rate will fall as unemployment increases. This might be because of the 'guardianship effect': as unemployment increases there are more people at home to deter criminals (Cohen *et al.*, 1981; Cohen and Felson, 1979), or it could be because unemployment reduces the wealth of victims (Cohen *et al.*, 1980).

Against this background there is a more fundamental debate over the meaning and interpretation of official crime statistics. A cursory glance at a criminology text reveals a long-standing concern over the 'dark figure' of hidden or unrecorded crime (Radzinowicz and King, 1977; Tierney, 1996). Clearly, if this level of unrecorded crime varies over time then official crime statistics will not reflect true changes in actual crime and as such, any estimated models of crime and economic incentives will be inherently biased. The purpose of this chapter is to take a further look at the 'dark figure'. In particular, we hypothesise that the divergence between the recorded crime rate and the true crime rate is related to variations in the economic cycle, as is the actual crime rate (although we recognise that a small part of the divergence will be due to changes in police recording practices (Taylor, 1999), or definitional changes).

To consider these issues further, we explore the influences on individual reporting inclinations using data from the British Crime Survey (BCS).[1] There are many aspects to consider in this analysis. Intuitively, one might expect that individuals would fail to report a crime if they perceive the outcome of reporting as negligible. For example, previous negative experience with the Criminal Justice System, personal prejudice, and a lack of confidence in the police all may affect an individual's reporting inclination. Similarly, it is possible that cultural and ethnic differences are likely to affect reporting rates given the varying perceptions of the police and officialdom across communities. To proceed with our analysis we next consider the literature on economic models of crime and then attempt to unravel the various hypotheses that have been put forward to explain why crimes are not reported. Following this, we consider the current data set and its suitability for our analysis. We then present our empirical methodology and discuss our results. We will show that once we take account of the non-random nature of victimisation, the probability of an incident being reported is largely driven by factors related to the economic cycle.

Literature Review

The motivation for this work comes from two sources. Firstly we consider the debate over the data used to analyse the relationship between economic incentives and the crime rate. This debate focuses on the nature of time series data and the validity of official crime statistics. The second literature we consider focuses on the determinants of individual reporting behaviour and the factors that might be associated with an individual's inclination to report a crime.

Crime and Economic Activity

The analysis of crime and criminal activity tends to be characterised by two opposing views. There are those who accept that official crime figures are prone to error, but proceed with the development of economic models of crime, focussing on the methodology used in time series analysis. For example, Elliot and Ellingworth (1998) argue that recent contributions to the literature have ignored the functional form of the variables used in the typical analysis. Pyle and Deadman (1994) improve on the pioneering work of Field (1990) by allowing for explicit modelling of long-run trends in variables, arguing that earlier work did not account for these long-run relationships. Hale (1998), on the other hand, in response to Deadman and Pyle, reconsiders the order of integration employed in time series models of crime, and the tendency for error correction models to be mis-specified. Although still ongoing, this debate has not overshadowed the general consensus that property crimes (e.g. burglary, theft and robbery) tend to be related to economic activity in some counter-cyclical way.

The second view, which characterises the criminological debate, tends to focus on the information contained in crime statistics, and in particular the correlation between recorded crime and actual crime. Often referred to as the 'dark figure', the volume of unrecorded crime can change as reporting and recording practices change. This in turn can lead to misleading claims about trends in the true crime rate based on official crime statistics. The causes and consequences of the 'dark figure' are well documented in the literature, as are attempts to overcome the problem (see for example Koffman, 1996 and Sparks *et al.*, 1977). The majority of the discrepancy is typically viewed as the result of under-reporting (Tierney, 1996), although other factors (such as definitional changes and the social or political construction of the shape of the 'crime problem') are also important and subject to vigorous debate in the literature (see for example, Maguire, 1997 and Taylor, 1999). Thus the focus of this chapter is the implication of changing levels of hidden crime for time-series models of crime.

To the researcher engaged in estimation of the determinants of crime, the well-established deficiency in criminal statistics would appear rather depressing. However, against this background, the seminal work of Myers (1980), and the material presented in Chapter Three and elsewhere in

Pudney *et al.* (2000), appears to offer some respite to those who estimate these models. Myers' original analysis was concerned with the impact of underreporting in a model of deterrence, and in particular, whether underreporting has any apparent effect on the magnitudes and signs of estimated coefficients. The conclusion of this analysis, carried out on a sample of US cities (the city was the level of aggregation for reporting outcomes), was that underreporting, and consequently the 'dark figure', was not a significant impediment in a simple economic model of deterrence. However, since this work there has been considerable enhancement in the sophistication of economic models of crime, and in the techniques used to estimate them (including error correction models and co-integration), which have been pursued against continual scepticism about the accuracy of recorded crime data.

Pudney *et al.* (2000) present a complex analysis of the relationship between crime, deterrence, and economic conditions that attempts to address the problem posed by hidden crime. The approach makes use of a variety of technically complex statistical methods, and involves a simulated maximum likelihood procedure in which the recording error and crime process are estimated simultaneously. The results suggest that although the biases that arise from recording errors are dynamically complex, they are of little practical significance. The implicit assumption in Pudney *et al.*, and most other work, is that the divergence between actual and reported (or recorded) crime is generated by a random process. The purpose of this analysis is to explore whether this is necessarily the case. To proceed, we begin by looking at the factors that might influence reporting activity.

The Determinants of Individual Reporting Behaviour

In a recent paper, Beki *et al.* (1999) presented an analysis of the crime rate in the Netherlands that appeared to take account of the 'dark figure'. This was achieved by including a number of regressors in their estimated crime equation that were believed to influence reporting inclination. Unfortunately, the choice of variables to control for underreporting does not appear to be guided by the available literature. Beki *et al.* include three variables for this purpose: housing tenure (rented or not), household contents insurance, and whether the individual has a telephone. Although the literature on underreporting is not large, there are clearly a greater number of factors to be considered. Notable contributions to this literature include Goldberg and Nold (1980), Myers (1980), Skogan (1994) and Sparks *et al.* (1977), all of which suggest that there are many factors that might influence the probability of an incident being reported. Goldberg and

Nold (1980), looking at burglary deterrence, include a model of the household's probability of reporting a crime given as a function of the loss involved, property damage, and the cost of reporting (although empirically they are not able to include the cost of reporting because their data set does not provide adequate information). More generally, Myers (1980) suggests that underreporting occurs because it sometimes just does not pay to report a crime. Whether or not a crime is reported, however, will also depend on a variety of individual attributes, experiences and personal circumstances specific to that incident. There appears to be some debate, however, as to the relative importance of these various factors. We proceed by considering the various hypothesised influences according to a number of groupings suggested by Skogan (1994) and Sparks *et al.* (1977).[2]

We first consider those influences on reporting inclination that can be considered socio-economic. This group of factors includes influences such as the age, gender and ethnicity of victims, their personal or household income, and labour market status. In general, these factors tend to impact on the likelihood of reporting an incident as a consequence of experience. For example, those on higher incomes tend to be less likely to have been previous victims and are thus more likely to report incidents (Skogan, 1994). Moreover, individuals who are older and on higher incomes are more likely to be insured than those on lower income or who are unemployed (Lewis, 1989), and hence are more likely to report an incident, particularly if it involves a loss. We also include location in this category, as victim surveys tend to suggest that certain social groups within certain areas (particularly the inner city) are more likely to be victims of crime and hence this will shape their tendency towards reporting incidents, probably downwards (Maguire, 1997).

The second group of factors relates to individuals' attitudes to the police and the criminal justice system. Individuals' attitudes towards the police tend to be shaped by various experiences, beliefs and prejudices, but it is likely that common experiences affect the likelihood of contacting the police in the light of an incident. For example, it is conceivable that an individual who is familiar with members of the police or is part of a neighbourhood watch scheme would have little hesitation in reporting an incident compared to someone who is less familiar with the way the police operate. On the other hand, if an individual perceives the police as ineffectual in dealing with burglary incidents, then they will see little point in contacting them. Indeed, Craig (1987), in an analysis of the deterrent impact of the police, claims that the probability of apprehension is a crucial element in determining whether a crime will be reported. Alternatively, individual reticence in reporting incidents may derive from a general fear or distrust of the police, or from a negative experience of law enforcement (Skogan, 1994). This reticence may derive from previous experience of being stopped by the police, or alternatively culpability may play a role in the decision to report an incident (Skogan, 1994).

The group of factors that tends to receive the greatest support in the literature relates to those influences that can be considered incident-specific. For example, an individual's inclination to report an incident may be influenced by the relationship between victim and offender (if known); the seriousness of the incident; or the loss (and/or damage) involved with the incident (although this is entangled with socio-economic factors as one would expect higher income households to experience greater losses in absolute terms). Other incident-specific influences include whether or not the victim thought the incident racially motivated, if the victim was at home at the time of the incident, and whether the incident occurred at night, all of which relate to the perceived threat or seriousness of the incident. Typically incident-specific influences involve some sort of assessment about the costs and benefits associated with reporting a specific incident. Goldberg and Nold (1980) allude to this type of assessment when they include the cost of reporting the incident in their reporting probability function.

The final group of influences relates to individual criminality. We have already mentioned that there are a number of factors relating to one's attitude towards the police that could conceivably influence the likelihood of reporting an incident. However, it may be the case that it is a victim's own criminal inclinations that affect the tendency not to report an incident (Sparks *et al.*, 1977). For example, an individual who regularly participates in drug misuse will be more reluctant to report an incident than a non-user, particularly if this increases the chance of direct contact with the police. Moreover, it may be the case that individuals involved in crime are less attached to 'normal society' in much the same way as other marginalised groups, and are thus unlikely to see the reporting of a burglary as an appropriate course of action.

In a more general sense, there is a certain amount of interconnection between many of the factors in the categories we have outlined. This makes it difficult to separate the impact of the various categories on the propensity to report a crime (although we can control for them individually). However, we can estimate a model of reporting behaviour in which individuals are assumed to rationally assess the costs and benefits of reporting an incident, even if their actual behaviour is not explicitly reflecting this assessment (Myers, 1980). This approach, in which incident specific factors, socio-economic differences, etc., are quantified as exogenous determinants of reporting behaviour, can help us establish whether factors that are associated with the economic cycle are dominant over other influences on reporting activity. We return to this issue when we discuss our methodology and results.

Data and Empirical Methodology

The British Crime Survey

To explore the under-reporting of crime we make use of data provided in the British Crime Survey (BCS). The BCS is an extensive victim survey that provides victimisation rates for a large number of categories of offence (the notable exclusions being fraud, drug offences and theft from businesses). It was first administered in 1982 and has been repeated in 1984, 1988, 1992, 1994, 1996 and 1998 (although at the time of writing the 1998 data were not available). More details of the BCS are given in Chapters 4 and 10. We restrict our analysis to the 1994 and 1996 surveys as data from previous years are not compatible due to differences in sampling and interview techniques.[3] With respect to the sample size, the 1994 survey yields a core sample of 14,500 adults, and the 1996 survey 16,350 adults. Both samples are increased by an ethnic minority booster sample of approximately 2000 Black and Asian adults. For more details of the sampling procedure for the 1994 survey see White and Malbon (1995), and for the 1996 survey see Hales and Stratford (1997).

In this chapter we are concerned with the reporting inclination of those individuals who have experienced some form of property crime over the year preceding the survey, in particular, residential burglary. This category of crime is the typical focus of the literature on predictive crime models, and is suitable for analysis as we are less likely to suffer from recall bias in our estimates. We use a modified version of the BCS definition of burglary: 'entering the respondent's dwelling as a trespasser with the intention of committing theft, rape, grievous bodily harm or unlawful damage [whether the intention is carried through or not]' (White and Malbon, 1995: 260). In our analysis, the respondent has been a victim of burglary if he or she answers yes to one of the following questions:

- Has anyone got into this house/flat without permission and stolen or tried to steal anything?

- Did anyone get into your house/flat without permission and cause damage?

- Have you had any evidence that someone has tried to get in without permission to steal or to cause damage?

The responses to these questions cover burglary, including unlawful damage, and attempted burglary. If interviewees respond that they have experienced a crime, they then complete a Victim Form. These are used to collect further information about all the incidents experienced during the year preceding the survey, up to a total of six (five for the 1994 survey). For each incident, the respondent is asked whether the police were informed and this provides us with our reporting data. There are, of course, many follow-ups to this primary question, depending on the interviewee's initial response. For example, if the incident was not reported, the respondent is asked to explain why not, and if the police were informed of the incident, the survey asks how it was reported and who contacted the police.

Modelling Reporting Inclination

There has been some previous analysis of the under-reporting of crime in the UK, however the methodology applied tends to be subject to some criticism. Skogan (1994) and MacDonald (2000) estimate reporting models using the sample of BCS crime incidents, where the dependent variable is a simple dichotomous measure of reporting (the incident was reported or not), regressed on a number of covariates capturing a number of the influences previously discussed. The approach taken in these papers is slightly problematic, because the observations in the data sample relate to 'incidents' rather than 'victims'.

If the sample consists of all possible incidents, it is likely that a proportion of these represent repeat victimisation (i.e. when interviewees have reported more than one burglary in the survey period). When this occurs there will be some form of event-dependency between observations as the experiences of one burglary might affect the reporting outcome of a subsequent burglary. Other than including a covariate that indicates repeat victimisation, there is no direct way of overcoming this problem. However, we can avoid the problem by taking an approach similar to Sparks *et al.* (1977), in which we estimate two alternative models. In the first model we look at the reporting of only the first recorded incident, ignoring any cases of repeat victimisation. Only considering the first incident experienced overcomes any problems of event-dependency, as any subsequent incidents are irrelevant to the first incident. As such the covariates used in the model will be directly related to the likelihood of reporting an incident, irrespective of whether later in the survey period a subsequent incident occurs. For our second model we consider whether the individual reports any of the incidents that have been experienced (which for the majority of individuals will be the only incident). By doing this we can include all data on incidents, but we have to revise all our incident-specific covariates so that they refer to all the incidents in a general sense (i.e. the reporting variable takes the value of 1 if any of the incidents are reported).

There are a number of other lesser problems to consider before we can proceed to our analysis. The first of these concerns those survey respondents who have experienced more incidents than there are available Victim Forms. If this occurs then we may loose information about these incidents if an individual experiences a lot of different types of crime in the survey period such that even if they have experienced only one burglary it does not get recorded on a Victim Form. Although we have no mechanism to overcome this problem, the number of observations we are likely to miss will be only a fraction of one per cent (Hales and Stratford, 1997). There is also a potential problem when interviewees experience a 'series' of incidents. This occurs when 'the same thing was done under the same circumstances and probably by the same people' (Hales and Stratford, 1997, p.3), in which case they are considered as one group (as would be the case in police recording practice). When this occurs, then a Victim Form is only completed for the last incident in the series and this one observation is used for the whole group. This might have implications for our model estimates as the details about just one incident mask the circumstances of several incidents. We overcome this problem by including a dummy variable to control for these anomalous observations. Furthermore, given that multiple incidents are likely to be influenced by social and economic conditions (see Chapter 8), this can be accounted for by first conditioning on the likelihood of being burgled, which is considered in the next section.

Empirical Methodology

The previous discussion highlighted our concern that the BCS observations are not a random sample from the universe of incidents. There are also reasons to question the non-random nature of victimisation in general. In Chapter Five and elsewhere (Osborn *et al.* 1992; Trickett *et al.* 1995), it has been shown that victimisation is highly correlated with a number of socio-economic factors, and these often overlap with the covariates that are likely to influence reporting behaviour. If this is the case then our data-generation process is characterised by non-random sample selection. In short, data on reporting activity is only observed when there is a burglary to report.

Although this sounds trivial, sample selection can result in considerable bias in our estimates. To overcome the problem we estimate a Bivariate Probit with Sample Selection (Greene, 1997).

To see how this is estimated let us first consider our primary model, which concerns individual reporting inclinations. As with many models in social science, we cannot observe an individual's tendency to report a crime, rather, we assume it to be an underlying latent process that drives the actual observed reporting outcome (i.e. whether the incident is reported or not). We let the latent variable r^* denote an individual's propensity to report a crime. This is related to the observed individual characteristics through the structural model:

$$r^* = x\beta + \varepsilon \tag{9.1}$$

where x is a row vector of personal and demographic attributes (predictors), β is the corresponding vector of parameters to be estimated, and ε is a normally distributed error term with mean zero and variance one, conditional on x, that captures the unobserved determinants of reporting inclination. The latent variable r^* drives the observed reporting outcome, r, through the measurement equation:

$$r = \begin{cases} 1 & \text{if } r^* > 0 \\ 0 & \text{if } r^* \leq 0 \end{cases} \tag{9.2}$$

Estimation of (9.1) as a probit model is straightforward, and provides us with direct measures of the impact of the various explanatory variables on the likelihood of reporting an incident. However, as expressed above, we can only estimate (9.1) if we observe a burglary. As being burgled is not necessarily a completely random event we must also estimate the probability of an individual being burgled. Suppose that the likelihood of being burgled is represented by the latent variable b^* which, in a similar fashion to the latent variable for reporting, is determined by:

$$b^* = z\gamma + \mu \tag{9.3}$$

where z is a row vector of personal and demographic attributes, γ is the corresponding vector of parameters, and μ is a normally distributed error term with mean zero and variance one, conditional on z. As with (9.1) above, the observed burglary outcome, b, takes the value of 1 if $b^* > 0$, and zero otherwise.

With this specification, we will observe a reporting outcome (r) only when $b = 1$ (i.e. $b^* > 0$). However, we must also allow for any unobserved characteristics that influence both r^* and b^*, in which case the error terms ε and μ will be correlated (i.e. the covariance parameter $\rho \neq 0$). We therefore estimate our model as a bivariate probit of the joint outcomes of (9.1) and (9.3), where the joint probability of being burgled and reporting that incident is given by:

$$\Pr(r_i = 1, b_i = 1) = \Phi(x\beta, z\gamma, \rho) \qquad (9.4)$$

where Φ is the cumulative distribution function for the standard bivariate normal distribution. Finally, to ensure that the bivariate model is fully identified, we must include at least one covariate in the burglary equation that is not in the reporting equation. In other words, we require a variable in z (termed an 'instrument') that influences the individual's likelihood of being burgled, but does not influence an individual's tendency to report an incident to the Police. We return to this issue in the next section.

Finally, we should note that the model given in (9.4) does not correspond exactly to the 'dark figure' of unreported crime. This is because the bivariate model gives us the probability of a victim reporting an incident and the probability of a non-victim reporting an incident if he or she were actually a victim. Fortunately, because the probability of being a victim is so low (below), we will find that the estimates from this bivariate model are very similar to the single probit model (9.1), which only considers those individuals in the sample who were victims. As such, in the next section we proceed to present the results of the bivariate model.

Results

In our sample of 34,850 respondents (18,333 from the 1996 survey and 16,517 from the 1994 survey), 2,820 (8.1 per cent) have been victims of burglary during the survey period (either once or more). Reporting rates vary according to how we define the sample, but on average 65 per cent of burglaries are reported (appendix Table 9.A.1 provides descriptive statistics for all the other variables used in our analysis). The selectivity-corrected probit estimates of the probability of reporting a burglary incident are given in Table 9.1. The coefficients indicate the impact of the corresponding explanatory variable on the probability of an incident being reported. The base characteristics for the models are: white, single, female, and in work. The uncorrected probit estimates of reporting are given in appendix Table 9.A.2. These reveal that sample selection tends to result in a slight upward bias in the size of the estimated coefficients and level of significance, although the same variables remain significant and the signs on the coefficients are typically unchanged. The estimated coefficients for the burglary selection equation are given in appendix Table 9.A.3. The selection equation is specified very simply, but it is interesting to note that living in an area perceived to have a drug problem has a positive impact on the probability of being victimised. Individuals located in an inner city area and those who have moved in the past year are also more likely to be burgled (the drug problem and recently moved variables are included as instruments so that the bivariate probit is fully identified).

In Table 9.1, we provide separate estimates for our two models. In Model 1 we consider the reporting of the first burglary experienced by individuals but ignore any subsequent incidents. Model 2 concerns all the incidents experienced by individuals, but with the variables coded so that they refer to *any* of the incidents (i.e. the reporting variable takes a value of one if any of the incidents have been reported). The models are specified simply with the set of covariates intended to reflect each of the categories identified earlier as likely influences on reporting, and where possible we have grouped the coefficients according to the categories of factors outlined earlier.

In general terms, the results in Table 9.1 are consistent across the two models. With respect to our socio-economic covariates, we find a significant positive association with age and reporting inclination. We also find that males are significantly less likely to report an incident than females. The results also suggest that individuals of Asian origin, when compared to the base group (White), have a stronger reporting inclination. These results are contrary to Sparks *et al.* (1977) who found that data on respondents themselves were of little use in predicting reporting (but it should be noted that the sample used was of known victims). Likewise, Skogan (1994) found gender and ethnicity insignificant in a logit model of reporting inclination. We also note that the variable capturing the effect of inner city location is not significant, although the signs on the coefficients are in the right direction (and as previously stated the variable is significant in the burglary selection equation).

Table 9.1   The probability of reporting a burglary

Covariates	Model 1 Coefficient	S.E.	Model 2 Coefficient	S.E
Socio-economic				
Age/100	0.546#	0.200	0.574#	0.204
Male	-0.181#	0.054	-0.171#	0.055
Married	0.071	0.054	0.077	0.054
Black	0.093	0.094	0.121	0.096
Asian	0.262#	0.090	0.256#	0.092
Other ethnic origin	-0.123	0.163	-0.156	0.163
Resident in inner city area	0.105	0.065	0.104	0.065
Household contents insurance	0.038	0.059	0.044	0.059
Unemployed	-0.195#	0.080	-0.237#	0.080
Other non-participant	-0.210#	0.064	-0.209#	0.065
Incident Specific				
Resulted in a loss of earnings	1.192#	0.273	1.189#	0.269
Involved a positively valued loss	1.036#	0.066	1.078#	0.070
Occurred at night	0.261#	0.052	0.277#	0.052
Occurred at weekend	0.112*	0.054	0.147#	0.055
Racially motivated	-0.068	0.334	-0.083	0.315
Victim responsible	-0.045	0.081	-0.096	0.079
Victim injured	0.978#	0.332	1.335#	0.369
Offender known	0.039	0.095	0.003	0.093
Incident covers a series	-0.307#	0.078	-0.223#	0.076
Attitudes to Police				
Worried about crime in area	0.180#	0.059	0.201#	0.059
Member of Neighbourhood Watch	0.040	0.088	-0.008	0.088
Believe police do very poor job	-0.277*	0.121	-0.246*	0.122
Criminality				
Taken any drug in past year[4]	-0.021	0.088	-0.014	0.088
Stopped by police more than twice	-0.173	0.486	-0.211	0.482
Constant	-1.300	0.278	-1.397	0.274
Correlation coefficient (ρ)	0.265	0.170	0.292	0.169
$N_{respondents\ (victims)}$	34850 (2756)		34850 (2820)	
χ^2 (d.f.)	1251 (47)		1283 (47)	
Log Likelihood	-11049		-10996	

Note: # = significant at 1% level, * = significant at 5% level.

A surprising result in Table 9.1 is that 'contents insurance' is not significant in either model. However, when insurance is interacted with 'loss' (not shown in these results) it becomes significant, although incidents involving loss when there is no contents insurance are also significantly associated with reporting.

Looking at the groups of influences as a whole, it is quite clear from our results that economic and incident specific factors tend to dominate the reporting decision. These findings are to some extent consistent with both Skogan (1994) and Sparks *et al.* (1977). In both models unemployment (and other non-participation) has a negative impact on the probability of reporting a burglary, and this is after having controlled for the probability of being burgled.[5] We also observe that incidents which involve a positively valued loss (due to loss of goods or damage to property) are significantly more likely to be reported than incidents that do not involve a loss. This is consistent with the results presented by Goldberg and Nold (1980). We also find that if the incident results in the victim incurring some loss of earnings then this has a significant positive impact on the probability of reporting. Although not well defined in the BCS Technical Manual, we assume that by reporting the incident, the individual believes that it is possible to recover the loss of earnings. The alternative definition of this variable is that the loss of earnings is a cost of reporting, but if this were the case, then we would expect that the sign on the coefficient would be in the other direction (i.e. if the act of reporting the incident resulted in a loss of earnings, say through time off work, then you would be less likely to report the incident).

To put these findings into context, we can consider the impact of these variables taking a value of one on the probability of reporting an incident. To do this we work out the probability of a given individual reporting an incident by substituting the estimated coefficients (β) from the bivariate probit results and the given characteristics (x) into the following equation (assuming a burglary has occurred):

$$\Pr(r = 1) = \Phi(\beta' x) \tag{9.5}$$

where Φ is the cumulative distribution function for the standard normal distribution. Thus, the probability of a 35-year-old individual with base characteristics (white, single, female, in work) reporting an incident is 0.14. However, should this individual be unemployed the probability of reporting an incident reduces to 0.09. On the other hand, if the incident resulted in the 35-year-old individual with base characteristics suffering a loss of earnings, the probability of reporting that incident increases to 0.53. Clearly this

reveals that loss of earnings has a much bigger impact on the probability of reporting an incident than does any difference in employment status. However, if we consider just those victims who have suffered a positively valued loss, the impact of labour market status becomes more apparent. Running a simple probit for reporting on just those victims who have experienced a loss (results not reported here), the probability of an individual with base characteristics reporting that incident is 0.65. If we make that person unemployed, then the chances of the incident being reported reduce to 0.54, (i.e. by 17 per cent).

Returning to our main results, other incident specific factors that significantly increase the probability of reporting include incidents that occur at night and those which result in the victim being injured. This is consistent with the conclusion drawn by Sparks *et al.* (1977) that the seriousness of the incident is important in determining whether it is reported or not. Finally we consider factors such as police antipathy and criminality. Our results suggest that individuals with a low opinion of the police are significantly less likely to report an incident than those who are neutral or positive about the police. Interestingly, being a member of a neighbourhood watch scheme appears to have no significant impact on reporting inclination (although the estimated coefficients are positive). However, we do observe that 'individuals' anxiety about burglary' has a significant positive coefficient in all the models. Surprisingly, our 'criminality' variables are not significantly associated with the probability of reporting an incident, although the signs on the coefficients are in the right direction. In this category we included recent (self-reported) drug use and frequent contact with the police due to being stopped for questioning or searching (although this does not necessarily imply criminality). In a previous analysis (MacDonald, 2000) we found drug users to be significantly less likely to report an incident. We do not find this association statistically significant in this analysis. This is perhaps due to the expanded set of covariates used here and the use of an improved estimation technique, however, we do observe that in the current results the sign on the estimated coefficients is negative in both models, as is the case in previous analysis.

Conclusion

The underreporting of crime is clearly a problem for any analyst who uses official crime statistics to comment on the crime rate. We began by hypothesising that variations in the under-reporting of property crime might be linked to the economic cycle, and proceeded to explore the factors that influence the 'dark figure' of hidden crime. Our literature review suggested that there are a number of factors that affect individuals' tendency to report an incident, including socio-economic differences, factors that are specific to the incident, individual attitudes towards the police, and individual 'criminality'. To estimate the impact of these various factors on reporting inclinations we used data from the British Crime Survey on individual experiences of burglary and estimated a bivariate probit model of reporting inclination, conditional on being burgled.

Many factors appear to be significant in explaining reporting inclination, although our results suggest that economic and incident-specific factors dominate the decision to report a burglary. In particular, we found significant associations between reporting inclination and several factors that are directly influenced by the economy. We found that labour market status has a significant impact on reporting, with non-participants and those not in employment being far less likely than those in work to report an incident. We also found that financial loss (as a result of stolen or damaged items) and loss of earnings have a strong positive impact on the probability of an individual reporting an incident. Other factors that significantly influence reporting inclination include an individual's dislike of the police (negative) and concern about burglary in the area (positive). Interestingly, we find no association between criminality factors and reporting inclination.

In conclusion, we have identified sufficient evidence to support our hypothesis that the reporting of burglary, and hence the divergence between the recorded crime rate and the true crime rate, is influenced by economic incentives. However, we have also found that incident-specific factors are also important in the reporting decision. Some of these factors are likely to be linked to the economic cycle, but some are clearly related to an individual's assessment of the costs and benefits of reporting an incident, once that incident has happened. However, although a certain proportion of the divergence between the true crime rate and the recorded rate is driven by factors that are not directly influenced by economic conditions (e.g. age, gender, time of incident, and suffering an injury), most of the variations in the 'dark figure' could be controlled for. What we have not determined, of course, is whether or not the variations in underreporting identified here will remain true over time. A natural extension to this analysis would be to estimate an economic model of criminal activity using time series data, which allows for variations in reporting activity to be simultaneously determined with the crime rate and influenced by the same variables used to proxy the economic cycle.

Notes

1. The British Crime Survey comes from Crown copyright records made available through the Home Office and the ESRC Data Archive, and has been used by permission of the Controller of Her Majesty's Stationery Office.
2. We note that Skogan (1994) and Sparks *et al.* (1977) look at the factors that influence the likelihood of reporting all types of incident. As we are focussing on property crime, some of the factors that they consider are less relevant to our discussion.
3. The differences in sampling and interview techniques are discussed in more detail in MacDonald (1998).
4. Questions about drug use are only asked of respondents under 60 years old. In the current model we simply set the 'drug use in the past year' variable equal to zero for all respondents aged 60 or over. This is justified by the fact that most research indicates that current drug use is concentrated among the young. It is interesting to note, however, that if we restrict our sample to just those respondents under 60 years old, this has no impact on the significance of the drug use coefficient but it results in a larger more significant coefficient on our unemployment variable.
5. In addition to the current model specification an alternative model was estimated which included several dummy variables to control for different household income bands. The results are not presented here to preserve space, but are available from the author on request. When we include income in the model, we find that those in the highest income bracket are significantly more likely than those on low income to report an incident. This complements the finding of a negative association between unemployment and reporting inclination.

References

Allen, R.C. (1996), 'Socioeconomic Conditions and Property Crime: A Comprehensive Review and Test of the Professional Literature', *American Journal of Economics and Sociology*, vol. 55, pp. 293-308.

Becker, G.S. (1968), 'Crime and Punishment: An Economic Approach', *Journal of Political Economy*, vol. 76, pp. 169-217.

Beki, C., Zeelenberg, K. and van Montfort, K. (1999), 'An Analysis of the Crime Rate in the Netherlands 1950-93', *British Journal of Criminology*, vol. 39, pp. 401-15.

Cantor, D. and Land, K.C. (1985), 'Unemployment and Crime Rates in the Post-World War II U.S.: A Theoretical and Empirical Analysis', *American Sociological Review*, vol. 50, pp. 317-32.

Cohen, L.E. and Felson, M. (1979), 'Social Trends and Crime Trends: A Routine Activity Approach', *American Sociological Review*, vol. 44, pp. 588-607.

Cohen, L.E., Felson, M. and Land, K.C. (1980), 'Property Crime Rates in the United States: A Macrodynamic Analysis, 1947-1977; with Ex Ante Forecasts for the Mid-1980s', *American Journal of Sociology*, vol. 86, pp. 90-118.

Cohen, L.E., Kluegel, J.R. and Land, K.C. (1981), 'Social Inequality and Predatory Criminal Victimisation: An Exposition and Test of a Formal Theory', *American Sociological Review*, vol. 52, pp. 505-24.

Craig, S.G. (1987), 'The Deterrent Impact of Police: An Examination of a Locally Provided Public Service', *Journal of Urban Economics*, vol. 21, pp. 298-311.

Ehrlich, I (1973) 'Participation in Illegitimate Activities: A Theoretical and Empirical Analysis', *Journal of Political Economy*, vol. 81, pp. 521-64.

Ehrlich, I. (1996), 'Crime, Punishment and the Market for Offenses', *Journal of Economic Perspectives*, vol. 10, pp. 43-67.

Elliot, C. and Ellingworth, D. (1998), 'Exploring the Relationship Between Unemployment and Property Crime', *Applied Economics Letters*, vol. 5, pp. 527-30.

Field, S. (1990), *Trends in Crime and Their Interpretation. A Study of Recorded Crime in Post-War England and Wales*, Home Office Research Study no. 119, Home Office, London.

Goldberg, G. and Nold, F.C. (1980), 'Does Reporting Deter Burglars? - An Empirical Analysis of Risk and Return in Crime', *Review of Economics and Statistics*, vol. 62, pp. 424-31.

Greene, W.H. (1997), *Econometric Analysis*, 3rd edition, Prentice Hall, London.

Hale, C. (1998), 'Crime and the Business Cycle in Post-War Britain Revisited', *British Journal of Criminology*, vol. 38, pp. 681-98.

Hales, J. and Stratford, N. (1997), *1996 British Crime Survey (England and Wales): Technical Report*, SCPR, London.

Koffman, L. (1996), *Crime Surveys and Victims of Crime*, University of Wales Press, Cardiff.

Lewis, H. (1989), *Insuring Against Burglary Losses*, Home Office Research and Planning Unit Paper 52, Home Office, London.

MacDonald, Z. (1998), *The Under-Reporting of Property Crime: A Microeconometric Analysis*, Discussion Papers in Public Sector Economics, 98/6, Department of Economics, University of Leicester.

MacDonald, Z. (2000), 'The Impact of Under-reporting on the Relationship Between Unemployment and Property Crime', *Applied Economics Letters*, vol. 6, forthcoming.

Maguire, M. (1997), 'Crime Statistics, Patterns and Trends: Changing Perceptions and Their Implications', in M. Maguire, R. Morgan and R. Reiner (eds), *The Oxford Handbook of Criminology*, Clarendon Press, Oxford , pp. 135-88.

Myers, S.L. (1980), 'Why are Crimes Underreported? What is the Crime Rate? Does it Really Matter?', *Social Science Quarterly*, vol. 61, pp. 23-43.

Myers, S.L. (1983), 'Estimating the Economic Model of Crime: Employment versus Punishment Effects', *Quarterly Journal of Economics*, vol. 98, pp. 157-66.

Osborn, D.R., Trickett, A. and Elder, R. (1992), 'Area Characteristics and Regional Variates as Determinants of Area Property Crime Levels', *Journal of Quantitative Criminology*, vol. 8, pp. 265-85.

Phillips, L., Votey, L.H. and Maxwell, D. (1972), 'Crime, Youth and the Labour Market', *Journal of Political Economy*, vol. 80, pp. 491-504.

Pudney, S., Deadman, D.F. and Pyle, D.J. (2000), 'The Relationship Between Crime, Punishment and Economic Conditions: Is Reliable Inference Possible When Crimes are Under-Recorded?', *Journal of the Royal Statistical Society Series A (Statistics in Society)*, vol. 163, pp. 81-97.

Pyle, D.J. (1998), 'Crime and Unemployment: What do Empirical Studies Show?', *International Journal of Risk, Security and Crime Prevention*, vol. 3, pp. 169-80.

Pyle, D.J. and Deadman, D.F. (1994), 'Crime and the Business Cycle in Post-War Britain', *British Journal of Criminology*, vol. 34, pp. 339-57.

Radzinowicz, L. and King, J. (1977), *The Growth of Crime: The International Experience*, Hamish Hamilton, London.

Raphael, S. and Winter-Ebmer, R. (1998), *Identifying the Effect of Unemployment on Crime*, Discussion Paper 98/19, University of California, San Diego.

Sjoquist, D.L. (1973), 'Property Crime and Economic Behaviour: Some Empirical Results', *American Economic Review*, vol. 63, pp. 439-46.

Skogan, W.G. (1994), *Contacts Between Police and Public: Findings From the 1992 British Crime Survey*, Home Office Research Study no. 134, Home Office, London.

Sparks, R.F., Genn, H.G. and Dodd, D.J. (1977), *Surveying Victims: A Study of the Measurement of Criminal Victimization, Perceptions of Crime, and Attitudes to Criminal Justice*, John Wiley, Chichester.

Taylor, I. (1997), 'The Political Economy of Crime', in M. Maguire, R. Morgan and R. Reiner (eds), *The Oxford Handbook of Criminology*, Clarendon Press, Oxford, pp. 265-303.

Taylor, H. (1999), 'A Crisis of 'Modernization' or Redundancy for the Police in England and Wales', *British Journal of Criminology*, vol. 39, pp. 113-135.

Tierney, J. (1996), *Criminology: Theory and Context*, Prentice Hall, London.

Trickett, A., Osborn, D.R. and Ellingworth, D. (1995), 'Property Crime Victimisation: The Roles of Individual and Area Influences', *International Review of Victimology*, vol. 3, pp. 273-95.

White, A. and Malbon, G. (1995), *1994 British Crime Survey: Technical Report*, OPCS Social Survey Division, London.

Witt, R., Clarke, A. and Fielding, N. (1999), 'Crime and Economic Activity', *British Journal of Criminology*, vol. 39, pp. 391-400.

Young, T.J. (1993), 'Unemployment and Property Crime: Not a Simple Relationship', *American Journal of Economics and Sociology*, vol. 52, pp. 413-15.

APPENDIX 9.1

Table 9.A.1 Descriptive statistics (continued over)

Variable	Mean	
Socio-economic		
Age/100	0.471	
Male	0.449	
Married	0.568	
White	0.834	
Black	0.068	
Asian	0.080	
Other ethnic origin	0.018	
Resident in inner city area	0.267	
Household contents insurance	0.570	
In work	0.503	
Unemployed	0.106	
Other non-participant	0.391	
Attitudes to Police		
Worried about crime in area	0.478	
Member of Neighbourhood Watch	0.110	
Believe police do very poor job	0.030	
Criminality		
Stopped by police more than twice	0.001	
Taken any drug in past year	0.062	
Incident Specific	Model 1	Model 2
Incident covers a series	0.123	0.131
Occurred at night	0.525	0.541
Involves a positively valued loss	0.630	0.656
Racially motivated	0.005	0.006
Resulted in a loss of earnings	0.032	0.037
Victim responsible	0.111	0.119
Victim injured	0.009	0.011
Occurred at weekend	0.659	0.674
Offender known	0.085	0.090

Table 9.A.1 Descriptive statistics (continued)

Variable	Mean
Variables used in burglary selection equation	
North of England	0.063
Yorkshire	0.098
North West England	0.119
East Midlands	0.077
West Midlands	0.109
East Anglia	0.036
South East	0.185
South West	0.079
Wales	0.048
London	0.185
Moved house in past year	0.110
Consider area to have drug problem	0.161
Rented accommodation	0.109
Flat	0.171
Detached house	0.184
Semi-detached house	0.303
Terraced house	0.325
Non-categorised house	0.018

Table 9.A.2 The probability of reporting a burglary – uncorrected estimates

Variables	Model 1 Coefficient	S.E.	Model 2 Coefficient	S.E.
Socio-economic				
Age/100	0.713[#]	0.170	0.751[#]	0.171
Male	-0.178[#]	0.056	-0.176[#]	0.056
Married	0.070	0.056	0.081	0.056
Black	0.099	0.098	0.124	0.099
Asian	0.255[#]	0.093	0.255[#]	0.094
Other ethnic origin	-0.163	0.167	-0.176	0.167
Resident in inner city area	0.046	0.057	0.044	0.058
Household contents insurance	0.037	0.061	0.054	0.061
Unemployed	-0.223[#]	0.081	-0.255[#]	0.081
Other non-participant	-0.224[#]	0.065	-0.226[#]	0.065
Incident specific				
Resulted in a loss of earnings	1.224[#]	0.277	1.236[#]	0.275
Involved a positively valued loss	1.026[#]	0.054	1.116[#]	0.055
Occurred at night	0.232[#]	0.053	0.282[#]	0.053
Occurred at weekend	0.071	0.056	0.154[#]	0.056
Racially motivated	-0.081	0.344	-0.076	0.327
Victim responsible	0.091	0.090	-0.101	0.082
Victim injured	0.999[#]	0.338	1.373[#]	0.376
Offender known	0.009	0.097	0.001	0.096
Incident covers a series	-0.238[#]	0.083	-0.234[#]	0.078
Attitudes to Police				
Worried about crime in area	0.179[#]	0.061	0.196[#]	0.061
Member of Neighbourhood Watch	0.036	0.091	-0.004	0.091
Criminality				
Believe police do very poor job	-0.297[*]	0.124	-0.270[*]	0.124
Taken any drug in past year	-0.044	0.091	-0.023	0.091
Stopped by police more than twice	-0.181	0.499	-0.199	0.499
Constant	-0.815	0.125	-0.937	0.127
$N_{victims}$	2756		2820	
χ^2 (d.f.)	541 (25)		656 (25)	
Log Likelihood	-1549		-1517	

Note: # = significant at 1% level, * = significant at 5% level.

Table 9.A.3 The probability of being burgled selection equation

	Model 1		Model 2	
	Coefficient	S.E.	Coefficient	S.E.
Age/100	-0.346$^\#$	0.058	-0.346$^\#$	0.058
Black	0.037	0.041	0.037	0.041
Asian	0.047	0.036	0.047	0.036
Other ethnic origin	0.086	0.070	0.086	0.070
Rented accommodation	0.053$^\$$	0.032	0.052$^\$$	0.032
Detached house	-0.001	0.038	-0.002	0.038
Semi-detached house	0.008	0.033	0.007	0.033
Terraced house	0.065*	0.030	0.065*	0.030
Non-categorised house	0.170*	0.071	0.171*	0.071
Consider area to have drug problem	0.217$^\#$	0.026	0.218$^\#$	0.026
Moved house in past year	0.254$^\#$	0.030	0.253$^\#$	0.030
Resident in inner city area	0.179$^\#$	0.024	0.179$^\#$	0.024
North of England	0.121$^\#$	0.046	0.122$^\#$	0.046
North West England	0.174$^\#$	0.037	0.174$^\#$	0.037
Yorkshire	0.163$^\#$	0.039	0.164$^\#$	0.039
East Midlands	0.035	0.045	0.037	0.045
West Midlands	0.056	0.039	0.057	0.039
East Anglia	-0.213$^\#$	0.068	-0.212$^\#$	0.068
South East	-0.128$^\#$	0.038	-0.125$^\#$	0.038
South West	-0.126$^\#$	0.049	-0.126$^\#$	0.049
Wales	-0.077	0.056	-0.076	0.056
Constant	-1.428	0.048	-1.428	0.048
$N_{respondents}$	34850		34850	
$N_{victims}$	2756		2820	

Note: # = significant at 1% level, * = significant at 5% level.

10. The Social and Economic Determinants of Illicit Drug Use

ZIGGY MACDONALD

Introduction

The prevention of illicit drug misuse has become a serious political issue in recent years. Public concern about the connection between drug use and crime, particularly property crime, has kept the drugs debate high on the media agenda. Yet the control of these substances presents a serious dilemma for policy makers, who must take into account the allocation of scarce public resources resulting from their interventions. In 1998 the Government launched its ten-year strategy for tackling drug misuse (Home Office, 1998). However there is a dearth of research focusing on the users of illicit drugs and their socio-economic characteristics. Against this background, and in the context of the general drugs debate, the economist Richard Stevenson has suggested that an appropriate policy would be to legalise all drugs in the UK, with a minimum of government regulation (e.g. to safeguard children) along the lines of that for alcohol (Stevenson 1990,1994a). The government view is at the other end of the spectrum, it being committed to reducing the prevalence and incidence of drug misuse via programmes of demand reduction and supply enforcement policies.

The legalisation-prohibition debate is complex and invariably suffers from a lack of supporting data, particularly in the UK context. In this chapter we analyse the survey data that is currently available to policy makers in the UK. We consider the British Crime Survey[1] (BCS), which is the primary source of UK drug use information, and observe serious limitations to what it can provide. We consider whether the information generated from just three drug use questions can allow sufficient analysis of important issues such as the initiation into drug abuse and the problem of escalating misuse. We also explore the relationship between alcohol abuse and drug misuse, and the pattern of drug use across income groups. We conclude by looking to future developments in the area of drug use surveys.

197

Previous Studies and Available Data

Research into the social and economic determinants of drug misuse tends to be characterised by a problematic lack of appropriate data. There have been a number of small, localised, studies, which typically focus on high risk groups or actual users, but it is difficult to draw inference about the population from these. For example Parker and Measham (1994) studied the drug experiences of 700 15-16 year olds in the north west of England, but concluded that due to marked social and cultural differences between regions, their results could not be projected onto other youth populations in the UK. This shortcoming of narrowly focussed samples is also apparent in the report produced by Campbell and Svenson (1992), who surveyed 457 university students about their current drug use. As one would expect, the results of this study are very difficult to extend to a larger population of young people, not least because of the unique environment students inhabit. Other research, of a more ethnographic nature, has tended to focus on a very small sample of drug users, but at a far greater level of detail (see for example O'Bryan, 1989). Although this type of research is useful in identifying the intricacies of 'drug culture', it tells us little about the prevalence and nature of drug use in the larger community.

More recently, surveys of arrestees have also helped build a picture of drug misuse (Bennett, 1998), but, like local surveys, such information is not representative of the whole population. Of course it could be argued that it is problem users, such as those involved in crime, who are the real concern for policy makers. However, having said this, those drug users arrested for crimes are not necessarily representative of all problem drug users. Moreover, as well as the costs of drug use in terms of acquisitive crime, we are also interested in the impact of drug use on the Health Service, on family formation, social integration, labour market productivity, education, etc. Indeed, although Bennett's work reveals a strong association between drug use and criminal activity, the analysis is carried out on information from 839 arrestees covering five police force areas and therefore cannot be regarded as national monitoring of drug use.

Although local research is revealing in some respects, national policy interventions should be influenced by national information. To achieve this, governments ought to invest in surveys of the general population in order to develop a representative picture across the country. In the US, drug use information is collected regularly at a national level via a number of household surveys, including the National Longitudinal Survey of Youth, the Monitoring the Future Survey, and the National Household Survey on Drug Abuse. In comparison to the US, the UK undertakes far less monitoring of drug use at a national level. The first purpose-designed survey of the general population was the 1992 'Four Cities Survey' (Leitner *et al.*, 1993), although this was not strictly a national survey as it involved only four UK cities (albeit with a relatively large sample of 5,000). Other sources of information at a national level include the Department of Health via its Regional Drug Misuse Database (Department of Health, 1996). Unfortunately, although this information may indicate something about underlying trends of consumption, such information only scratches the surface of the scale and nature of drug use at a national level. For example, although the Regional Drug Misuse Database collects information on the use of a wide variety of drugs, this information is only received from those individuals who present themselves to community-based agencies for problem drug misuse. Apart from these sources of information, the only other major source of drug misuse information in the UK is the British Crime Survey (BCS).

The British Crime Survey

Questions about individuals' use of certain controlled drugs were introduced into the BCS in 1992, and have been included in the subsequent surveys of 1994, 1996 and 1998. In this chapter we restrict our analysis to the 1994 and 1996 data. The 1998 data is yet to be placed in the public domain, and the 1992 survey is generally considered unsuitable for analysis and comparison with the 1994 and 1996 surveys (Ramsay and Percy, 1997). This is primarily because of the change to Computer-Assisted Personal Interviewing in 1994,[2] but also because of inconsistencies in variables between 1992 and 1994. The BCS drug use questions are only presented to interviewees aged 16-59, via a self-completion questionnaire. The survey population is determined using the Postcode Address File as a sampling frame. For the 1994 survey, this yields a core sample of 14,500 adults, and the 1996 survey 16,350 adults. In both years, the core sample is increased via an ethnic minority booster sample of approximately 2,000 Black and Asian adults. For more details of the sampling procedure for the 1994 survey see White and Malbon (1995), and for the 1996 survey see Hales and Stratford (1997). After losses for non-response and missing information, our pooled sample consists of 22,128 individuals (9,952 for 1994 and 12,176 for 1996). Ramsay and Percy (1996) and Ramsay and Spiller (1997) present non-technical summaries of the 1994 and 1996 data, respectively. In this chapter we present a more technical analysis of the pooled data for the two samples, emphasising the potential shortcomings of the BCS questionnaire design.

Observational Problems

BCS respondents are asked three questions about their use of 13 of the most commonly abused drugs, plus the bogus drug Semeron (put in the survey to test for false claiming). Excluding Semeron, ten of the drugs can be broadly categorised under three classes, as given in the 1971 Misuse of Drugs Act. Class A or 'hard' drugs (cocaine/crack, ecstasy, heroin, LSD, magic mushrooms [classified when 'prepared for use' i.e. dried], and methadone) have stiffer penalties for their possession and/or intent to supply, whereas Class B and Class C drugs (taken together to represent 'soft drugs', these include amphetamines, cannabis and unprescribed tranquillisers) involve smaller penalties. Respondents are asked the following questions about their use of each drug:

1. 'Have you ever taken [DRUG] even if it was a long time ago?'
2. 'In the last 12 months have you ever taken [DRUG]?'
3. 'In the last month have you taken [DRUG]?'

These three questions are seen as something of a 'gold standard' for large-scale drug use surveys. In effect, these questions provide information about an individual's lifetime prevalence of drug use, including recent and current use.

Although in principle information at this level of detail should be useful for policy makers, there are serious shortcomings in such limited questioning. Putting to one side the usual problems associated with surveys that omit marginalised groups, the major shortcoming with the BCS questions is that they are asked in the wrong order. Ignoring for the moment the one month recall question, assume we are interested in an individual's drug use in two periods: past use (in the time prior to the past year) and recent use (in the last 12 months prior to the interview). This is a natural line of inquiry if one is concerned about initiation into drug use or its duration. Given the order that the questions are asked of interviewees, it is impossible to separate recent drug use from past drug use because, by definition, if an individual has used drugs in the past 12 months, then he or she has also used drugs 'ever'. The outcome is that we can only observe three rather than four possible usage outcomes:

- no drug use ever (answer NO to the 'ever' question);

- only past drug use (answer YES to the 'ever' question, NO to the 'last year' question); and
- current drug use (answer YES to both questions).

A simple reordering of the BCS questions would yield far more information about individual drug use histories. Thus, if the first question concerns drug use in the last 12 months, and the second question concerns use in the period prior to the past 12 months, we observe four outcomes rather than three:

- no drug use ever (answer NO to both questions);
- past drug use, no current use (answer NO to the 'last year' question, YES to the 'prior to last year' question);
- current drug use, no past use (answer YES to the 'last year' question, NO to the 'prior to last year' question); and
- past and current drug use (answer YES to both questions).

With this observational regime we can properly isolate current drug use from that in the past, and better address the issue of escalating drug use (considered in more detail later).

In not asking the questions in the reverse order there is a serious identification problem for econometric estimation of drug use transitions between past and current use. A more detailed discussion of these statistical issues can be found in Chapter Eleven and elsewhere in MacDonald and Pudney (2000). In addition, whereas we can observe whether an individual has only used drugs in the past, we know nothing about the frequency of use (whereas in the US National Longitudinal Survey of Youth this information is collected). This last point is important if policy makers make a distinction between problem drug misuse and the occasional 'recreational' use of drugs.

These observational problems present a number of hurdles to overcome if we are to make effective use of the BCS drug use information. However, to dismiss the information outright is unduly pessimistic. These questions are not unique to the BCS (for example the US Monitoring the Future Survey uses them), and some level of understanding about drug use can be achieved from the data. To explore what can be achieved, we begin by presenting a summary of drug use for the pooled 1994 and 1996 data in Table 10.1.

Table 10.1   A summary of illicit drug use (%)*

N = 22,128	Any drug	'Hard' drugs	'Soft' drugs
Ever used	26.3	9.1	25.3
	(0.30)	(0.19)	(0.29)
Only used in past	16.7	6.9	15.9
	(0.25)	(0.17)	(0.25)
Used in past year	9.6	2.2	9.4
	(0.20)	(0.10)	(0.20)
Used in past month	5.6	0.9	5.5
	(0.16)	(0.07)	(0.15)

* standard errors in parenthesis.

The figures in Table 10.1 suggest that over a quarter of the sample have tried at least one illicit drug at some point in their life (indeed, for respondents aged 25 or less, this figure rises to almost 40 per cent). Although there is likely to be some element of under-reporting in the survey given the sensitive nature of the subject (Hoyt and Chaloupka, 1994; McAllister, 1991), the figures in Table 10.1 reveal something about the possible level of drug use in the UK. Focussing on the most recent periods, almost six per cent of this adult sample has consumed drugs in the month prior to the survey, with ten per cent reporting consumption in the past year. These figures have some similarity to those reported in 'The Four Cities Survey', where up to 24 per cent of the main sample had used an unprescribed drug at some point in their life, with the figure reducing to nine per cent for recent use (i.e. use in the past year).

Finally, Table 10.1 reveals some interesting patterns of soft and hard drug use. The ratio of those who report current soft drug use (i.e. in the past month) to those reporting ever taking soft drugs (which by default will include the former) is much higher than the ratio for current hard drug use (0.22 compared to 0.10). Similarly, the ratio of past soft drug use only to ever used soft drugs (0.63) is considerably lower than the ratio for hard drug use (0.76). This suggests that soft drug use is more enduring than hard drug use.

Empirical Methodology

Modelling Drug Use

One of the aims of this chapter is to explore the extent to which the BCS drug use data can be used to estimate a model of drug use, which we can use to predict drug use for an individual with given characteristics. Becker and Murphy's (1988) theoretical model of rational addiction has become popular with economists investigating the price sensitivity of the demand for various illicit or addictive goods (see for example Chaloupka, 1991; Grossman and Chaloupka, 1998; and Stevenson, 1994b). The Becker-Murphy model focuses on the interdependency of past, current and future consumption of addictive drugs. This approach requires panel data and detailed information over time on drug prices. Unfortunately such detailed information is not available for the UK (in order to get price information, Grossman and Chaloupka use the US Drug Enforcement Administration's System to Retrieve Information from Drug Evidence).

To explore the determinants of drug use, we use an approach similar to that presented in Sickles and Taubman (1991), who studied illicit drug use in the US by using data from the National Longitudinal Survey of Youth. Constrained utility maximisation leads to a demand for each consumption good (including drugs), which is a function of income, prices, endowments and tastes (which are allowed to vary by socio-economic status). For our purposes, the demand response of an individual is restricted to a binary choice as the questions asked in the survey only elicit yes-no answers. Thus, we are studying only demand at the extensive, rather than intensive, margin (i.e. we can look at whether an individual has used drugs, but not how often or how much). Although price is of less relevance at this level of demand, the lack of price data does require us to assume that prices are the same for all individuals.

Logit Estimation

As we only observe a binary outcome as our measure of drug use (used drugs or not), we must employ a discrete regression model (Maddala, 1983), rather than the more usual ordinary least squares (OLS) regression (which requires that the dependent variable is continuous and normally distributed). To do this we assume that individuals have an underlying propensity to consume drugs, denoted by the response variable, d^*. This unobserved propensity is defined by the regression relationship:

$$d^* = \beta' x + \mu \tag{10.1}$$

where x is a row vector of personal and demographic attributes (predictors), β is the corresponding vector of parameters we wish to estimate, and μ is a normally distributed error term with mean zero and variance one, conditional on x. The error term represents the unobserved variation in the determinants of drug use.

We cannot observe an individual's propensity to consume drugs, rather we observe a binary response variable, d, that takes the value of one if the respondent answers yes to a drug use question, and zero otherwise. The individual's propensity to consume drugs, given by the latent variable, d^*, drives this observed drug use outcome through the measurement equation:

$$d = \begin{cases} 1 & \text{if } d^* > 0 \\ 0 & \text{if } d^* \leq 0 \end{cases} \tag{10.2}$$

In other words, the observed binary outcome is equal to 1 if the respondent reports 'yes' to drug use (i.e. if the unobserved propensity, d^*, is greater than zero) and zero otherwise.

Estimation of (10.1) through a logit regression is straightforward, and provides us with a set of estimated coefficients (β) that can be interpreted individually as the impact on the probability of drug use for a one unit change in the variable associated with that coefficient, given the characteristics (x). Unlike OLS regression, we cannot interpret the logit coefficients directly as the amount by which the dependant variable will change for a one-unit change in the associated variable. Rather, we have to calculate the predicted probability of drug use for an individual with a certain set of characteristics compared to the base characteristics used in the regression. After estimating β, the probability that the ith individual with given characteristics x_i, will answer yes to drug use is given by:

$$\Pr(d = 1) = \frac{e^{(\beta' x)}}{1 + e^{(\beta' x)}} \tag{10.3}$$

where $\beta' x$ is the product of the estimated coefficients and characteristics of interest.

Results

We present estimates for a number of different models of drug use. We consider the determinants of past drug use (where there is no current use), current drug use, and escalating drug use. It is in estimating the latter of these models where we encounter the greatest problems resulting from the ordering of the BCS dug use questions. Beyond these models, we also consider the association between alcohol consumption and drug use, and the variation in drug use across income groups. These models also reveal problems with the BCS that are generated elsewhere in the general questionnaire design.

Past Drug Use

To begin our analysis we look at the factors associated with the probability of only using drugs in the past period (i.e. at least 12 months before the survey). As we are dealing with past drug use, we only include socio-economic determinants that cannot realistically be regarded as exogenous variables. For example, we cannot include current income in the model, as this is unlikely to reflect the individual's income at the time the past consumption occurred. A good starting point is to take a very simple model that only includes age, education, ethnicity and gender as explanatory variables for drug use in the past. In line with previous studies (Sickles and Taubman, 1991), a lifestyle variable is included to capture religious practice, as this is likely to be fairly constant over time. For full details of all the variables used in all models reported in this chapter see Appendix Table A1. Simple logit estimates for this past use model are given in Table 10.2. Two sets of results are presented. The first estimate has the dependent variable 'used hard drugs in the past only', and the second has the dependent variable 'used soft drugs in the past only'. We separate the two classes of drugs because of clear differences in their characteristics, and hence in what might explain why individuals consume them. For the models reported in Table 10.2 the base categories are 'White', 'no formal qualifications' and 'female' (a year dummy is also included in all the regressions reported in this chapter but is not shown in the results).

Briefly, the results suggest that being male and having higher qualifications positively influence the likelihood of past hard and soft drug use, compared to the base. We find no significant positive association between race and past drug use, a result that is consistent with a number of other studies (for example, Leitner *et al.*, 1993). This is interesting, as although it is widely accepted that ethnic minority communities are over-represented in areas of high social deprivation, and these areas appear to have the biggest concentration of drug-related problems, there is no evidence in this data to suggest a positive association between ethnic groups and drug use. If anything, our results suggest that being of Black or Asian origin has a significant negative association with past drug use, as does age and religious practice. This peculiarity of the drug scene in the British ethnic communities is discussed in more detail in Pearson and Patel (1998).

Table 10.2 The determinants of past drug use: logit estimates using the full sample

Covariate	Past hard drug use		Past soft drug use	
	Coefficient	|t|	Coefficient	|t|
Religious practice	-0.457*	3.783	-0.217*	3.011
Male	0.581*	10.526	0.228*	6.060
Age	-0.047*	17.330	-0.012*	7.077
Degree	0.499*	5.527	0.962*	15.465
Further education	0.291*	3.061	0.538*	8.030
'A' Level/equivalent	0.109	1.082	0.508*	7.186
'O' Level/equivalent	0.041	0.482	0.383*	6.444
Clerical/Low GCSE	-0.066	0.585	0.244*	3.107
Other qualification	-0.070	0.439	0.123	1.153
Black	-0.526*	4.778	-0.237*	3.428
Asian	-1.235*	8.314	-1.044*	10.886
Other origin	-0.222	1.264	-0.349*	2.698
Constant	-1.260	10.214	-1.637	18.569
Observations	22128		22128	
χ^2 (d.f.)	613.08 (13)		553.76 (13)	
Log Likelihood	-5423.81		-9426.43	

Notes: * significant at the 1% level (two-tailed test).

The figures in Table 10.2 also indicate that older individuals are less likely to have taken any drugs in the past. However, in the absence of any cohort-specific 'cultural' factors, one would expect that an older individual is at least as likely as a younger person to have taken drugs in his or her lifetime (although there will be a much lower probability of current use).

As this is not the case, these results must be picking up a cohort effect, with the higher reporting rate of younger respondents explained by the greater availability of drugs and acceptance of their use now compared with 20 or 30 years ago. Indeed, specific work on cohort effects (e.g. Parker and Measham, 1994) has shown that young people today are more likely to be in 'offer' situations and more likely to have tried drugs than have young people a decade ago. To explore this further we split the sample into those aged 16-29 and those aged 30-59 and repeated the regression estimates.[3] The choice of split in age groups is driven by a common finding that individuals tend to 'mature out' of drug use around the ages of 28 to 35 (Kandel, 1980; Labouvie, 1996; Ramsay and Percy, 1996). Of course we are not able to test this maturation theory directly with the BCS data because we cannot observe at what age the last drug episode occurred. The results, not presented here, pick up the cohort effect for past use of soft drugs. For the younger cohort, age has a significant positive influence on the likelihood of past soft drug use although there is no significant association for the past use of hard drugs. The older cohort, however, still exhibits the significant negative association of age with past drug use. In both cases, other significant coefficients remain the same.

Current Drug Use

So far we have considered the determinants of all past consumption, but it is perhaps more relevant to consider the factors that influence recent drug consumption. To do this, we extend the past drug use model by including variables that capture socio-economic factors such as income, location, marital status, family composition and alcohol abuse, all of which are likely to have some influence on the current choice about drug consumption. The inclusion of income and alcohol abuse in the model present a potential endogeneity problem, but this will be considered in more detail later. Unlike Stenbacka *et al.* (1993), we are unable to include characteristics such as truancy, father's alcohol habits, 'emotional control' and 'drunkenness', which are argued to be better predictors of illicit drug use than socio-economic variables. This is primarily because such information is not available in the BCS, but it is also because the inclusion of these 'behavioural variables' is likely to introduce a further endogeneity problem. As such we estimate a more straightforward model here, the results of which are given in Table 10.3.

Table 10.3   The determinants of current drug use: logit estimates using the full sample

Covariate	Recent hard Coefficient	|t|	Recent soft Coefficient	|t|
Religious practice	-0.459#	1.904	-0.519*	4.443
Male	0.675*	6.579	0.609*	11.413
Age	-0.107*	15.053	-0.089*	27.512
Degree	0.108	0.572	0.391*	4.117
Further education	0.046	0.245	0.148	1.530
'A' Level/equivalent	0.138	0.836	0.195$	2.124
'O' Level/equivalent	-0.043	0.293	0.027	0.342
Clerical/Low GCSE	-0.163	0.856	-0.014	0.141
Other qualification	0.143	0.526	-0.158	1.018
Black	-0.397$	2.381	-0.240*	2.779
Asian	-1.236*	4.989	-1.200*	9.421
Other origin	0.332#	1.423	0.056	0.381
Household Type 1	0.533*	3.189	0.193$	2.251
Household Type 2	0.451*	2.638	0.251*	3.160
Household Type 3	0.043	0.231	-0.079	0.826
Household Type 4	-0.158	0.937	0.050	0.577
Household Type 6	-0.153	0.773	-0.189$	1.963
Inner City	0.290*	2.815	0.297*	5.351
Drinker	0.441*	3.645	0.678*	10.922
Married	-1.039*	6.699	-0.742*	9.901
Income 1	0.169	0.997	0.057	0.623
Income 2	0.322#	1.779	0.162#	1.691
Income 3	0.143	0.787	0.031	0.335
Income 5	-0.163	0.865	-0.056	0.624
Income 6	0.021	0.107	0.003	0.031
Unemployed	0.376*	3.426	0.298*	4.896
Constant	-1.147	3.584	0.049	0.305
Observations	22128		22128	
χ^2 (d.f.)	916.92 (27)		2468.39 (27)	
Log Likelihood	-1919.53		-5656.14	

Notes: * significant at 1% level;
$ significant at 5% level;
# significant at 10% level (two-tailed tests).

We estimate the current use model separately for soft and hard drugs with the following characteristics as the base: single, White, female, no formal qualifications, in work, living in a two adult plus one or two children household, an average household income of £15,000-£19,999 per year, non-attendance at church/synagogue, etc. Unemployment is also used as a regressor, as our lowest income category includes interviewees who spontaneously responded 'none' when quizzed about their income, or provided a zero response. This category might not truly reflect relative social deprivation, so the inclusion of unemployment should capture the variation in drug use not captured by our very low-income regressor.

Looking briefly at the results for both hard and soft drugs, compared to the base categories, being male, on low income, unemployed, located in an inner city area, and a frequent drinker are all positively associated with drug consumption. Having a degree or 'A' levels is also associated with current soft drug use. Factors with a negative association with current drug use, include religious practice, being older, Black or Asian, or married. To put these results into perspective, a comparison of predicted probabilities for current use of soft drugs is presented in Table 10.4. These are calculated for different individuals with given characteristics (x) using the significant parameter estimates (β) from the logit regression and substituting them into equation (10.3).

Table 10.4 Selected predicted probabilities of current soft drug use

More likely		Less likely	
Base	*0.174*	*Base*	*0.174*
+ male	0.279	+ religious	0.112
+ unemployed	0.333	+ age 35	0.027
+ inner city	0.401	+ married	0.013
+ drinker	0.569	+ Asian	0.003

The first line of figures in Table 10.4 gives the probability of an 18-year old individual with base characteristics currently taking class B/C drugs. We then go down the table cumulatively adding characteristics that increase the probability of current soft drug use compared to this base (i.e. we make the individual male, then a male who is unemployed, etc.). We then go in the other direction, starting at the base, cumulatively adding characteristics that reduce the probability of current drug use. This approach is quite illuminating. For example, we see that whereas a married

Asian woman, aged 35 and religiously orientated has a probability of current drug use of less than 0.1 per cent (p=0.003), a single, White, unemployed male, located in the inner city, who is a frequent drinker has at least a 60 per cent chance of being involved in current drug use (p=0.569).

Income and the Demand for Drugs

In our current drug use model we included income as a regressor for drug use. Although not particularly significant (possibly because unemployment is capturing the effect of low income), the inclusion of income in the model presents a potential endogeneity problem (as does unemployment). This type of problem is discussed in more technical detail in Chapter Eleven, and elsewhere in MacDonald and Pudney (2000). The essence of the problem is the possible simultaneity of drug use and income, and the potential unobserved heterogeneity, which raises questions about the direction of causality in a single equation drug-use function. Put simply, just as drug use is likely to have an impact on an individual's earnings, income is likely to affect consumption of drugs in just the same way as any other good. This problem is also characterised by the existence of unobserved heterogeneity, which reflects the possibility that the some of the unobserved attributes that affect income could be the same unobserved characteristics that influence an individual's decision to take drugs. The net effect of these possible influences is that without taking them into account, our logit estimates are likely suffer a downward bias.

This endogeneity problem is typically overcome by jointly estimating separate equations for income and drug use. However, the BCS only provides information on household income, given in income bands, which makes estimation of a separate income equation particularly complex and beyond the scope of this chapter. Moreover, total household income is probably less relevant for individual drug use. For example, an individual with a well-off parent, and hence high household income, but no personal income may still be involved in drugs. Having said this, it is quite likely that total household income can act as a proxy for relative deprivation in the most general sense. Although we should be aware of these problems, it is still worthwhile exploring the pattern of drug use across income groups. Our results so far suggest that an individual with a low household income is more likely to be involved in drugs than an individual with a relatively higher household income. This may reflect the lifestyle of those who might be considered economically inactive. The significant positive association between unemployment and recent drug use supports this, although the direction of this association is open to debate. To explore this further, in

Figure 10.1 we graph the probability of participation in soft drug use across all income groups.

In Figure 10.1 we see that, after an initial fall in the predicted probability of past soft drug use between very low income and the next income group, the trend of past soft drug use becomes positively related to income. Thus those individuals with the highest current household income (£30,000 plus) have the highest predicted probability of having taken soft drugs in the past but not recently. With respect to more recent use, as expected, the trend is reversed and it is individuals from low-income households who have the highest probabilities of drug use. Although not shown here, these patterns are observed for hard drug use as well.

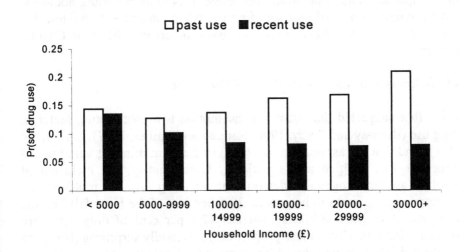

Figure 10.1 The probability of soft drug use by income group

The relationship between household income and past soft drug use might be explained by exploring the impact of university education. Our earlier regression results indicate a positive association between higher education and past drug use. It is also well established that higher education is positively associated with higher wages. Thus, assuming individuals who have taken drugs in their past are active in the labour market, if their reported drug use occurred during their time at university then we would expect high income earners to have a high reported rate of past drug use. A simple way to explore this is to consider the educational background of past drug users according to their current income group, and *vice versa*. The first observation from the sample is the symmetrical difference in education attainment of high and low-income groups. Considering the whole sample, 55 per cent of the high-income group have a degree and seven percent have no formal qualifications, whereas only five percent of the low-income group have a degree but 39 per cent have no formal qualifications. However, when we compare the sample of past soft drug users to non-users, 47 per cent of the high-income group with a history of past soft drug use have a degree, whereas only 33 per cent of the non-users in this income group have a degree. Similarly, 50 per cent of those with a degree who have used soft drugs in their past are in the highest income group compared to 44 per cent of non-users with a degree who are in this group. Although this simple analysis is far from conclusive, it is quite revealing about the labour market impact of past soft drug use when educational attainment is taken into account. We explore this issue in greater detail in Chapter Eleven.

The Relationship between Alcohol and Drug Abuse

It is often suggested that alcohol consumption is a contributing factor in drug use (Ramsay and Percy, 1996; Ramsay and Spiller, 1997). Earlier, we also found that the association between our frequent drinking variable and drug use was positive and significant. Unfortunately, the inclusion of alcohol as an exogenous determinant of drug use is problematic.[4] Comparing drug users to non-users, 20.6 per cent of the latter fall into the category of frequent drinkers, whereas 47.4 per cent of drug users are frequent drinkers. Given these proportions, it is hardly surprising that when frequent drinking is introduced into a regression equation as an exogenous determinant of drug use, it is always a significant and the coefficient positive. However, there is a serious danger that single-equation estimates will be biased because, as with income and drug use, it is most likely that alcohol consumption and drug use are endogenously determined. The essence of the problem is that drug use and alcohol abuse might simply be the jointly determined outcome of a given, unobserved, lifestyle. We can test this empirically by jointly estimating an equation for alcohol abuse and one for drug use. This bivariate probit model requires that each equation be of the form of equation (10.1), with normally distributed error terms of mean zero and unit variance. Estimated separately, we assume that the covariance of the error terms (ρ) is zero (i.e. the two models are unrelated and alcohol abuse can be used as an exogenous variable to explain drug use). The purpose of the bivariate model is to test the hypothesis that the error covariance is zero (either by a simple t-test or Log Likelihood test). If the hypothesis is rejected then we can say that the outcome that an individual is a drug user and the outcome that the individual is an alcohol abuser are jointly determined by some unobserved underlying process. If this is the case then alcohol abuse should not be included in a single equation model of drug use.

To test this we jointly estimated a model for current soft drug use and a model for frequent/heavy drinking using a bivariate probit regression. As we are only interested in the covariance parameter, we do not present the full results of the bivariate probit regression here. The estimated coefficients for current soft drug use were very similar to the estimates provided earlier (in Table 10.3) using the single equation model that included alcohol abuse. The only real difference was the size of the parameter estimates (this would have a slight effect on the predicted probabilities of current drug use), but the same variables were significant with the same sign. What is important is the covariance parameter, ρ, which was positive and significant at the one per cent level (with a 't' value of 11.4). This result provides us with sufficient reason to believe that drug use and heavy drinking are jointly determined and not independent events. We should therefore be sceptical about introducing a variable to capture alcohol abuse as an explanatory variable in a drug use equation. Unfortunately, given the data limitations, we have been unable to identify the underlying process that drives the joint outcomes of heavy drinking and drug use.

Escalating Drug Misuse

To conclude our analysis we consider the issue of escalating drug use. It has been suggested that the use of cannabis, and other soft drugs, is at the beginning of an initiation process into harder drugs (Stenbacka *et al.*, 1993). The role of soft drugs, particularly cannabis, as a 'stepping stone' to hard drug use may be justification alone for not considering any change in law with respect to possession of soft drugs. However, in trying to explore this issue we encounter a serious drawback arising from the BCS observational deficiencies highlighted earlier. To properly address the issue of escalating drug use, we need an observational regime about individuals' drug use along the following lines:

1. no drug use;
2. soft drug use in the past, no hard drug use in the past; and
3. current hard (and soft) drug use.

This observational regime would represent a logical escalation in drug use, which we could use to determine the factors associated with escalating drug misuse. Unfortunately, we are not able to observe the second outcome. The only way we can identify past drug use is as previously defined: 'past use only'. This means that we cannot observe soft drug users who have not used hard drugs in the past but are currently using them (and possibly soft drugs). Of course, if the questions were asked in the reverse order, the regime presented above would be observable because we can separate use in the past year from use in the period prior to the last year.

In the absence of an appropriate observational regime, our options are rather limited if we want to model escalating drug use. We can observe the number of past (only) soft drug users who are currently hard drug users (22 out of 2,525), but we exclude all those individuals who have used soft drugs in the past and soft drugs (plus hard drugs) in the current period. Therefore, to proceed with our analysis, we look at escalating drug use in a slightly different way. Rather than considering escalation dynamically, we consider the difference in probability of a given individual being in one of three drug use states, as indicated by the categorical variable, d_e, that takes one of three values:

$d_e = 0 \Rightarrow$ no drug use
$d_e = 1 \Rightarrow$ soft drugs only (class B/C)
$d_e = 2 \Rightarrow$ hard and soft drugs.[5]

This categorical variable replaces the binary variable (used or not) in equation (10.1), which can now be estimated as an ordered logit model. The ordered logit is for all purposes the same as the logit model except that the dependent variable must consist of mutually exclusive categories that are defined in ascending order. However, to calculate the relative probabilities of no drug use, soft drug use only, and hard drug use, we have to use a slightly modified version of equation (10.3) to generate the following three equations:

$$\Pr(d_e = 0) = \frac{1}{1 + e^{(\beta'x - k_1)}} \tag{10.4}$$

$$\Pr(d_e = 1) = \frac{1}{1 + e^{(\beta'x - k_2)}} - \frac{1}{1 + e^{(\beta'x - k_1)}} \tag{10.5}$$

$$\Pr(d_e = 2) = 1 - \frac{1}{1 + e^{(\beta'x - k_2)}}$$

(10.6)

where k_1 and k_2 are the estimated values of the unobserved thresholds at which the categorical variable increases. Substituting a given set characteristics (x) and the parameter estimates (β) into equations (10.4)-(10.6) provides the predicted probability of a given individual being in the given drug use states.

The ordered model was estimated for reported drug usage in the past year. Given the results of the bivariate probit model in the previous section, we have excluded the frequent drinking variable from this model (although this makes little difference to the estimated coefficients for the other regressors). The results are presented in Table 10.5.

The signs on the coefficients for the ordered logit model are essentially the same as for the simple logit model. What is interesting to observe are the marginal probabilities of different scales of drug use for the various individuals identified earlier as likely drug users. Some comparative probabilities, calculated using equations (10.4)-(10.6), are presented in Table 10.6. These probabilities are calculated with respect to the same base as those calculated for Table 10.4. That is: single, non-church-going, White, female, no formal qualifications, employed, living in a two adult plus one or two children household, aged 18, with an average household income of £15,000-£19,999 per year. Again, we cumulatively add characteristics to the base that increase the probability of drug use, then cumulatively add characteristics that reduce this probability.

Table 10.5   Ordered logit estimates of the probability of drug use

Covariate	Coefficient	|t|
Religious practice	-0.594*	5.197
Male	0.687*	13.148
Age	-0.088*	27.781
Degree	0.411*	4.410
Further education	0.139	1.461
'A' Level/equivalent	0.227*	2.521
'O' Level/equivalent	0.036	0.463
Clerical/Low GCSE	0.007	0.075
Other qualification	-0.164	1.067
Black	-0.301*	3.552
Asian	-1.290*	10.377
Other origin	0.002	0.013
Household Type 1	0.257*	3.061
Household Type 2	0.294*	3.776
Household Type 3	-0.046	0.488
Household Type 4	0.040	0.468
Household Type 6	-0.196$^\$$	2.067
Inner City	0.302*	5.558
Married	-0.761*	10.392
Income 1	0.061	0.680
Income 2	0.182$^\$$	1.935
Income 3	0.056	0.603
Income 5	-0.047	0.528
Income 6	0.089	0.956
Unemployed	0.291*	4.897
Threshold 1 (k_1)	-0.295	
Threshold 2 (k_2)	1.365	
Observations	22128	
χ^2 (d.f.)	2462.93 (26)	
Log Likelihood	-6917.92	

Notes: * significant at 1% level;
$^\$$ significant at 5% level.

Table 10.6 Selected predicted probabilities of the level of drug use in the past year

	No drug use	Soft drugs only	Hard/soft drugs
Base	*0.783*	*0.167*	*0.050*
+ Male	0.646	0.259	0.095
+ Low income	0.576	0.301	0.123
+ All adult household	0.503	0.339	0.158
Base	*0.783*	*0.167*	*0.050*
+ Religious	0.868	0.104	0.028
+ Black	0.898	0.081	0.021
+ Married	0.950	0.040	0.010

The figures in Table 10.6 reveal some interesting comparisons. For example, we see that whereas a single White male, on low income living in an all adult household, has a 16 per cent chance of current involvement in hard drugs (p=0.158), a Black, married female, with the same base characteristics except religious practice, has an almost 100 per cent chance of not being involved in current drug consumption. It is also worth noting that as the probability of drug use increases, the ratio of soft drug to hard drug use decreases. This suggests that an individual with a high probability of soft drug use has a higher relative probability of hard drug use. In this respect we reveal something about one aspect of escalating use. Clearly there comes a point when the level of drug use is such that the distinction between soft and hard drugs becomes less relevant to the individual user. Unfortunately, because of the way the BCS questions are presented, we cannot extend our analysis much beyond this. We can, however, make a passing observation about the pattern of migration in the other direction, that is, from multiple drug use to single drug use. In our sample there are 2,123 individuals who reported any drug use in the past year. Of these, 61 per cent reported only using cannabis during this time. Of these cannabis only users, a third had used class A drugs at some point in their life. Although not particularly conclusive, this does suggest that individuals who have used hard drugs at some point in their life do not necessarily continue to do so. Of course, because we know nothing about frequency of use, we cannot tell whether this illustration simply reflects a number of soft drug users who at some point in their life had brief spells of recreational or one-off hard drug use.

Conclusions

The purpose of this chapter was to explore the social and economic determinants of illicit drug use, focusing on evidence provided by survey data. Our illicit drug use information came from the British Crime Survey, although, we observed that the nature of the BCS questions is somewhat limiting. Excluding issues of under-reporting and misrepresentation, in only asking interviewees three drug use questions, the BCS questionnaire design limits analysis of UK drug use to that at the extensive margin. In particular we know nothing about the frequency of drug use and the quantities consumed, nor do we know the age at which this consumption is initiated. Moreover, the BCS questions only allow us to observe a limited number of drug use states. We can observe whether an individual has never consumed drugs, consumed drugs in the past but not recently, or has consumed drugs recently. What would be useful to policy makers, however, is more information about individuals' circumstances at the point of initiation into drug use. In the context of the BCS information, if we were able to identify those individuals who have not consumed drugs in the past but have consumed recently, we would be better positioned to comment on the initiation process. We have shown that this could be achieved by simply reordering the BCS drug use questions. Although this change would make comparisons between future surveys and those that have already taken place slightly cumbersome, the added value of such a change in policy terms far outweighs this problem. In addition to these limitations, the shortcomings in BCS questionnaire design prevent us from analysing the processes of 'maturing out' of drug use and escalation in drug use. We are also restricted in what analysis we can present in terms of drug use and individual earnings. This is because of the way income information is gathered in the BCS.

However, to conclude that the BCS drug use information is wholly inadequate for policy needs is somewhat pessimistic. Although the information provided by the BCS has nothing like the detail that some of the US surveys provide, in the absence of this detail we have been able to identify some underlying patterns of drug use in the UK. Perhaps it is this prevalence information that is of greatest value. For example, the BCS information reveals drug use to be quite widespread. Our results suggest that around 25 per cent of the adult population between the ages of 16 and 59 have tried at least one illicit drug in their lifetime, with one in ten adults reporting the use of drugs in the past year. The data also shows that these proportions increase dramatically if we consider the under 25 age group. In addition, we can observe that there is a greater prevalence of soft drugs than there is hard drugs, but the factors influencing consumption of either class of drug are similar. In particular, when we consider individuals who have used drugs in the past but have not done so in the past year, we find that young White males have the highest probability of use. This combination of individual attributes, when combined with low income and inner city location, also has a significant influence on the likelihood of current drug consumption. In general, family stability (e.g. marriage), religious practice and, to some extent, being of ethnic minority origin (particularly Asian) tend to significantly reduce the probability of the use of both classes of drugs.

We briefly considered the relationship between alcohol abuse and drug use, and presented evidence to suggest that these two outcomes are jointly determined and hence driven by some unobserved process. This result implies that the relationship between alcohol consumption and drug use is more than a simply causal one, and thus requires further research. For example, one way to explore this association might be to take account of whether initiation into alcohol and drug abuse occur at different points in an individual's life (Burgess and Propper, 1998). We also considered the relationship between income and drug use. Our results suggest that those on a higher income tend to have a higher frequency of past drug use compared to those on lower incomes, although current drug use tends to be concentrated in the latter group. Finally, we used the BCS data to explore the issue of escalating drug use. Although we are limited in what we can observe, we have shown that as the probability of drug use increases, the probability ratio of soft to hard drug decreases. This result suggests that as the tendency to take drugs increases, the distinction between soft and hard drug consumption blurs, perhaps indicating a greater acceptance of hard drugs for those individuals who see drug use as 'normal'.

In conclusion, although the BCS is somewhat limited, some detail about drug use in the UK can be derived from it. Our main concern is with the order of the drug use questions in the BCS. Perhaps the most unfortunate outcome of relying on the addition of some simple 'yes-no' type drug use questions to an existing household survey, is that policy makers cannot really know the true extent of hard drug use, particularly at the intensive margin. Although it might be argued that surveys of this type will never reveal much about problem drug misuse because they tend to omit marginalised groups, there is a lot to be gained from a well designed household survey. The British Crime Survey is a useful source of information for policy makers, but if governments are to continue using survey data to guide policy interventions, then perhaps a national drug abuse survey for the UK should be seriously considered.

Notes

1. The British Crime Survey comes from Crown copyright records made available through the Home Office and the ESRC Data Archive and has been used by permission of the Controller of Her Majesty's Stationery Office
2. In this respect, O'Muircheartaigh and Campanelli (1998) note that 'the interviewer is seen as one of the principal sources of error in data collected from structured face-to-face interviews' (p. 63). As such the data from 1994 onwards will be subject to totally different sources of error than the 1992 survey.
3. We have also estimated additional models that contain age-race interaction terms in order to capture the differences between young and old ethnic groups. However, the inclusion of these interaction terms makes very little difference to the results so they are not included here.
4. Apart from the issue of simultaneity, the inclusion of alcohol into the model is also problematic because the questions used to generate this information differ between survey years. In the 1994 survey, interviewees are asked about their level of drinking, with possible responses such as: 'drink a moderate amount', 'drink quite a lot', etc. The 1996 survey, however, uses the same questions as the General Household Survey and the Health Survey of England. These questions generate responses in terms of daily consumption (e.g. 'once or more a day', '5 or 6 days a week'). To overcome this we have constructed a drinking frequency variable that takes the value of one if the interviewee reported 'drinking heavily'/'drink quite a lot' (1994 responses) or 'once or more a day'/'5 or 6 days a week' (1996 responses), and zero otherwise.
5. The scope of this variable could be improved with a fourth category that captures 'hard drugs only'. Unfortunately the lack of observations in this category renders its inclusion inappropriate for modelling.

References

Becker, G. and Murphy, K. (1988), 'A Theory of Rational Addiction', *Journal of Political Economy*, vol. 96, pp. 675-700.

Bennett, T. (1998), *Drugs and Crime: the Results of Research on Drug Testing and Interviewing Arrestees*, Home Office Research Study 183, Home Office, London.

Burgess, S.M. and Propper, C. (1998), *Early Health Related Behaviours and Their Impact on later Life Chances: Evidence from the US*, Centre for Analysis of Social Exclusion, CASE paper 6, London School of Economics.

Campbell, R.L. and Svenson, L.W. (1992), 'Drug Use Among University Undergraduate Students', *Psychological Reports*, vol. 70, pp. 1039-42.

Chaloupka, F.J. (1991), 'Rational Addictive Behaviour and Cigarette Smoking', *Journal of Political Economy*, vol. 99, pp. 722-42.

Department of Health. (1996), *Drug Misuse Statistics*, Department of Health Statistical Bulletin 1996/24, Department of Health Statistics Division, London.

Grossman, M. and Chaloupka, F.J. (1998), 'The Demand for Cocaine by Young Adults: A Rational Addiction Approach', *Journal of Health Economics*, vol. 17, pp. 427-74.

Hales, J. and Stratford, N. (1997), *1996 British Crime Survey (England and Wales): Technical Report*, SCPR, London.

Home Office. (1998), *Tackling Drugs to Build a Better Britain: the Government's Ten-Year Strategy for Tackling Drugs Misuse*, HMSO, London.

Hoyt, G.M. and Chaloupka, F.J. (1992). 'Effect of Survey Conditions on Self-Reported Substance Use', *Contemporary Economic Policy*, vol. 12, pp. 109-21.

Kandel, D. (1980), 'Drug and Drinking Behaviour Among Youth', *Annual Review of Sociology*, vol. 6, pp. 235-83.

Labouvie, E. (1996), 'Maturing Out of Substance Abuse: Selection and Self-Correction', *Journal of Drug Issues*, vol. 26, pp. 457-76.

Leitner, M., Shapland, J. and Wiles, P. (1993), *Drugs Usage and Drugs Prevention - The Views and Habits of the General Public*, HMSO, London.

MacDonald, Z. and Pudney, S. (2000), 'Analysing Drug Abuse with British Crime Survey Data: Modelling and Questionnaire Design Issues', *Journal of Royal Statistical Society - Series C (Applied Statistics)*, vol. 49, pp. 95-117.

Maddala, G. (1983), *Limited Dependent and Qualitative Variables in Econometrics*, Cambridge University Press, Cambridge.

McAllister, I. and Makkai, T. (1991), 'Correcting for the Underreporting of Drug Use in Opinion Surveys', *The International Journal of the Addictions*, vol. 26, pp. 945-61.

O'Bryan, L. (1989), 'Young People and Drugs', in S. MacGregor (ed.), *Drugs and British Society: Responses to a Social Problem in the Eighties*, Routledge, London, pp. 64-76.

O'Muircheartaigh, C. and Campanelli, P. (1998), 'The Relative Impact of Interviewer Effects and Sample Design Effects on Survey Precision', *Journal of the Royal Statistical Society - Series A (Statistics in Society)*, vol. 161, pp. 63-77.

Parker, H. and Measham, F. (1994), 'Pick 'n' Mix: Changing Patterns of Illicit Drug Use Amongst 1990s Adolescents', *Drugs: Education, Prevention and Policy*, vol. 1, pp. 5-13.

Pearson, G. and Patel, K. (1998), 'Drugs, Deprivation, and Ethnicity: Outreach Among Asian Drug Users in a Northern English City', *Journal of Drug Issues*, vol. 28, pp. 199-24.

Ramsay, M. and Percy, A. (1996), *Drug Misuse Declared: Results of the 1994 British Crime Survey*, Home Office Research Findings, No. 33, Home Office, London.

Ramsay, M. and Percy, A. (1997), 'A National Household Survey of Drug Misuse in Britain: A Decade of Development', *Addiction*, vol. 92, pp. 931-37.

Ramsay, M. and Spiller, J. (1997), *Drug Misuse Declared in 1996: Latest Results from the British Crime Survey*, Home Office Research Study 172, Home Office, London.

Sickles, R. and Taubman, P. (1991), 'Who Uses Illegal Drugs?', *American Economic Review*, vol. 81, pp. 248-51.

Stenbacka, M., Allebeck, P. and Romelsjo, A. (1993), 'Initiation into Drug-Abuse: The Pathway From Being Offered Drugs to Trying Cannabis and Progression to Intravenous Drug Abuse', *Scandinavian Journal of Social Medicine*, vol. 21, pp. 31-39.

Stevenson, R. (1990), 'Can Markets Cope With Drugs?', *Journal of Drug Issues*, vol. 20, pp. 659-82.

Stevenson R. (1994a), *Winning the War on Drugs: To Legalise or Not?*, Hobart Paper 124, Institute of Economic Affairs.

Stevenson R. (1994b), 'Harm Reduction, Rational Addiction, and the Optimal Prescribing of Illegal Drugs', *Contemporary Economic Policy*, vol. 12, pp. 101-8.

White, A. and Malbon, G. (1995), *1994 British Crime Survey: Technical Report*, OPCS Social Survey Division, London.

APPENDIX 10.1

Table 10.A.1   Variable descriptions and descriptive statistics

Variable	Description	Mean	Sd. Err
Age	Chronological age	36.69	0.077
A recent	Has used class A drug in past year	0.022	0.001
A past only	Has used class A drug in past only	0.069	0.002
B recent	Has used class B/C drug in past year	0.094	0.002
B past only	Has used class B/C drug in past only	0.159	0.002
Religious practice	Belongs to church/synagogue/mosque/etc.	0.104	0.002
Degree	Degree or higher qualification	0.136	0.002
Further education	Teaching/nursing, HND, BTEC	0.126	0.002
'A' Level/equivalent	A levels, ONC, C\&G advanced	0.109	0.002
'O' Level/equivalent	High grade GCE/GCSE ,CSE (1), craft	0.245	0.003
Clerical/Low GCSE	Low grade GCE/GCSE/CSE (2-5), clerical	0.091	0.002
Other qualification	Other qualification	0.047	0.001
No qualifications	No formal qualifications	0.246	0.003
Asian	Asian	0.078	0.002
Black	Black	0.087	0.002
Other origin	Chinese or 'other' origin, or none	0.023	0.001
White	White	0.812	0.003
Household Type 1	Single adult household	0.150	0.002
Household Type 2	2 adult household	0.256	0.003
Household Type 3	1 = 3 or more adult household	0.140	0.002
Household Type 4	Lone parent household	0.149	0.002
Household Type 5	Two adults plus 1 or 2 children	0.223	0.003
Household Type 6	1= other household type	0.145	0.002
Drinker	Drinks a lot or heavily	0.502	0.003
Inner City	1 = lives in inner city area	0.268	0.003
Married	Married	0.595	0.003
Male	Male	0.461	0.003
Income 1	Total household income (THI) < £5000	0.090	0.002
Income 2	(THI) £5000-£9,999	0.138	0.002
Income 3	(THI) £10,000-£14,999	0.153	0.002
Income 4	(THI) £15,000-£19,999	0.160	0.002
Income 5	(THI) £20,000-£29,999	0.190	0.003
Income 6	(THI) £30,000 +	0.170	0.003
Unemployed	Currently unemployed	0.304	0.003

11. The Labour Market Consequences of Illicit Drug Use

ZIGGY MACDONALD AND STEPHEN PUDNEY

Introduction

In this chapter we consider the impact of illicit drug use on labour market outcomes. This is a growing area of social research, encouraged in part by the availability of suitably large data-sets in recent years. The impact of alcohol consumption on earnings has received particular attention, but there is also concern about the effects of illicit drug use on labour market outcomes. Culyer (1973) originally highlighted this issue whilst considering whether drug use should be a genuine concern for social policy makers. This concern typically centres on the productivity of drug users. Since the work of Becker (1964) and Grossman (1972) there has been a common belief among economists that a strong relationship exists between health and earnings. Apart from genetic and dietary factors that might affect this relationship, economists have been concerned about the impact of substance use or abuse on labour market outcomes, which can be considered to be an indirect effect of this consumption upon physical and mental health. If drug users are more likely to experience chronic absenteeism and frequent spells out of the labour market, then assuming that workers receive the value of their marginal product as pay, this reduced productivity will manifest itself through lower wages.

Recent research in this area has raised questions about the relationship between illicit drug use and productivity. It is argued that single-equation models will suffer from bias arising from the simultaneity of drug use and wages, and from the existence of unobserved heterogeneity. This naturally raises questions about the direction of causality in a wage equation that has a measure of drug use as an explanatory variable. If drugs are a normal consumption good, but also have a negative impact on wages (and hence income), then the endogeneity issue is clear as this implies simultaneous causation between drug use and wages.

223

In addition to the potential for simultaneous causation between drug use and wages, there is also some likely heterogeneity because unobserved attributes that affect wages or employment outcomes may overlap with the characteristics that influence an individual's choice to take drugs. For example, there might be some unobserved characteristic, such as a high rate of time preference, which tends to cause individuals to select high paying jobs without consideration for investment in human capital, but also, according to Becker and Murphy (1988), making them more likely to be attracted to drugs.

The purpose of this chapter is to investigate these issues using data for the UK. The majority of previous research in this area has used data from the US. However, the British Crime Survey (BCS)[1] yields sufficient information to consider the relationship between illicit drug use and labour market outcomes from a UK perspective. In the following section we discuss the relevant literature in this area, making reference to recent research that focuses on the impact of alcohol abuse on labour market outcomes. We then consider the BCS data set, its advantages and shortcomings, and discuss the sample properties. Following this, we develop our empirical model, which includes a joint model covering past and current drug use together with unemployment and occupational attainment. We then present our estimation results, and complete the chapter with our concluding remarks.

Brief Review of Literature

In taking a brief overview of the substance abuse-labour market outcomes literature, it is quite clear that the various findings are far from unequivocal. To illustrate this we will focus on two aspects of the relationship between drug use and labour market outcomes: the impact of illicit drug use on labour supply, and the association between drug use and wages.

Drug Use and Labour Supply

The relationship between substance abuse and labour supply has not generated any consensus in the literature. There is the obvious debate (typically between sociologists and economists) over the direction of causality. For example, although most economists would argue that substance abuse will impact on labour supply, perhaps through some detrimental effect on health, it has been argued that it is unemployment that tends to foster drug use, rather than the reverse (Peck and Plant, 1987).

Where there is agreement over the likely direction of causality, the results of empirical work leave the impact of substance use on labour supply open to question. For example, in considering alcohol abuse and labour supply, Mullahy and Sindelar (1991,1996) find a statistically significant negative association between these variables, whereas Kenkel and Ribar (1994) do not (although they find a small statistically significant negative association between heavy drinking and the labour supply of males). The different conclusions that are drawn from these studies may relate to the different definitions of labour supply that are used. However, Kaestner (1994a), using the same data set as Kenkel and Ribar (the US National Longitudinal Survey of Youth - NLSY), finds a negative association between marijuana (cannabis) or cocaine use and the hours of labour supplied by young males.

All the studies mentioned above allow for the endogeneity of drug use and labour market outcomes. Against this, Zarkin *et al.* (1998a) suggest that substance abuse and hours worked are not endogenously determined. Following extensive tests for exogeneity of substance abuse variables, they estimate a single equation model of labour supply for a sample of 18 to 24 year old men taken from the US National Household Survey on Drug Abuse. They find no significant relationship between past month labour supply and the use of cigarettes, alcohol or cocaine in the past month. They conclude that there is little evidence to support a robust labour supply-drug use relationship. Similarly, although Kaestner's (1994a) cross-sectional results support a negative relationship between drug use and hours of labour supplied, his longitudinal estimates do not support any systematic effect of drug use on labour supply.

Drug Use and Attainment

There is a growing body of empirical evidence in the labour economics literature that suggests that once endogeneity is accounted for, the relationship between substance abuse and wages is typically positive. Kaestner (1991), using data from the NLSY, finds that increased frequency of cocaine or marijuana is associated with higher wages, a finding consistent across gender and age groups. Likewise, Gill and Michaels (1992) and Register and Williams (1992) find very similar results. These results echo those that have been found for the relationship between alcohol and wages. For example, Berger and Leigh (1988), using data from the US Quality of Employment Survey and taking account of self-selection, found that drinkers receive higher wages, on average, compared to non-drinkers. More recently, French and Zarkin (1995), Heien (1996), Hamilton and

Hamilton (1997) and MacDonald and Shields (2000) present results that support a quadratic relationship between drinking intensity and wages.[2]

Although the majority of the reported research suggests a positive relationship between substance use and wages, there is some work that questions this general view. Kaestner (1994b), using two waves of the NLSY, provides cross sectional results that are generally consistent with the previous studies, but longitudinal estimates that suggest that the wage-drug use relationship varies according to the type of drug and individual. For example, there is a positive relationship between cocaine use and wages for females, but a negative relationship between marijuana use and wages for males. In addition, Kandel *et al.* (1995), using a follow-up cohort of the NLSY, find a positive relationship between drug use and wages in the early stages of an individual's career, but a negative relationship later on in the career (in the mid-thirties). However, Burgess and Proper (1998), using the same data source, are not able to replicate this finding. Their results suggest that adolescent alcohol and soft drug use have little or no effect on the earnings of men in their late 20s or 30s, although they do find that early hard drug use has a significant negative impact.

Data and Sample Characteristics

Researchers in the US are fortunate to have several different sources of drug misuse information. In contrast, the UK undertakes very little monitoring of drug use at a national level (see Chapter 10). The only major source of comparable drug misuse information in the UK is the British Crime Survey (BCS). The BCS is a household victimisation survey, representative of the adult population of England and Wales.[3] Information on drug misuse has been collected in the 1992, 1994, 1996 and 1998 sweeps of the BCS, although the 1992 survey is not suitable for comparison with later surveys (Ramsay and Percy, 1997) and the 1998 survey is not in the public domain at the time of writing. In this analysis we pool the 1994 and 1996 data, which after losses for incomplete records, and exclusion of those aged over 50, leaves us with a sample of 13,908 individuals with complete drug use and labour market information (6,404 for 1994 and 7,504 for 1996).

Self-Reported Data

The BCS drug use information is self-reported, which is the norm for this type of analysis. The difficulties associated with self-reported data are widely recognised, particularly when the subject matter is sensitive. Indeed, Hoyt and Chaloupka (1994) concluded that previous research that has used the NLSY is particularly vulnerable to the large reporting errors that accompany the substance use measures. Typically we expect some variation in under-reporting between socio-economic groups. For example, in an analysis of the NLSY, Mensch and Kandel (1988) found that, compared to individuals with a relatively heavy use of drugs, light users tend to under-report their consumption, as do females and ethnic minorities. There is also evidence to link survey conditions to individual reporting behaviour. Hoyt and Chaloupka (1994) find that the presence of others during the administration of the survey, the use of telephone interviews and self-administration of the survey can all lead to mis-reporting. Moreover, O'Muircheartaigh and Campanelli (1998) report that the interviewer can be the biggest source of error in survey data.

There is little we can do to overcome some of the potential sources of reporting error in our sample, although the use of a laptop computer, which is passed over to the interviewee following some brief instructions from the interviewer, might abate some of the problems. This method of eliciting information offers the same level of anonymity as sealed booklet methods (McAllister and Makkai, 1991). Indeed, it is claimed that the change to computers for self-reporting in the BCS resulted in the identification of some groups of users (such as heroin users from the Asian community) that had previously not reported any drug consumption (Ramsay and Percy, 1997). In general, any drug use data collected via surveys are likely to miss certain high-risk groups and be subject to a variety of sources of error. We recognise this as a problem but take some comfort from the data collection method used in the BCS.

Drug Use Information

Using a laptop computer, BCS interviewees aged 16 to 59 are required to answer questions about their experience of 14 commonly abused drugs (including a bogus drug Semeron, put in the survey to test for false claiming). Survey respondents are asked whether they have ever taken any of the listed drugs, taken any in the past 12 months or in the past month. There are number of ways to categorise the drugs, for example we could group them according the perceived harm associated with their use (MacDonald and Pudney, 1999). However, in line with Chapter 10 and our previous analysis (MacDonald and Pudney, 2000), we group the drugs according to their classification in the Misuse of Drugs Act, 1971. Thus we define two groups of drugs: 'hard' and 'soft'; reflecting the common perception of their differing risk. In the hard category we include class A drugs: cocaine/crack, ecstasy, heroin, LSD, magic mushrooms and unprescribed methadone. The remaining drugs (amphetamines, cannabis and unprescribed tranquillisers), which are either class B or C drugs, comprise our soft drug category. Although this grouping of the drugs might not reflect the combinations in which they are commonly used, we have found that alternative (subjective) categories make little difference to the results.

In Table 11.1 we summarise the frequency of reported use of the drugs listed in the BCS by men and women for two age cohorts: those aged 16 to 25, and those aged 26 to 50. The split by age reflects a common finding in the literature that suggests individuals tend to 'mature out' of drug use in their late 20s or early 30s (Gill and Michaels, 1991; Labouvie, 1996; MacDonald, 1999; Ramsay and Percy, 1996). Thus we would expect drug use to be more prevalent in the youngest group. We also anticipate a cohort effect, stemming from the increasing prevalence of the youth drug 'culture' over time (Parker and Measham, 1994).

Table 11.1   Past and present illicit drug use (%)*

	Age 16-25		Age 26-50	
	Females	Males	Females	Males
Soft drugs				
Ever used	35.10	47.26	20.03	31.47
	(1.35)	(1.41)	(0.55)	(0.60)
Only used in past	15.87	16.52	14.65	21.98
	(1.03)	(1.05)	(0.48)	(0.53)
Recently used	19.20	30.74	5.38	9.49
	(1.11)	(1.30)	(0.31)	(0.38)
Hard drugs				
Ever used	3.27	6.20	2.48	4.21
	(0.50)	(0.68)	(0.21)	(0.26)
Only used in past	2.23	3.49	1.94	3.10
	(0.42)	(0.52)	(0.19)	(0.22)
Recently used	1.04	2.70	0.54	1.11
	(0.29)	(0.46)	(0.10)	(0.13)
Observations	1255	1259	5357	6037

* Standard errors in parentheses.

The figures in Table 11.1 reveal that the use of soft drugs is far more prevalent than hard drugs for both age cohorts, but there is a clear pattern of diminishing use (both ever and recent) from the younger to the older group and from males to females. In particular, the figures suggest that almost half of the young men in the sample have tried a soft drug at some point in their life, whereas the figure reduces to under a third for the older group. Moreover, for both men and women, the proportion of the older group reporting any use ever is almost the same as the proportion of the younger group who report recent use. In terms of the gender divide, it is quite clear that men have a much higher rate of reported drug use then do women, but the age difference is still important. For example, about one in five young women report recent use of soft drugs whereas the rate is just over one in twenty for older women. We also observe that for younger men and women, a much greater proportion report recent use of soft drugs than use only in the past. This observation is reversed for the older group, where the rate of use in the past only is more than double the rate of recent use.

Labour Market Information

We consider first the impact of drug use on the risk of unemployment. Kaestner (1994a) and Zarkin *et al.* (1998b) consider the drug use-employment relationship by focusing on labour supply as measured by the number of hours worked. In this analysis we focus on employment status rather than hours worked. In Table 11.2 we summarise drug use according to employment status for the current sample. BCS respondents are classified as employed if they confirm that they were in paid employment or self-employment in the previous week (full-time or part-time). In our analysis, the unemployed category includes all those respondents who were not employed at the time of the survey, but reported that they were currently looking for work. Thus we exclude individuals in full-time education, those who are sick or disabled, retired or looking after the home/family.

Table 11.2 reveals a sharp contrast in the reported drug use rates between the employed and the unemployed. In all cases, there appears to be a much higher prevalence of drug use amongst the unemployed group. This is in sharp contrast to the data from the NLSY, where there is no significant differential between the level of drug use of those in work and those who are unemployed (Kaestner, 1994a). In the current sample, the proportion of unemployed men reporting recent use of hard drugs is higher than the proportion of the employed men reporting any use ever.

Table 11.2   Summary of drug use by employment status (%)*

	Females		Males	
	Employed	Unemployed	Employed	Unemployed
Soft drugs				
Ever used	22.39	30.56	33.30	43.55
	(0.53)	(2.32)	(0.58)	(1.72)
Recently used	7.53	15.40	11.44	26.54
	(0.33)	(1.82)	(0.40)	(1.53)
Hard drugs				
Ever used	2.49	4.80	3.88	9.77
	(0.20)	(1.08)	(0.24)	(1.03)
Recently used	0.60	1.51	1.01	4.34
	(0.10)	(0.61)	(0.12)	(0.71)
Observations	6216	577	6467	820

* Standard errors in parentheses.

Turning our attention to the relationship between drug use and occupational attainment for those who are in work, the majority of research into this relationship has made use of individual data on earnings. Unfortunately, individual wages are not observed in the BCS. The survey provides detail of total household income (coded in bands) but it is unlikely that household income is relevant for individual drug use. To proceed, we require a measure of occupational attainment relevant to each individual. As it is difficult to define and rank occupations objectively, we use an approach due to Nickell (1982) and recently used by Harper and Haq (1997) and MacDonald and Shields (2000). We rank occupations using the average earnings associated with an individual's occupation. In other words, we define occupational success in terms of relative levels of average hourly pay for the occupation in question. It is thus to be interpreted as a measure of the labour market status of the individual's occupation, rather than as an indicator of his or her actual wages, or of success within an occupation.

We calculate the mean hourly wage associated with each occupation using pooled data from the UK Quarterly Labour Force Survey (QLFS) for 1993, 1994 and 1995 (12 quarterly surveys in all). The QLFS codes occupation to the 3-digit level of the Standard Occupational Classification, which gives 899 possible occupation categories. These occupational codes are also used in the BCS, allowing us to map the mean hourly wage from each occupational category in the QLFS to individual occupations in the

BCS. Given that there are nearly 900 occupations defined in the survey we treat the associated mean hourly wage as a continuous variable in our analysis.

A casual look at the distribution of occupational status by drug-use status reveals an interesting feature in the current sample, which reflects findings from other data. Average occupational status for those who have ever used drugs is higher than that for those who report no drug use ever. This result holds for men and women, for the younger and older cohorts, and for any category of drug use. This last observation suggests two potentially opposing outcomes of drug use: unemployment or enhanced occupational attainment. These two associations may represent opposite causal links: drug use may raise the risk of unemployment; whereas occupational success (and high income) may raise the demand for drugs. We consider these outcomes further in the following sections, focusing on the difference between past and current drug use.

The Empirical Model

In order to accommodate the dynamic nature of drug use, we consider an individual's life as consisting of two periods, based on the time dimensions offered by the BCS drug use questions. The past period finishes 12 months before the survey interview, and the current period covers the 12 months preceding the interview.[4] These two periods allow us to define past and current drug use. The levels of drug use in these two periods are represented by a pair of trichotomous indicators d_t ($t = 1, 2$). We let $d_t = 0$ indicate no drug use, $d_t = 1$ indicate the use of 'soft' drugs only and $d_t = 2$ indicate the use of 'hard' (or hard and soft) drugs. We define two indicators of labour market outcomes: current unemployment u (a binary indicator) and, for those in work, occupational attainment a (a continuous variable). Both relate only to the current period.

Before we can define our empirical model, we first have to confront a serious observational problem stemming from the design of the questionnaire used in the BCS, which was alluded to in Chapter Ten. The respondent is asked only whether he or she has ever used drugs, and, if so, whether or not within the last year. This questionnaire structure has the unfortunate feature that if a respondent reports drug use in the current period, we do not know whether there was any use in the past period. Thus d_1 and d_2 are only partially observable. Nevertheless, it is possible to estimate a suitable model by means of an iterative maximum likelihood method.

First, we define a latent variable d_1^* that represents an individual's past propensity to consume drugs. This drives the observed indicator of actual drug use, d_1, through an ordered probit mechanism:

$$d_1^* = x_1\beta_1 + \varepsilon_1 \tag{11.1}$$

$$d_1 = r\psi(C_{1r} \le d_1^* < C_{1r+1}), \quad r = 0, 1, 2 \tag{11.2}$$

where $\psi(\Xi)$ is the indicator function, equal to 1 if the event Ξ occurs and 0 otherwise; $C_0 = -\infty, C_3 = +\infty$, and C_1, C_2 are unknown threshold parameters; x_1 is a row vector of personal and demographic attributes, β_1 is the corresponding vector of parameters, and ε_1 is a N(0,1) random error.

The second stage of the model determines current drug use, current unemployment and occupational attainment jointly, but conditional on past drug use. This is achieved through a system of three latent variables (d_2^*, u^*, and a^*) representing the individual's unobserved current propensities to consume drugs, to be unemployed, and to do well when employed. These are generated by the following multivariate regression structure:

$$d_2^* = x_2\beta_2 + \xi_1\delta_{21} + \xi_2\delta_{22} + \varepsilon_2 \tag{11.3}$$

$$u^* = x_3\beta_3 + \xi_1\delta_{31} + \xi_2\delta_{32} + \varepsilon_3 \tag{11.4}$$

$$a = x_4\beta_4 + \xi_1\delta_{41} + \xi_2\delta_{42} + \varepsilon_4 \tag{11.5}$$

where $x_2...x_4$ are row vectors of personal and demographic attributes, $\beta_2... \beta_4$ are the corresponding vectors of parameters, and $\varepsilon_2... \varepsilon_4$ are errors with a trivariate normal distribution with zero means, unit variances and unrestricted correlations, conditional on x = {x_1, x_2, x_3} and d_1. The variables ξ_1 and ξ_2 are binary indicators defined as $\xi_r = \psi(d_1 = r)$, where the estimated coefficients represent the impact of past drug use on current drug use, unemployment and attainment.

The observable counterparts of these latent variables are the indicators of current drug use d_2, unemployment u and occupational attainment a. The latent variables (11.3) and (11.4) are assumed to generate the observed states by means of the following relationships:

$$d_2 = r\psi(C_{2r} \le d_2^* < C_{2r+1}), \ r = 0, 1, 2 \tag{11.6}$$

$$u = \psi(u^* > 0) \tag{11.7}$$

where the C_{2r} are threshold parameters subject to normalising restrictions as before.

There are nine joint outcomes for d_1 and d_2, which cover all the possible combinations of drug use over our two time periods. Unfortunately, given the questionnaire design problems highlighted earlier, we can only observe six of the possible outcomes:

1. No use of drugs ever;
2. No current use, only soft drugs in past;
3. No current use, hard drugs in past;
4. Current use of soft drugs, no hard drugs ever;
5. Current use of soft drugs, past use of hard drugs; and
6. Current use of hard drugs.

For a more details of these drug use combinations, and a full discussion of how the outcome probabilities are constructed, see MacDonald and Pudney (2000). For our purposes, we note that the probabilities require evaluation of (at most) bivariate normal probabilities.[5] These probabilities are then used to construct the following log-likelihood function, which we maximise numerically using GAUSS MAXLIK software.

$$\ln L = \sum_{i=1}^{n} \{\ln \Pr(d_{1i}|x_{1i}) + \ln \Pr(d_{2i}, u_i, a_i|x_{2i}, x_{3i}, x_{4i}, d_{1i})\} \tag{11.8}$$

Results

In our analysis we provide separate estimates for our two age groups and for men and women. For a description of all the variables used in this analysis and their mean values see appendix Tables 11.A.1 and 11.A.2 respectively. In the estimated models we use the drug use categories that are embedded in UK law, which we defined earlier. We begin by briefly discussing the results for the ordered probit estimates of past and current drug use.

Past and current drug use

Following Sickles and Taubman (1991), the past drug use component of the model (11.1)-(11.2) is specified relatively simply to include only basic demographic variables, plus religious practice and some simple age-race interactions. This choice of covariates reflects the need to include only exogenous factors that are unlikely to be affected by past drug use.[6] The current drug use component is also specified as a simple ordered probit, but with an expanded set of covariates describing the current demographic nature of the individual and his or her household, current drinking habits, and also the lag effect of past drug use. The results for the past and current drug use components are summarised in Tables 11.3 and 11.4.

Table 11.3   The probability of past drug use

	Age 16-25		Age 26-50	
	Females	Males	Females	Males
Age/10	0.216	0.346**	-0.190***	-0.297***
	(0.178)	(0.167)	(0.031)	(0.027)
Black	0.938	2.514*	-0.043	-0.722*
	(1.520)	(1.419)	(0.439)	(0.393)
Asian	-3.364*	0.149	-0.330	-0.605
	(1.943)	(1.024)	(0.584)	(0.465)
Black*age	-0.504	-1.186*	-0.031	0.156
	(0.716)	(0.639)	(0.126)	(0.113)
Asian*age	1.302	-0.330	-0.036	-0.043
	(0.862)	(0.477)	(0.167)	(0.129)
Church	-0.168	-0.223	-0.270***	-0.202***
	(0.157)	(0.193)	(0.073)	(0.070)
Y1996	0.012	0.031	-0.096**	0.043
	(0.091)	(0.083)	(0.043)	(0.037)
C_{11}	1.118	1.125	0.065	-0.566
	(0.391)	(0.369)	(0.119)	(0.103)
C_{12}	1.627	1.526	0.810	0.115
	(0.390)	(0.369)	(0.117)	(0.103)
Observations	1255	1259	5357	6037

Notes: standard errors in parenthesis
   *** significant at 1% level;
   ** significant at 5% level;
   * significant at 10% level (two-tailed tests).

The results in Table 11.3 reveal an important aspect to the impact of age on drug use. Note that the age effect here represents a combination of factors: the effect of ageing on demand; a cohort effect; and the fact that the implicitly defined 'past' period lengthens as we consider older cohorts. We find a significant negative association between age and past drug use for the older cohort, but for the younger cohort the association is positive, although more noticeable for the first model. The positive association of drug use with age for the younger group (significant only for males) presumably reflects the effect of the passage of time - older people have simply had more time in which to take drugs. The negative coefficient on age for the older cohort, however, probably reflects a cohort effect (mentioned previously): that when those in the older cohort were of a typical drug taking age, drug use was far less widespread and they were much less likely to be in 'offer' situations.

Concentrating on our other variables, the results presented here are in line with those given in Chapter Ten. The impact of religious attendance appears particularly important for the older cohort, with a significant reduction in the probability of past drug use for those who report regular attendance at a Church, Mosque, Synagogue, etc. However, this association is not statistically significant for the younger cohort, although the sign on the coefficient is negative for all estimates. Where we observe ethnic differences, the interaction between ethnicity and age is quite complex, but few of the estimated coefficients are statistically significant.

The results in Table 11.4 relate to drug use in the current period. As with past drug use, age is an important factor, however, in all cases there is a significant negative association between age and current drug use. We also find that young female Asians and older male Asians are less likely than their White counterparts to have consumed any drug in the past year. Although this is mostly the case for individuals of Black origin, we do find that older Black men are more likely than Whites to have consumed drugs in the past year. Other factors with statistically significant estimated coefficients include the impact of marriage (-ve)[7], location in the inner city (+ve), living in rented accommodation (+ve) and alcohol consumption (+ve).

Finally, we find that the estimated lag effect (δ_{22}) of past hard drug use in the current drug use model turns out to be positive and statistically significant for all estimates. In other words, an individual who has consumed hard drugs in the past is much more likely to be currently consuming these drugs than someone who had not consumed hard drugs in the past.[8]

Table 11.4   The probability of current drug use (continued over)

	Age 16-25		Age 26-50	
	Females	Males	Females	Males
Age/10	-0.532**	-0.840***	-0.454***	-0.463***
	(0.226)	(0.190)	(0.053)	(0.043)
Black	-0.476*	-0.037	-0.157	0.314***
	(0.270)	(0.170)	(0.217)	(0.121)
Asian	-0.633***	-0.235	-0.126	-0.499***
	(0.241)	(0.152)	(0.196)	(0.158)
Educat 1	0.226	0.127	0.214***	-0.075
	(0.223)	(0.169)	(0.114)	(0.080)
Educat 2	-0.062	-0.089	0.195*	-0.162*
	(0.231)	(0.165)	(0.116)	(0.089)
Educat 3	0.152	0.239	-0.100	-0.036
	(0.208)	(0.147)	(0.134)	(0.093)
Educat 4	0.036	0.162	-0.093	-0.140
	(0.182)	(0.130)	(0.108)	(0.086)
Educat 5	0.145	0.095	-0.139	-0.037
	(0.215)	(0.171)	(0.145)	(0.107)
Educat 6	-0.756*	-0.125	-0.011	-0.236
	(0.414)	(0.279)	(0.230)	(0.170)
Household 1	-0.582***	0.323*	-0.112	0.087
	(0.190)	(0.176)	(0.106)	(0.108)
Household 2	0.202	0.346**	0.092	0.033
	(0.175)	(0.147)	(0.117)	(0.093)
Household 3	0.170	0.019	-0.098	-0.075
	(0.141)	(0.128)	(0.160)	(0.131)
Household 4	0.491**	-0.116	-0.087	0.013
	(0.203)	(0.229)	(0.112)	(0.104)
Household 5	0.238	0.069	-0.066	-0.052
	(0.244)	(0.182)	(0.122)	(0.092)
Married	-0.770***	-0.258*	-0.484***	-0.408***
	(0.160)	(0.138)	(0.093)	(0.089)
Inner-City	-0.041	0.200**	0.151**	0.164***
	(0.114)	(0.093)	(0.075)	(0.058)
Rented	0.411***	0.139	0.406***	0.218***
	(0.123)	(0.117)	(0.080)	(0.073)
Church	-0.193	-0.476*	-0.218	-0.177
	(0.203)	(0.265)	(0.145)	(0.129)
Freqdrnk	0.384***	0.310***	0.327***	0.245***
	(0.133)	(0.108)	(0.081)	(0.061)

Table 11.4 **The probability of current drug use (continued)**

	Age 16-25		Age 26-50	
	Females	Males	Females	Males
Y1996	0.262**	0.258**	0.101	0.195***
	(0.120)	(0.105)	(0.078)	(0.069)
Lagged drug effects:				
δ_{22}	1.371***	1.240***	1.181***	1.219***
	(0.134)	(0.220)	(0.100)	(0.156)
C_{21}	0.181	0.234	0.065	0.138
	(0.444)	(0.457)	(0.234)	(0.225)
C_{22}	1.158	1.913	1.138	1.268
	(0.453)	(0.508)	(0.238)	(0.251)
Observations	1255	1255	5357	5357

Notes: standard errors in parenthesis
*** significant at 1% level;
** significant at 5% level;
* significant at 10% level (two-tailed tests).

Labour market status and occupational attainment

The variables in the binary probit for unemployment and the regression for occupational attainment (mean hourly occupation wage) are similar to those specified for the current drug use probit, except that we exclude religious attendance and housing tenure (rented). The results for unemployment and occupational attainment are summarised in Tables 11.5 and 11.6 respectively. It is here that the different experiences of men and women become particularly apparent.

Table 11.5   The probability of current unemployment (continued over)

	Age 16-25		Age 26-50	
	Females	Males	Females	Males
Age/10	-0.518*	-0.114	-0.095*	-0.086**
	(0.274)	(0.207)	(0.048)	(0.037)
Black	0.356*	0.498***	0.383***	0.242***
	(0.190)	(0.171)	(0.093)	(0.083)
Asian	0.813***	0.077	0.036	0.267***
	(0.160)	(0.138)	(0.175)	(0.085)
Educat 1	-0.706***	-0.851***	-0.559***	-0.798***
	(0.273)	(0.192)	(0.120)	(0.080)
Educat 2	-0.596**	-1.090***	-0.510***	-0.686***
	(0.241)	(0.177)	(0.122)	(0.081)
Educat 3	-0.733***	-0.748***	-0.220***	-0.797***
	(0.217)	(0.156)	(0.118)	(0.099)
Educat 4	-0.691***	-0.921***	-0.248***	-0.368***
	(0.183)	(0.134)	(0.088)	(0.071)
Educat 5	-0.207	-0.583***	-0.413***	-0.290***
	(0.207)	(0.157)	(0.131)	(0.094)
Educat 6	-0.565	-0.283	-0.045	-0.143
	(0.391)	(0.242)	(0.147)	(0.105)
Household 1	0.197	-0.098	-0.061	-0.203*
	(0.193)	(0.206)	(0.108)	(0.105)
Household 2	0.104	-0.064	0.066	-0.232***
	(0.196)	(0.150)	(0.112)	(0.081)
Household 3	-0.200	-0.018	-0.058	-0.380***
	(0.171)	(0.132)	(0.140)	(0.105)
Household 4	0.339*	0.325	-0.134	-0.119
	(0.194)	(0.248)	(0.110)	(0.102)
Household 5	0.010	0.444***	0.025	-0.059
	(0.252)	(0.178)	(0.111)	(0.073)
Married	-0.352**	-0.207	-0.646***	-0.690***
	(0.168)	(0.150)	(0.092)	(0.078)
Inner-City	0.293**	0.296***	0.291***	0.408***
	(0.117)	(0.097)	(0.071)	(0.053)
Freqdrnk	-0.272	0.069	-0.031	-0.125**
	(0.177)	(0.119)	(0.081)	(0.058)
Y1996	-0.438***	-0.103	-0.278***	-0.151***
	(0.125)	(0.110)	(0.071)	(0.058)

Table 11.5   The probability of current unemployment (continued)

	Age 16-25		Age 26-50	
	Females	Males	Females	Males
Lagged drug effects:				
Soft (δ_{31})	0.327*	0.178	0.119	0.010
	(0.181)	(0.152)	(0.094)	(0.073)
Hard (δ_{32})	0.476***	0.450***	0.078	0.342***
	(0.181)	(0.120)	(0.152)	(0.076)
Constant	0.335	-0.221	-0.685	-0.048
	(0.544)	(0.441)	(0.217)	(0.173)
ρ_{du}	0.119	0.115*	0.157**	0.200***
	(0.091)	(0.064)	(0.067)	(0.043)
Observations	1255	1259	5357	6037

Notes: standard errors in parenthesis
   ***   significant at 1% level;
   **   significant at 5% level;
   *   significant at 10% level (two-tailed tests).

Table 11.6   Determinants of occupational attainment (continued over)

	Age 16-25		Age 26-50	
	Females	Males	Females	Males
Age/10	0.236***	0.233***	0.025***	0.041***
	(0.035)	(0.038)	(0.006)	(0.005)
Black	-0.023	-0.073**	-0.010	-0.063***
	(0.029)	(0.033)	(0.014)	(0.014)
Asian	0.108***	-0.098***	0.027	-0.062***
	(0.031)	(0.026)	(0.017)	(0.014)
Educat 1	0.399***	0.362***	0.577***	0.486***
	(0.042)	(0.039)	(0.014)	(0.014)
Educat 2	0.218***	0.150***	0.435***	0.269***
	(0.042)	(0.038)	(0.015)	(0.014)
Educat 3	0.146***	0.131***	0.283***	0.235***
	(0.039)	(0.035)	(0.015)	(0.014)
Educat 4	0.092	0.039	0.192***	0.147***
	(0.038)	(0.033)	(0.012)	(0.013)
Educat 5	0.085	0.037	0.103***	0.069***
	(0.043)	(0.040)	(0.017)	(0.018)
Educat 6	0.082	0.010	0.123***	0.044**
	(0.061)	(0.052)	(0.019)	(0.021)
Household 1	0.142***	0.029	0.105***	0.067***
	(0.030)	(0.038)	(0.014)	(0.018)
Household 2	0.073**	0.038	0.078***	0.023**
	(0.029)	(0.030)	(0.013)	(0.012)
Household 3	0.051**	0.015	0.024	0.003
	(0.024)	(0.026)	(0.015)	(0.015)
Household 4	-0.008	0.049	-0.002	-0.004
	(0.033)	(0.048)	(0.015)	(0.017)
Household 5	-0.046	0.002	0.031**	0.028**
	(0.035)	(0.040)	(0.012)	(0.011)
Married	-0.007	0.013	-0.001	0.053***
	(0.024)	(0.028)	(0.012)	(0.014)
Inner-City	-0.013	-0.019	-0.021**	-0.055***
	(0.018)	(0.021)	(0.009)	(0.009)
Freqdrnk	-0.015	0.034	0.040***	0.024***
	(0.020)	(0.021)	(0.009)	(0.008)
Y1996	-0.035**	0.001	-0.011	-0.011
	(0.017)	(0.019)	(0.008)	(0.008)

Table 11.6   Determinants of occupational attainment (continued)

	Age 16-25		Age 26-50	
	Females	Males	Females	Males
Lagged drug effects:				
Soft (δ_{41})	0.019	-0.002	0.036***	-0.018*
	(0.024)	(0.027)	(0.011)	(0.010)
Hard (δ_{42})	0.051*	-0.013	0.022	-0.019
	(0.026)	(0.025)	(0.015)	(0.013)
Constant	0.993	1.144	1.406	1.532
	(0.078)	(0.081)	(0.029)	(0.028)
ρ_{dw}	0.076	0.000	0.032	-0.019
	(0.055)	(0.055)	(0.033)	(0.030)
Mean LL	-1.361	-1.813	-1.005	-1.347
Observations	1255	1259	5357	6037

Notes: standard errors in parenthesis
*** significant at 1% level;
** significant at 5% level;
* significant at 10% level (two-tailed tests).

The impact of socio-economic factors on unemployment and occupational attainment are more or less as expected. The educational variables are highly significant in both sets of estimates, particularly for the older cohorts. Looking at the impact of age, the results suggest that older respondents are less likely to be currently unemployed and tend to be in occupations with a higher wage. In all cases, those of Black origin tend to have a higher probability of being currently unemployed, and Black men tend to have lower wages when compared to Whites. The results for Asians vary according to gender, but only in terms of the statistical significance of the estimated coefficients. Young Asian women and older Asian men tend to have a higher probability of unemployment than Whites, whereas the estimated coefficients for young Asian men and older Asian women are positive but not significant. However, when we consider wages these results are reversed, and it is young Asian women who tend to have higher wages than Whites, whereas Asian men (young or old) tend to have lower wages (the estimated coefficient for older women is not statistically significant). Marriage appears to be negatively associated with current unemployment but is not found to be important in the determination of wages, although the coefficient on marriage is significant and positive for older men. Residence in the inner city is positively associated with current unemployment, but for the older cohort there is a statistically significant positive association with wages. We also observe that older individuals who report frequent alcohol consumption tend to have higher wages. This is consistent with the literature although we do not distinguish between frequent drinking and problem drinking, and nor do we allow for alcohol consumption to be endogenously determined (see MacDonald and Shields, 2000).

Focusing on the relationship between drug use and labour market outcomes, the lagged effects of past drug use vary according to age, gender and the groups of drugs considered. Looking first at participation, we see that the past use of soft drugs tends not to be significantly associated with current unemployment, except for young women where the association is positive, but of marginal significance. However, past use of hard drugs has a significant positive impact on the probability of current unemployment, except for older women, where the estimated coefficient is not significantly different from zero. Overall, there is sufficient evidence to support the view that use of hard drugs is associated with long-term damage to employment prospects. In addition to the lagged effects, Table 11.5 also shows significant correlations between current drug use and unemployment, except for young women, although it is difficult to unravel this association.

Finally, looking at the impact of drug use on attainment for those in work, there is little evidence of any systematic relationship. Whereas there is a negative relationship between the past use of soft drugs and the wages of older men, we observe a positive association between these variables for older women. On the other hand, we find no significant association between past soft drug use and wages for the younger cohort, and no association between past hard drug use and wages for any group considered. The one exception is curious as we find a positive association between the past use of hard drugs and the wages of young women (although the estimated coefficient is small and of marginal significance). These results are generally in line with the literature (e.g. Kaestner, 1994b), and are partially supported by the correlation between current drug use and wages, although in all cases, except for young women, the estimated correlation coefficient is not significant.

Overall, a summary of the results is quite revealing. We find no evidence of a negative association between past hard drug use and occupational attainment, but nor is there any evidence to suggest a significant positive relationship with hard drug use and attainment, except for young women. We do find a slight positive association with past soft drug use and occupational attainment for older women, but a negative association for older men. Where the impact of drug use on labour market outcome is most apparent is with respect to unemployment. In all cases, past hard drug use is positively associated with unemployment, and in most cases the estimated coefficient is significant. Although the impact of past soft drug use is less apparent, in most cases the coefficient is positive, and for young women it is statistically significant.

Concluding Remarks

The aim of the research presented in this chapter was to explore the relationship between illicit drug use and two labour market outcomes: unemployment and occupational attainment. To do this we used data from the British Crime Survey and estimated a joint model covering past and current drug use together with unemployment and occupational attainment.

The most important aspect of our analysis concerns the impact of drug use on unemployment, which suggests long-term harm to employment prospects. We suggest that taking the relationship between drug use and unemployment into account may in part explain why recent work has failed to find any significant negative relationship between drug use and earnings. We have shown that drug use (particularly hard drugs) greatly increases the risk of unemployment, and any association with earnings for those in work therefore misses much of the impact. The strong evidence of the adverse affects of drug use on employment prospects overwhelms the mild estimated positive association between past soft drug use and occupational attainment for women. For this reason, we believe that policy conclusions should be concerned with the implications of drug use for unemployment rather than the impact on the productivity of those who are in work.

Productivity related aspects of drug use are mentioned in the Government's drugs strategy (Home Office, 1998), and as a consequence have recently been the subject of a UK Health and Safety Executive initiative, concerned with substance abuse in the workplace. However, although we recognise that drug use in the workplace ought to be discouraged, we suggest that there should be more emphasis on the link between drug use and unemployment (and other features of social exclusion), which although recognised in the strategy, has received less attention than workplace issues. Although we have not focused on other aspects of drug use in the workplace (as, for example, in Kaestner and Grossman's (1998) work on workplace accidents), productivity issues appear to be of less importance than employment outcomes. One possibility is to tie in drug rehabilitation with Welfare to Work for those unemployed individuals who are identified as dependent on hard drugs. Whatever the policy intervention, it is quite clear that there could be a significant reduction in the social costs associated with drug use by those on low incomes, particularly if an expensive 'drug habit' is financed through alternative means.

Notes

1. The British Crime Survey comes from Crown copyright records made available through the Home Office and the ESRC Data Archive, and has been used by permission of the Controller of Her Majesty's Stationery Office.
2. Although, in a later study, Zarkin *et al.* (1998b) suggest that the relationship between drinking and wages is linear, and that the returns to wages are positive across a wide range of alcohol consumption levels.
3. For more details of the sampling procedure for the 1994 survey see White and Malbon (1995), and for the 1996 survey see Hales and Stratford (1997).
4. Given that the BCS also asks about drug use in the past month, we could elaborate our model and work with three periods: up to one month ago; one to twelve months ago; and more than twelve months ago. However, the one-month period gives few additional observations between drug-use categories, and it greatly complicates the analysis. Thus we lose little by ignoring the one-month response.
5. Further details (in the form of a GAUSS procedure) are available on request from the authors.
6. The inclusion of religious practice does not strictly fall into this category, but it is likely that in most cases religious orientation is formed at an age before experimentation with drugs typically begins.
7. We also note that conditioning our estimates on education, marriage and household formation is problematic as there is a possibility that these are themselves related to drug use (Burgess and Propper, 1998; Kenkel and Ribar, 1994). However, it is only our model for current (rather than past) drug use that is conditional on family and education variables, and it seems reasonable to regard these variables as predetermined with respect to the current period.
8. Note that we have excluded the lagged effect of past soft drug use on current drug use by setting the coefficient δ_{21} to zero. When δ_{21} is estimated, the result is poorly determined (taking negative values in some cases), with large standard errors and statistically insignificant. Imposing the restriction $\delta_{21} = 0$ has no appreciable impact on the other estimated parameters.

References

Becker, G. and Murphy, K. (1988), 'A Theory of Rational Addiction', *Journal of Political Economy*, vol. 96, pp. 675-700.

Becker, G.S. (1964), *Human Capital*, University of Chicago Press, Chicago.

Berger, M. and Leigh, J. (1988), 'The Effect of Alcohol Use on Wages', *Applied Economics*, vol. 20, pp. 1343-51.

Burgess, S.M. and Propper, C. (1998), *Early Health Related Behaviours and Their Impact on later Life Chances: Evidence from the US*, Centre for Analysis of Social Exclusion, CASE paper 6, London School of Economics.

Culyer, A. (1973), 'Should Social Policy Concern Itself with Drug Abuse?', *Public Finance Quarterly*, vol. 1, pp. 449-56.

French, M. and Zarkin, G. (1995), 'Is Moderate Alcohol Use Related to Wages? Evidence From Four Worksites', *Journal of Health Economics*, vol. 14, pp. 319-44.

Gill, A. and Michaels, R. (1991), 'The Determinants of Illegal Drug Use', *Contemporary Policy Issues*, vol. 9, pp. 93-105.

Gill, A. and Michaels, R. (1992), 'Does Drug Use Lower Wages?', *Industrial and Labor Relations Review*, vol. 45, pp. 419-34.

Grossman, M. (1972), 'On the Concept of Human Capital and the Demand for Health', *Journal of Political Economy*, vol. 80, pp. 223-55.

Hales, J. and Stratford, N. (1997), *1996 British Crime Survey (England and Wales): Technical Report*, SCPR, London.

Hamilton, V. and Hamilton, B. (1997), 'Alcohol and Earnings: Does Drinking Yield a Wage Premium?', *Canadian Journal of Economics*, vol. 30, pp. 135-51.

Harper, B. and Haq, M. (1997), 'Occupational Attainment of Men in Britain', *Oxford Economic Papers*, vol. 49, pp. 638-50.

Heien, D. (1996), 'Do Drinkers Earn Less?', *Southern Economic Journal*, vol. 63, pp. 60-68.

Home Office. (1998), *Tackling Drugs to Build a Better Britain: the Government's Ten-Year Strategy for Tackling Drugs Misuse*, HMSO, London.

Hoyt, G.M. and Chaloupka, F.J. (1994). 'Effect of Survey Conditions on Self-Reported Substance Use', *Contemporary Economic Policy*, vol. 12, pp. 109-21.

Kaestner, R. (1991), 'The Effects of Illicit Drug Use on the Wages of Young Adults', *Journal of Labor Economics*, vol. 9, pp. 381-412.

Kaestner, R. (1994a), 'The Effect of Illicit Drug Use on the Labour Supply of Young Adults', *Journal of Human Resources*, vol. 29, pp. 126-55.

Kaestner, R. (1994b), 'New Estimates of the Effects of Marijuana and Cocaine Use on Wages', *Industrial and Labor Relations Review*, vol. 47, pp. 45470.

Kaestner, R. and Grossman, M. (1998), 'The Effect of Drug Use on Workplace Accidents', *Labour Economics*, vol. 5, pp. 267-94.

Kandel, D., Chen, K. and Gill, A. (1995), 'The Impact of Drug Use on Earnings: A Life-Span Perspective', *Social Forces*, vol. 74, pp. 243-70.

Kenkel, D.S. and Ribar, D.C. (1994), 'Alcohol Consumption and Young Adults' Socioeconomic Status', *Brookings Papers on Economics Activity: Microeconomics*, pp. 119-75.

Labouvie, E. (1996), 'Maturing Out of Substance Abuse: Selection and Self-Correction', *Journal of Drug Issues*, vol. 26, pp. 457-76.

MacDonald, Z. (1999), 'Illicit Drug Use in the UK: Evidence from the British Crime Survey', *British Journal of Criminology*, vol. 39, pp. 585-608.

MacDonald, Z. and Pudney, S. (1999), *The Wages of Sin? Illegal Drug use and the Labour Market*, Discussion Papers in Public Sector Economics, 99/6, University of Leicester.

Macdonald, Z. and Pudney, S. (2000), 'Analysing Drug Abuse with British Crime Survey Data: Modelling and Questionnaire Design Issues', *Journal of Royal Statistical Society - Series C (Applied Statistics)*, vol. 49, pp. 95-117.

MacDonald, Z. and Shields, M. (2000), 'The Impact of Alcohol Use on Occupational Attainment in England', *Economica*, forthcoming.

McAllister, I. and Makkai, T. (1991), 'Correcting for the Underreporting of Drug Use in Opinion Surveys', *International Journal of the Addictions*, vol. 26, pp. 945-61.

Mensch. B.S. and Kandel, D.B. (1988), 'Underreporting of Substance Abuse in a National Longitudinal Youth Cohort', *Public Opinion Quarterly*, vol. 52, pp. 100-24.

Mullahy, J. and Sindelar, J.L. (1991), 'Gender Differences in Labor Market Effects of Alcoholism', *American Economic Review*, vol. 81, pp. 161-65.

Mullahy, J. and Sindelar, J.L. (1996), 'Employment, Unemployment and Problem Drinking', *Journal of Health Economics*, vol. 15, pp. 409-34.

Nickell, S. (1982), 'The Determinants of Occupational Attainment in Britain', *Review of Economic Studies*, vol. 49, pp. 43-53.

O'Muircheartaigh, C. and Campanelli, P. (1998), 'The Relative Impact of Interviewer Effects and the Sample Design Effects on Survey Precision', *Journal of the Royal Statistical Society - Series A (Statistics in Society)*, vol. 161, 63-77.

Parker, H. and Measham, F. (1994), 'Pick 'n' Mix: Changing Patterns of Illicit Drug Use Amongst 1990s Adolescents', *Drugs: Education, Prevention and Policy*, vol. 1, pp. 5-13.

Peck, D.F. and Plant, M.A. (1987), 'Unemployment and Illegal Drug Use', in T. Heller, M. Gott and C. Jeffery (eds), *Drug Use and Misuse: A Reader*, Wiley, Chichester.

Ramsay, M. and Percy, A. (1996), *Drug Misuse Declared: Results of the 1994 British Crime Survey*, Home Office Research Findings, no. 33, Home Office, London.

Ramsay, M. and Percy, A. (1997), 'A National Household Survey of Drug Misuse in Britain: A Decade of Development', *Addiction*, vol. 92, pp. 931-37.

Register, C. and Williams, D. (1992), 'Labor Market Effects of Marijuana and Cocaine Use Among Young Men', *Industrial and Labor Relations Review*, vol. 45, pp. 435-48.

Sickles, R. and Taubman, P. (1991), 'Who Uses Illegal Drugs?', *American Economic Review*, vol. 81, pp. 248-51.

White, A. and Malbon, G. (1995), *1994 British Crime Survey: Technical Report*, OPCS Social Survey Division, London.

Zarkin, G., Mroz, T., Bray, J. and French, M. (1998a), 'The Relationship Between Drug Use and Labor Supply for Young Men', *Labour Economics*, vol. 5, pp. 385-409.

Zarkin, G., French, M., Mroz, T. and Bray, J. (1998b), 'Alcohol Use and Wages: New Results from the National Household Survey on Drug Abuse', *Journal of Health Economics*, vol. 17, pp. 53-68.

APPENDIX 11.1

Table 11.A.1   Variable descriptions

Covariate	Description
Age/10	Age at time of survey/10
Ethnicity	Base = white and 'other' (inc. Chinese)
Asian	Asian (Indian, Pakistani, Bangladeshi)
Black	Black (African, Caribbean, other)
Education	Base = no formal qualifications
Educat 1	Degree or higher
Educat 2	Teaching/nursing, HND, BTEC
Educat 3	A levels, ONC, CG advance
Educat 4	High grade GCE/GCSE ,CSE grade 1
Educat 5	Low grade GCE/GCSE/CSE, clerical
Educat 6	Other qualification
Family structure	Base = other household type
Household 1	Single adult household
Household 2	Two adult household
Household 3	Three or more adult household
Household 4	Lone parent household
Household 5	Two adults plus one or two children
Married	Married or cohabiting
City	Lives in inner city area
Rented	Lives in rented accommodation
Church	Belongs to church/synagogue/mosque, etc.
Freqdrnk	Regular drinker
Y1996	Year dummy
Soft ever	Ever used soft drugs
Soft recent	Recent use of soft drugs
Hard ever	Ever used hard drugs
Hard recent	Recent use of hard drugs
Unemployed	Currently unemployed
Mean. hr. wage	Mean hourly occupational wage

Table 11.A.2   Descriptive statistics (means)

Covariate	Age 16-25		Age 26-50	
	Females	Males	Females	Males
Age/10	2.15	2.14	3.71	3.71
Ethnicity				
Asian	0.10	0.13	0.05	0.08
Black	0.07	0.07	0.09	0.07
Education				
Educat 1	0.11	0.10	0.16	0.20
Educat 2	0.11	0.13	0.13	0.17
Educat 3	0.17	0.16	0.10	0.12
Educat 4	0.40	0.31	0.28	0.20
Educat 5	0.11	0.12	0.09	0.08
Educat 6	0.03	0.04	0.04	0.05
Family structure				
Household 1	0.11	0.12	0.14	0.18
Household 2	0.29	0.23	0.25	0.24
Household 3	0.29	0.35	0.10	0.09
Household 4	0.09	0.06	0.17	0.09
Household 5	0.09	0.11	0.29	0.32
Married	0.32	0.22	0.67	0.73
City	0.27	0.27	0.23	0.23
Rented	0.18	0.17	0.09	0.10
Church	0.09	0.06	0.12	0.09
Freqdrnk	0.19	0.26	0.22	0.32
Y1996	0.52	0.51	0.55	0.54
Soft ever	0.33	0.44	0.22	0.31
Soft recent	0.19	0.30	0.06	0.09
Hard ever	0.14	0.23	0.06	0.11
Hard recent	0.05	0.10	0.01	0.02
Unemployed	0.11	0.19	0.05	0.10
Mean. hr. wage	5.60	6.04	6.36	7.34

12. Income Tax Evasion: A Theoretical Analysis

ALI AL-NOWAIHI AND DAVID PYLE

Introduction

A most unusual paradox exists in the literature on income tax evasion. This is the theoretical result that, assuming non-increasing absolute risk aversion, an increase in the income tax rate will lead to an increase in the amount of income declared to the tax authority (Yitzhaki, 1974). This result follows from standard portfolio theory if we think of tax evasion as an investment in a risky asset. Unfortunately, this result is completely at variance with all known evidence about the effect of a tax change, whether this is from experimental studies (Baldry, 1987, Friedland, Maital and Rutenberg, 1978) or econometric analysis of income tax returns (Clotfelter, 1983; Crane and Nourzad 1990). Despite the fact that Yitzhaki's results accords with neither common sense nor evidence, it has dominated the tax evasion literature for more than quarter of a century.

Gordon (1989), extending Benjamini and Maital (1985), showed that the theory could be made compatible with the evidence by incorporating psychic (or stigma) costs into the utility function. More specifically, Gordon assumed decreasing absolute risk aversion and a constant marginal disutility of evasion. In these circumstances an increase in the tax rate would increase evasion, provided that the marginal disutility of evasion is sufficiently high. The explanation for this is that an increase in the tax rate will make 'honesty more expensive' and the resulting substitution effect will be in the opposite direction to the 'income effect'. If the marginal disutility of evasion is sufficiently high, then the former will dominate the latter. Gordon (1989, p 804) concludes, '...additively separable preferences, constant marginal disutility from behaving dishonestly and individuals differentiated only by an honestly characteristic, yield a model in which taxpayers dichotomise into two groups. The first consists of the more dishonest, typically all evaders, who display conventional [i.e. Yitzhaki] comparative static behaviour. By contrast, the 'honest' group contains non-evaders and small evaders, and under decreasing absolute risk aversion, the latter evade more if the tax rate rises....'.

More recently Yaniv (1999) has attacked the problem in an entirely different way by abandoning the subjective expected utility approach in favour of prospect theory. He models advanced tax payments systems and shows that, in a prospect theoretic framework, as long as the declaration is sufficiently large, an increase in the tax rate would decrease the tax declaration. We show below that to obtain such a result it is not necessary to abandon the expected utility model.

Instead, in this chapter we seek to extend Gordon's result to general neo-classical utility functions. In particular, we drop the assumptions of additively separable preferences, constant marginal disutility of evasion and individuals differentiated only by an honesty characteristic. We then show that an increase in the tax rate will increase evasion if the subjective probability of detection is either sufficiently low or sufficiently high. Individuals in the latter category will be necessarily small evaders. However, those in the former category, i.e. those with a low subjective probability of detection, can be either small or large evaders. Individuals with subjective probabilities of detection in the intermediate range will exhibit a Yitzhaki-type response. To explain observed aggregate behaviour, we have to assume that few consumers have subjective probabilities of detection in the intermediate range, or that the utility functions are such that this intermediate range is empty. Simulation results using a logarithmic utility function suggest that tax evasion will increase with an increase in the income tax rate for plausible parameter values.

However, first we present a simple introduction to the theoretical literature on the economics of income tax evasion, which explains the work of Allingham and Sandmo (1972) and Yitzhaki (1974) and provides the background to the theoretical modelling which follows in the later sections of the paper.

A Simple Model of Taxpayer Non-Compliance

The first rigorous economic analysis of an individual's decision to evade payment of income tax was due to Allingham and Sandmo (1972). The impetus for this research came from two related literatures: first, the newly emerging work on the economics of crime (Becker, 1968), and second, the economic analysis of risk and uncertainty (Arrow, 1971). Deliberate under-reporting of income to the tax authority is inherently risky and also illegal. Therefore, it seems natural to apply the analytical tools developed in these other fields to answer the question 'how much of my income should I declare to the tax authority, given that I might get caught and punished if I fail to declare everything that I earn?'

In the approach proffered by Allingham and Sandmo individuals are assumed to be rational, amoral and risk averse. It is further assumed that they attempt to maximise expected utility that is dependent solely upon their income. In other words they neither derive pleasure from taking a risk and getting away with it nor suffer pangs of remorse from cheating on their tax obligations. We will consider in a later section how stigma (or guilt) can be built into the individual's decision framework.

Each individual's actual income (I) in the time period is assumed to be fixed. A constant tax rate (t) is paid on declared income (D). The probability of being investigated by the tax authority is given by p, which is also assumed to be constant. Finally, if a taxpayer is caught evading, she must pay a penalty on her undeclared income (i.e. $I - D$) of F per unit of undeclared income. The penalty rate (F) is assumed to be greater than the tax rate. If she is not caught then her net income after tax will be given by

$$W = I - tD \tag{12.1}$$

However, if she is caught her net income after taxes and penalties will be given by

$$Z = I - tD - F[I - D] = I(1 - F) - D[t - F] \tag{12.2}$$

Of course, if $D = I$, then $Z = W = (1 - t) I$.

The individual's opportunity locus is shown in Figure 12.1 by the line *AB*. AB is linear because we have assumed that F and t are fixed constants. At point A, all income is declared to the tax authority, i.e. $D = I$, so that net income will be the same in both states of the world (the states of the world are (i) being caught for income tax evasion and (ii) getting away with income tax evasion). At B, no income is declared, so that if unsuccessful, income falls to $I(I - F)$. However, if she gets away with it then net income will be I. Clearly the slope of AB is given by $1 - F/t$. Where the taxpayer locates on AB indicates the extent of her involvement in tax evasion.

The taxpayer's expected utility is simply a weighted average of her utility in the two situations which can arise, i.e. caught or not caught for evasion, the weights being given by p and $1-p$ respectively, i.e.

$$EU = (1 - p)U(W) + pU(Z), \tag{12.3}$$

where $U(.)$ is her utility function.

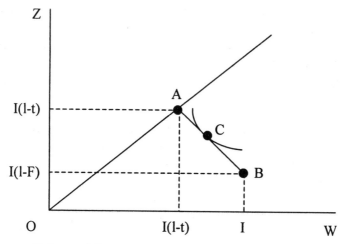

Figure 12.1   The opportunity locus

If at the moment she declares all of her income, but she can increase her expected utility by not declaring some income, then the economic approach suggests that she will evade. It is fairly easy to show that she will decide to evade if the expected penalty on undeclared income (pF) is less than the tax rate payable on declared income (t). This would occur if the derivative $dEU/dD < 0$, when evaluated at $D = I$. The first derivative is,

$$\frac{dEU}{dD} = -t(1-p)U'(W) - (t-F)pU'(Z) < 0$$

where $U'(.)$ is the first derivative of the utility function.

Clearly when $D = I$, $W = Z$ and so, $U'(W) = U'(Z)$ and the condition for 'entry' into income tax evasion then simplifies to

$$-t(1-p) - p(t-F) < 0,$$

which can be further simplified to

$$pF < t.$$

If the individual is risk averse then she will have indifference curves in Z, W space that are convex to the origin (see Pyle, 1983, p. 19). Assuming an interior optimum, the individual would be maximising expected utility at point like C in Figure 12.1.

An interior optimum (i.e. involving some undeclared income) will occur when:

$$\frac{dEU}{dD} = -t(1-p)U'(W) - (t-F)pU'(Z) = 0 \tag{12.4}$$

The second order condition for a maximum is automatically satisfied by the assumption that individuals are risk averse ($U''(.) < 0$).

To determine what will happen to the optimal declaration of income (D^*) when the tax rate (t), the penalty (F) and the probability of detection (p) change, we need to differentiate equation (12.4) above with respect to t, F and p in turn and solve for

$$\frac{\partial D^*}{\partial t}, \frac{\partial D^*}{\partial F} \text{ and } \frac{\partial D^*}{\partial p} \text{ respectively}$$

The results of this exercise are as follows,

$$\frac{\partial D^*}{\partial t} \text{ cannot be signed unambiguously}$$

$$\frac{\partial D^*}{\partial F} > 0$$

$$\frac{\partial D^*}{\partial p} > 0$$

For more detail on the proofs of these results see Pyle (1989, pp. 91-2). Fortunately, they can all be shown fairly easily diagrammatically.

Consider, first, the effect of an increase in the tax rate (t). This is shown in Figure 12.2. An increase in the tax rate, say from t to t', merely slides the point A along the certainty line to A'. The new opportunity locus becomes $A'B$. The change from AB to $A'B$ clearly involves both an income (or wealth) effect and a substitution effect. Unfortunately, these effects work in opposite directions and so we cannot be sure what the overall outcome will be. The substitution effect tends to increase the desire to evade (because the financial gain is greater), but, if we assume decreasing absolute risk aversion, the income effect will have the opposite effect as the tax increase makes people poorer (people on lower incomes are less willing to take a risk of a given size).

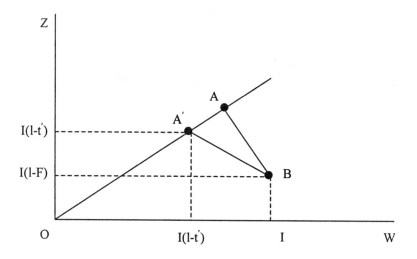

Figure 12.2   An increase in the rate of income tax, t

The effect of a change in the penal rate of tax (F) can be analysed in a similar fashion. Examination of Figure 12.3 shows that increasing F moves point B down vertically to B'. The effect is again to change both the slope and position of the opportunity locus. However, in this case the income and substitution effects work in the same direction, i.e. discouraging risk and moving C' closer to A than is C. So that, increasing the penal rate of tax discourages income tax evasion.

Finally, an increase in the probability of detection (p) will not affect the opportunity locus, but will alter the slope of the indifference curves. The slope of an indifference curve is given by

$$\frac{dZ}{dW} = \frac{-(1-p)U'(W)}{pU'(Z)}$$

As W and Z are independent of p, an increase in p will flatten the indifference curves. Consider the old optimum at C. The new indifference curve passing through C will cut the budget constraint AB. The optimum must, therefore, move to the left and the individual declares more of her income (see Figure 12.4).

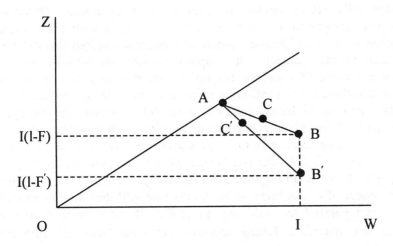

Figure 12.3   An increase in the penal rate of tax, F

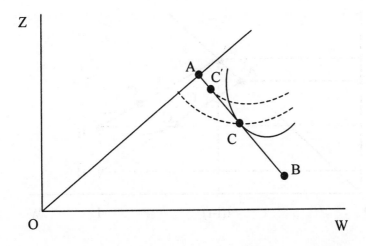

Figure 12.4   An increase in the probability of detection, p

Yitzhaki (1974) tried to remove the ambiguity concerning the effect of a change in the tax rate. He argued that under many countries' tax laws penalties for income tax evasion are levied on evaded tax, i.e. $t(I-D)$, and not on evaded income, i.e. $(I-D)$. Under this formulation of the penalty it is possible to show that $\partial D^*/\partial t > 0$ i.e. an increase in the tax rate will encourage individuals to declare more income for tax purposes. This result looks distinctively odd and certainly does not accord with either casual empiricism or the considerable volume of empirical research that has been undertaken in this subject.   It happens because the penalty paid on undeclared income (Ft) and the tax rate (t) are now proportional to each other, so that there is no substitution effect if the tax rate is changed. A rise in the tax rate now produces a pure income effect. It reduces the taxpayer's income and, if we assume decreasing absolute risk aversion, she will declare more of her income in order to reduce risk. This can be seen more clearly in Figure 12.5. Under this formulation of the penalty, the slope of the opportunity locus (in Figure 12.5) is given by $-(Ft-t)/t = 1-F$ which is independent of t. An increase in the tax rate will then simply shift AB inwards and parallel to itself, say to $A'B'$. If we assume decreasing absolute risk aversion, falling income will mean that C' (the new optimum) involves declaring more income than is declared at C.

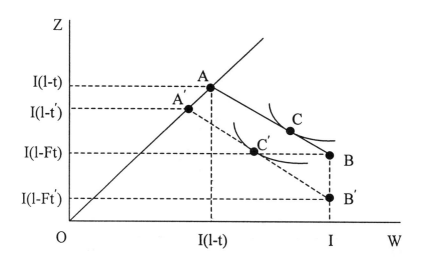

Figure 12.5   An increase in the income tax rate (Yitzhaki case)

A Formal Model of Income Tax Evasion in the Presence of Stigma

In the previous section, we argued that the prediction of the theoretical model concerning the effect of a change in the rate of income tax does not accord with empirical evidence concerning its effect. In the remainder of this chapter we will attempt to adapt the theoretical model so that it produces a more convincing prediction. We have decided to approach this by incorporating so-called 'stigma costs' into the individual's decision calculus.

As before, we consider an individual with income I who pays tax at the rate t on declared income D. If she decides to evade and is not caught, then her net income after tax will be,

$$W(D) = I - tD \qquad (12.5)$$

However if she is caught, she must pay a penalty of F (>1) per unit of evaded tax. Her net income after tax and penalties will be given by,

$$Z(D) = I - tD - Ft[I - D] = (F - 1)tD + (1 - Ft)I \qquad (12.6)$$

We assume that the tax-payer values both income and honesty and that her preferences are represented by the utility function $U(Y, D)$, where Y is net income (Y = either W or Z) and we measure honesty by the amount of declared income, D. Let the probability of detection be p, then the tax-payer's expected utility is given by:

$$u(D) = pU(Z(D), D) + (1 - p)U(W(D), D) \qquad (12.7)$$

$U = U(Y)$ gives Yitzhaki's model while $U = V(Y) + vD$ gives Gordon's model.

To simplify notation, we shall use a subscript variable to denote differentiation with respect to that variable. For example, U_Y, U_{YY}, U_{YD} denote $\partial U / \partial Y$, $\partial^2 U / \partial Y^2$ and $\partial^2 U / \partial Y \partial D$ respectively. We shall also use U_W and U_Z to denote U_Y evaluated at $Y = W$ and $Y = Z$ respectively, and so on. Unfortunately this notion cannot be used consistently. Thus we shall use $U_D(W)$ and $U_D(Z)$ to denote U_D evaluated at $Y = W$ and $Y = Z$, respectively. We make the following assumptions:

A1   I, t, F, p (and v in the case of Gordon's model) are exogenous.

A2   There exist D_0, Y_0 such that $0 \le D_0 \le I$, $0 \le Y_0 \le I$ and

> **A2.1**   in the region defined by $D_0 \le D \le I$ and $Y_0 \le Y \le I$, $U(Y,D)$ is continuous with continuous first and second order partial derivatives,

> **A2.2**   if $D_0 \le D \le I$ then $Y_0 \le Z(D) \le I$,

> **A2.3**   if $D < D_0$ then for some D_1 ε $[D_0,I]$: $u(D) < u(D_1)$.

A3 $U_Y > 0$, $U_D \ge 0$, $U_{YD} \ge 0$

A4   either:

> **A4.1** $U_{YY} < 0$, $U_{YD} = U_{DD} = 0$, or

> **A4.2** $U_{DD} < 0$, $U_{YD} = U_{YY} = 0$, or

> **A4.3** $U_{YY} < 0$, $U_{DD} < 0$, $U_{YY}U_{DD} > (U_{YD})^2$

A5   and finally:

> **A5.1** $U_D(W(I),I) < t\, U_Y(W(I),I)$

> **A5.2** $U_D(W(D_0), D_0) > t\, U_Y(W(D_0), D_0)$

The assumptions given in A2-A4 are slightly weakened versions of standard neo-classical assumptions that $U(Y,D)$ be strictly concave (A4.3) and twice continuously differentiable. By (A2.1), we require that $U(Y,D)$ be twice differentiable in a region $D_0 \le D \le I$, $Y_0 \le Y \le I$.

Assumption (A2.2) guarantees that the bounds are compatible in the sense that if $D_0 \le D \le I$ then $Y_0 \le Z(D) \le I$ and, hence, also $Y_0 \le W(D) \le I$. Assumption (A2.3) guarantees that an optimising tax-payer will always choose a D in the region where $U(Y,D)$ is twice differentiable.

Finally, assumption (A5.1) excludes the case of a tax-payer who is so honest that she will never evade. This can be seen by setting equation (12.14), in the Appendix, to be less than zero at $D = I$ and then simplifying. By contrast, (A5.2) implies that a tax-payer who is sufficiently honest will declare $D > D_0$ even if she faces a zero probability of being caught. This follows also from equation (12.14) in the Appendix, but this time setting $p = 0$ and requiring that $u_D > 0$ when $D = D_0$

We assume that the tax-payer chooses the optimal level of declared income, which we denote by $\hat{D}$, so as to maximise expected utility, $u(D)$, given by (12.7) above. From our assumption it follows that $u_{DD} < 0$ and, hence, $\hat{D}$ is unique. From the maximum theorem it follows that $\hat{D}$ is a continuous function of the parameters I, t, F, p (and v in the case of Gordon's model). For $D_0 < \hat{D} < I$, $\hat{D}$ satisfies $u_D = 0$, from which it follows that $\hat{D}$ is a differentiable function of the parameters. Letting x be any one of these parameters, it follows that

$$\hat{D}_x = -u_D / u_{DD} \text{ , evaluated at } D = \hat{D}.$$

Hence

$$sign\ \hat{D}_x = sign\ u_{\hat{D}_x}\ (\text{when } D_0 < \hat{D} < I\ ). \tag{12.8}$$

In more familiar notation: sign $\partial \hat{D} / \partial x = \partial^2 u / \partial D \partial x$ evaluated at $D = \hat{D}$. This can be used to derive the following comparative static results (see the appendix for details).

Theorem 1 (The Gordon Case)[1]

Assume:

    (a)   a constant marginal disutility of evasion, i.e. $U_D = v$, a constant.
    (b)   Non-increasing absolute risk aversion (with respect to income).
    (c) $pF < 1$.

Then there exist v^*, k such that $0 \leq v^* < k$ and

    (i) $v < k \Rightarrow \hat{D} < I, v \geq k \Rightarrow \hat{D} = I$;
    (ii) $p > 0 \Rightarrow v^* > 0$ and $0 \leq v < v^* \Rightarrow \hat{D}_t$ (Yitzhaki case);
    (iii) $v = v^* \Rightarrow \hat{D}_t = 0$; and
    (iv) $v^* < v < k \Rightarrow \hat{D}_t < 0$.

Theorem 2

(i)   there exists a probability P_{max} such that $0 < P_{max} \le 1$ and
        $0 \le p < P_{max} \Rightarrow D_0 < \hat{D} < I;$

(ii)   there exists $P_1 \varepsilon(0, P_{max}]$ such that $\hat{D}_t < 0$ for $p\varepsilon[0, P_1);$

(iii)   there exists $P_2 \varepsilon[0, P_{max})$ such that $\hat{D}_t < 0$ for $p\varepsilon(P_2, P_{max});$

(iv)   if the marginal utility of income, U_Y, is constant then $\hat{D}_t < 0$
        when $0 \le p \le P_{max}.$

Theorem 3

Consider the case $0 \le p < P_{max}$, then

(i) $\hat{D}_p > 0;$

(ii)   if $U_{ZD} < -t(F-1)U_{zz}$, then $\hat{D}_F > 0;$

(iii)   if $U_{ZD} < -t(F-1)U_{zz}$ and $tF > 1$, then $\hat{D}_t > 0.$

By Theorem 3(i), the amount of tax declared will be an increasing function of the probability of detection. By Theorem 2(ii, iii), the amount of tax declared will be a decreasing function of the tax rate, provided the (subjective) probability of detection is either sufficiently low or sufficiently high. If the marginal utility of income is constant, then the amount declared will be a decreasing function of the tax rate for all probabilities (Theorem 2(iv)).

Simulation Results for a Logarithmic Utility Function

Consider a tax-payer who declares some, but not all, of her income and who values honesty as well as net income. Faced with a rise in the tax rate, she will evade more if her (subjective) estimate of the probability of detection is either sufficiently low or sufficiently high (Theorem 2(ii), (iii)). This will be her response for all probability values in the special case of risk neutrality with respect to income (Theorem 2 (iv)). In this section we examine the pattern of responses for the case of logarithmic utility:

$$U(Y,D) = a \ln Y + b LnD, \quad a, b > 0 \tag{12.9}$$

Although this is also a special case (it has the property of constant relative risk aversion) it is more interesting than the constant marginal utility of income case. Moreover, (12.9) appears to provide quite a severe test of the hypothesis that $\hat{D}_t < 0$ for two reasons. First, because $U_{WD} = U_{ZD} = 0$. If these were positive, they would contribute negatively to $\hat{D}_t$ (see (12.16), below). Second, $U_{ZZ}/U_Z \to -\infty$ as $Z \to 0$ and, hence, for small positive Z, $-U_{ZZ}$ will contribute a large positive term to $\hat{D}_t$.

For simplicity, we assume that

$$a + b = 1 \text{ and } I(\text{income}) = 1 \tag{12.10}$$

Neither of these restrictions entail any significant loss of generality. This is because $a + b = 1$ can be achieved by a positive affine transformation (i.e. by dividing (12.9) by $a + b$); and because (12.9) exhibits constant relative risk aversion, allowing us to normalise income to any positive value.

The following theorem, Theorem (4), establishes an algorithm for calculating the intervals $[0, p_1)$ and $(p_2, P_{\max})$ on which $\hat{D}_t < 0$.

Theorem 4

Suppose that

$$b < t < b + \frac{a}{F} \tag{12.11}$$

If $Ft < 1$, put $\delta = \frac{1}{2}$, otherwise $\delta = \frac{(F-1)b + Ft - 1}{2(F-1)b}$

Let $D_0 = \frac{\delta b}{t}$ and $Y_0 = (F-1)tD_0 + 1 - Ft$

Then assumptions (A2) – (A5) hold and Theorems 2, 3 follow with

$$P_{\max} = \frac{t - b}{atF} \tag{12.12}$$

Let:

$$g = \frac{tF - 1}{F - 1}$$

$$B = a[p + (1 - p)g] + b(1 + g)$$

$$C = bg$$

$$d = \sqrt{B^2 - 4C}$$

$$x = \frac{B + d}{2}$$

Then, for $0 \le p < P_{max}$

$$\hat{D} = \frac{x}{t}$$

$$W = 1 - x$$

$$Z = (F - 1)(x - g)$$

$$u_{\hat{D}_t} = \frac{pa(F - 1)[tF - (F - 1)x]}{Z^2} - \frac{(1 - p)ax}{W^2} - \frac{b}{x} \tag{12.13}$$

Condition (12.11) is necessary (as well as sufficient) for $\hat{D}_t < 0$ on a non-empty interval $(0, P_1)$. For example, consider the case $a = 0.9$ (therefore $b = 0.1$), $t = 0.3$ and $F = 4.5$. Then $t = b + a/F$ and (12.11) is violated. For $p = 0$, (12.13) gives $u_{\hat{D}} < 0$. However, $Z \to 0$ and $p/Z^2 \to +\infty$ as $p \to 0$ (while W and x remain bounded away from zero as $p \to 0$). Consequently, $u_{\hat{D}_t} \to +\infty$ .as $p \to 0$. Hence, the continuity argument used in the proof of Theorem (2) fails here. For this example, there does not exist a $P_1 > 0$ such that $\hat{D}_t < 0$ on $[0, P_1)$.

Fortunately, (12.11) is not a stringent condition. The left hand side of (12.11), i.e. $b < t$, is equivalent to $P_{max} > 0$ (from (12.12)). This condition is needed to avoid the (mathematically trivial) case of a tax-payer who is so honest, she never evades tax. The right hand side of (12.11) will be satisfied, for example, whenever $Ft \leq 1$. Since, typically, $F \leq 2$ and $t \leq 0.5$, this is not a stringent condition either.

Condition (12.11) 'works' by ensuring that Z remains bounded away from zero as $p \rightarrow 0$. In turn, this ensures that $u_{\hat{D}_t}$ is continuous at $p = 0$. It then follows from $u_{\hat{D}_t} < 0$ at p = 0, that the same holds on some non-empty interval $[0, P_1)$. Taking $P_1 \leq P_{max}$ we get that $D_0 < \hat{D} < 0$ on $[0, P_1)$. Hence, we can use (12.8) to deduce that $\hat{D}_t < 0$ on $[0, P_1)$

The following Theorem, Theorem 5, provides an interpretation of the constant b in the logarithmic utility function (12.9).

Theorem 5

Consider the logarithmic utility function (12.9) with $a + b = 1$. Then $\hat{D} = b I/t$ at $p = 0$, i.e., b is the proportion of income paid in tax when the tax-payer's subjective probability of being detected for evasion is zero.

Theorem (2) establishes the existence of non-empty intervals $[0, P_1)$ and (P_2, P_{max}) such that evasion will rise with a rise in the tax rate, if the tax-payer's subjective probability of detection lies in one of these ranges. To determine the size of these intervals for plausible parameter values, we carried out a large number of computer simulations, a selection of which are reported in Table 12.1 below. The simulations are for the logarithmic utility function (12.9) under the normalisation condition (12.10). The simulations were carried out using the PC-MATLAB software. The programme implements Theorem (4): it calculates $u_{\hat{D}_t}$ (see (12.13)) for values of p from zero to P_{max} in steps of size 0.001 (0.0001 for simulations 7-9). This step size could not be reduced because of memory limitations. Intervals $[0, P_1)$ and (P_2, P_{max}) were then found for which $u_{\hat{D}_t} < 0$. Note that when the intervals overlap, i.e. $P_1 > P_2$, then $\hat{D}_t < 0$ for the whole range $[0, P_{max})$.

Table 12.1   Simulation results for a logarithmic utility function

	b	t	F	P_1	P_2	P_{max}	D_1	D_2
1	0.02	0.2	2	0.4590	0.4582	0.4592	0.9989	0.9929
2	0.05	0.3	2	0.4380	0.4376	0.4386	0.9978	0.9942
3	0.1	0.4	2	0.4160	0.4157	0.4167	0.9984	0.9960
4	0.2	0.5	2	0.3750	0.3750	0.3750	1	1
5	0.3	0.6	2	0.3570	0.3561	0.3571	0.9998	0.9987
6	0.5	0.7	2	0.2850	0.2847	0.2857	0.9995	0.9988
7	0.1	0.3	3.5	0.2116	0.2115	0.2116	0.9999	0.9996
8	0.1	0.3	4	0.0116	0.0879	0.1852	0.4052	0.6948
9	0.1	0.3	4.4	4×10^{-4}	0.0910	0.1684	0.3452	0.7557
10	0.01	0.3	2	0.1560	0.4742	0.4882	0.0686	0.9373
11	0.001	0.3	2	0.1400	0.4978	0.4988	0.0065	0.9915
12	10^{-4}	0.3	2	0.1390	0.4999	0.4999	6.5×10^{-4}	0.9959
13	10^{-5}	0.3	2	0.1380	0.5000	0.5000	6.5×10^{-5}	0.9954
14	10^{-10}	0.3	2	0.1380	0.5000	0.5000	6.4×10^{-10}	0.9953
15	0.01	0.25	1.5	0.4950	0.6125	0.6465	0.2501	0.7571
16	0.001	0.25	1.5	0.4430	0.6627	0.6647	0.0194	0.9765
17	10^{-4}	0.25	1.5	0.4400	0.6665	0.6665	0.0019	0.9958
18	10^{-6}	0.25	1.5	0.4390	0.6667	0.6667	1.9×10^{-5}	0.9940
19	10^{-10}	0.25	1.5	0.4390	0.6667	0.6667	1.9×10^{-9}	0.9940
20	0.01	0.4	2	0.0450	0.4844	0.4924	0.0334	0.9753
21	0.001	0.4	2	0.0400	0.4982	0.4992	0.0033	0.9963
22	10^{-4}	0.4	2	0.0390	0.4999	0.4999	3.3×10^{-4}	0.9972
23	10^{-5}	0.4	2	0.0390	0.5000	0.5000	3.3×10^{-5}	0.9970
24	10^{-10}	0.4	2	0.0390	0.5000	0.5000	3.3×10^{-10}	0.9970

Recall that b is the weight placed by the tax-payer on honesty, t is the tax-rate, F is the penalty and for subjective probabilities of detection greater than P_{max}, the tax-payer declares all income, i.e. $D = I (= 1)$. Also recall that $P_{max} = 0$ for $b \geq t$, i.e. the taxpayer never evades for $b \geq t$ (see (12.12)). In Table 12.1 $D_1 = \hat{D}(P_1)$ and $D_2 = \hat{D}(P_2)$, i.e. the proportions of income declared for these subjective probabilities of detection. From Theorem 3 (i) recall the $\hat{D} > 0$ for $p \; \varepsilon \,[0, P_1)$ and $p \; \varepsilon \,(P_2, P_{max})$. Hence $\hat{D}_t < 0$ for $\hat{D}_t \; \varepsilon(0, D_1)$ and $\hat{D} \; \varepsilon \,(D_1, 1)$.

Note that $P_1 > P_2$ (and $D_1 > D_2$) for simulations one to six. Hence $\hat{D}_t < 0$ for the full range $[0, P_{max})$ of the reported parameter values. This result still holds when b is increased or t or F is reduced beyond the reported values, provided that (12.11) is not violated.

Typically, $F \leq 2$. Nevertheless, simulations seven to nine study the effect of increasing F beyond 2. In this case, $\hat{D}_t < 0$ on the whole range $[0, P_{max})$ for $b = 0.1$, $t = 0.3$ and $F = 3.5$, but the intervals $[0, P_1)$ and (P_1, P_2) shrink rapidly as F increases to 4.4. At $F = 4.5$, $P_1 = 0$, as discussed above. However, even at $F = 4.4$, the intervals $[0, D_1)$ and $(D_2, 1)$ remain substantial. This is because of the high penalty, F.

Simulations 10-24 show that $[0, P_1)$ does not shrink to zero as $b \rightarrow 0$. The reason is that $u_D = b/D$. Hence for any fixed positive b, no matter how small, $u_D \rightarrow +\infty$ as $D \rightarrow 0$. Hence, as long as the tax-payer puts some value on honesty, no matter how little, there will be an interval $[0, P_1)$ on which evasion rises with a rise in the tax-rate. Moreover, the interval $[0, P_1)$ can remain sizeable even as $b \rightarrow 0$, as in simulations 15-19. However, except for simulation 15, the intervals $[0, D_1)$ and $(D_2, 1)$ for small b, appear too small, to be practically significant.

Conclusions

In this chapter we have considered a tax-payer who values honesty as well as net income. We have assumed that her preferences are given by a standard neo-classical utility function, that she is an expected utility maximiser, and that she declares some, but not all, of her income.

We have proved that she will declare less income the higher the tax rate (as is empirically observed) provided that her subjective evaluation of the probability of detection is either sufficiently low or sufficiently high (Theorem 2(ii), (iii)). The explanation of this result is simple. We may view tax evasion as, partly, an investment in a risky asset. It then follows from standard portfolio theory that under non-increasing absolute risk aversion, an increase in the tax rate will increase the amount of declared income (Yitzhaki, 1974). However, an increase in the tax rate will also make honesty more expensive. The resulting substitution effect will be in the opposite direction to the portfolio effect. If the (subjective) probability of detection is sufficiently small then the income effect will be relatively unimportant. The substitution effect will dominate, leading to an increase in evasion in response to an increase in the tax rate. At the other extreme, if the (subjective) probability of detection is sufficiently high the quantity evaded will be small. Again, the income effect will be small and, hence an increase in the tax rate will cause an increase in evasion.

Our simulation results for a logarithmic utility function suggest that, in fact, an increase in the tax rate will cause an increase in income tax evasion for a large range of realistic parameter values.

Note

1.   The formal proofs for all the theorems presented here are available from the authors.

References

Allingham, M.G. and Sandmo, A. (1972), 'Income Tax Evasion: A Theoretical Analysis', *Journal of Public Economics*, vol. 1, pp. 323-38.

Arrow, K.J. (1971), *Essays in The Theory of Risk Bearing*, Markham, Chicago.

Baldry, J.C. (1987), 'Income Tax Evasion and The Tax Schedule: Some Experimental Results', *Public Finance*, vol. 42, pp. 355-84

Becker, G.S. (1968), 'Crime and Punishment: An Economic Approach', *Journal of Political Economy*, vol. 76, pp. 169-217.

Benjamini, Y and Maital, S. (1985), 'Optimal Tax Evasion Policy: Behavioural Aspects', In W. Gaertner and A. Wenig (eds), *The Economics of The Shadow Economy*, Springer-Verlag, Berlin.

Clotfelter, C.T. (1983), 'Tax Evasion and Tax Rates: An Analysis of Individual Returns', *Review of Economics and Statistics*, vol. 65, pp. 363-73.

Crane S.E. and Nourzad F. (1990), 'Tax Rates and Tax Evasion: Evidence from California Amnesty Data', *National Tax Journal*, vol. 43, pp. 189-99.

Friedland, N., Maital, S. and Rutenberg, A. (1978), 'A Simulation Study of Income Tax Evasion', *Journal of Public Economics*, vol. 10, pp. 107-16.

Gordon, J.P.F. (1989), 'Individual Morality and Reputation Costs As Deterrents to Tax Evasion', *European Economic Review*, vol. 33, pp. 797-805.

Pyle, D.J. (1983), *The Economics of Crime and Law Enforcement*, Macmillan, Basingstoke.

Pyle, D.J. (1989), *Tax Evasion and The Black Economy*, Macmillan, Basingstoke.

Yaniv, G. (1999), 'Tax Compliance and Advance Tax Payments: A Prospect Theory Analysis', *National Tax Journal*, vol. 52, pp. 753-64.

Yitzhaki, S. (1974), 'A Note on Income Tax Evasion: A Theoretical Analysis', *Journal of Public Economics*, vol. 3, pp. 201-02.

13. Income Tax Evasion: An Experimental Approach

STEPHEN PUDNEY, DAVID PYLE AND TOLGA SARUC

Introduction

Following on from the work of Allingham and Sandmo (1972), a considerable amount time and effort has been devoted by economists to the study of income tax evasion, from both theoretical and empirical perspectives. However, the study of tax evasion has attracted interest from many different disciplines, such as sociology, psychology, anthropology as well as economics. Researchers from these different areas have emphasised different aspect of tax evasion. For example, sociological models have tended to be more concerned with the perception of sanctions, fear of social disapproval and attitudes to taxation (See Kinsey, 1986; Hessing *et al.*, 1988b). In this chapter we focus upon the work of economists.

Economists have assumed that the tax declaration decision is made in conditions of uncertainty, by taxpayers who are rational, amoral expected utility maximisers. Some of the theory of the income tax decision has been analysed in the previous chapter. Here, we consider the empirical evidence linking both the decision to evade and the extent of any evasion to economic and deterrence variables, in particular the income tax rate, the level of income, the probability of being audited and the severity of the punishment if caught for tax evasion.

The data we have used to analyse the tax declaration decision have been obtained from a series of tax 'experiments' conducted with Turkish citizens. The experimental approach has been used before in the area of income tax evasion, partly because of the difficulty in obtaining reliable information in other ways, e.g. from surveys and income tax returns. A weakness of the survey method, which relies upon individuals telling investigators about their participation in tax evasion, is that income tax evaders may either fail to respond or may respond in a dishonest manner to enquiries about their tax affairs. Hessing *et al.* (1988a) and Elffers *et al.* (1987) have explored the limitations of the survey method in their studies.

267

Both studies reported insignificant correlations between respondents' self-reports of tax evasion and officially documented behaviour.

The problem confronting analysis of income tax returns is that reliable inference requires the sample to be random. In many jurisdictions the detailed analysis that has been carried out into taxpayers' fiscal affairs by the internal revenue service (and which might form the basis of researchers' samples) has been of a group who are thought to be tax evaders, and who do not constitute a random sample of income tax payers. One possible exception to this is the US data generated as part of the Taxpayer Compliance Measurement Programme (TCMP), which has been analysed by Clotfelter (1983), Dubin *et al.* (1987) and Witte and Woodbury (1985) amongst others. However, TCMP data are not entirely problem free; IRS audits have more ability to detect overreported deductions than underreported income where the burden of proof is the responsibility of IRS. Also, TCMP audits do not include non-reporters. Moreover these audits measure both taxpayers' intentional evasion and unintentional mistakes, and in determining the voluntary compliance rate, overpayments and underpayments are combined. See Long and Swingen (1991) for a more detailed criticisms of TCMP data.

The Experimental Methodology

A major advantage of the experimental approach is that the possible explanatory variables can be manipulated and controlled directly. However, one drawback is that individuals involved in the experiment may not behave as they would in real life. For example, participants may try to guess the objective of the experiment and either behave in ways which they think that the experimenter wishes them to or attempt to sabotage the experiment. As a consequence, some investigators have tried to mask the real objective of the experiment within a business game (Webley *et al.*, 1991). Webley and Halstead (1986) found that subjects who perceived the experiment as a tax declaration were almost entirely honest, while subjects who considered the experiment as a game in general declared only part of their income. They stated that the use of computers was strongly associated with the playing of games by participants. Also, they criticised previous experimental studies, where the instructions asked subjects to maximise their net income and where the purposes of the experiment were transparent. However, Robben *et al.* (1990) found no evidence that subjects who guessed the correct purpose of the experiment were more likely to underreport their income.

Davis and Swenson (1988) have argued that using neutral terms rather than loaded language may discourage role-playing by subjects. Beck *et al.* (1991) carried out experiments in abstract settings by using 'neutral terms' such as surcharge and check rather than 'loaded terms' like tax rate and audit. However, Alm, *et al.* (1992b) carried out an experiment with 48 students in which some sessions were run twice, once with neutral instructions and once with loaded instructions and it would appear that the use of neutral or loaded instructions did not make any difference to the outcome.

Another potential disadvantage of the experimental approach is that some aspects of the 'real life' evasion decision are difficult to incorporate into the experiment. For example, how can one mimic the social stigma (or shame) of either failing to declare all of one's income or being exposed as a cheat. Nevertheless, given the difficulties of obtaining reliable data by other means, it may be worthwhile using experimental observations as a means of generating supplementary information about individual behaviour in this sphere of activity.

Literature Review

The basic design of experiments in the tax evasion literature has been similar. Usually, they have been played with student subjects, who are given a 'paper' income (referred to as gross income) and then asked to decide how much of that income to report to the 'tax authority'. Participants pay taxes on reported income only, but reported income is audited with some probability usually known in advance by the participants. If subsequently a participant is found to have failed to declare everything, then he/she pays a fine at a known predetermined rate. The process of declaring income and auditing declarations continues for a certain number of rounds and at the end of the experiment subjects are rewarded in relation to their net income over the period of the experiment.[1] During the experiment the effect of various policy parameters, such as the tax rate, fine rate and the probability of audit can be seen by changing their values in certain rounds. In the following sections we review a number of studies under these different parameters.

Tax Rate

In Allingham and Sandmo's original theoretical analysis of income tax evasion, the predicted effect of a change in the income tax rate was ambiguous and depended upon the relative sizes of the income and substitution effects (Allingham and Sandmo, 1972). However, Yizhaki (1974) showed that, for the individual taxpayer at least, if the penalty was related to the amount of unpaid tax (rather than to undeclared income), then an increase in the tax rate would unambiguously reduce the extent of evasion. This result arose because an increase in the tax rate in these circumstances produced only an income effect, which made taxpayers worse off. As a result, they preferred to take less risk and hence reduced evasion (see Chapter Twelve). Yitzhaki's theoretical result seems to fly in the face of commonsense and empirical work was aimed at testing the effect of tax rate changes upon evasion. Of course, Yitzhaki's result could be consistent with evidence of a negative association between the tax rate and the amount of income declared for income tax purposes at the aggregate level (for example, if the higher tax rate encourages more people to engage in evasion, this may offset the reduced amount of evasion by those already evading). Here, we review only studies which have adopted an experimental methodology and which examine individual behaviour rather than aggregate evidence (see Pyle (1991) for a review of studies which have used different approaches).

The study of Friedland, *et al.* (1978), which involved 15 Israeli psychology students, showed that increasing the tax rate (from 25 per cent to 50 per cent) led to a dramatic increase both in the probability of underreporting and in the extent of the underreporting of income. Baldry (1987) conducted a similar experiment with 49 students in Australia and also found that the amount of tax evasion by those who decided to evade was increased by an increase in the marginal tax rate, but that changes in the marginal tax rate were not significantly related to the propensity to evade (i.e. whether or not evasion took place). Alm, *et al.* (1992a), in an experiment with 15 students, also found that a higher tax rate led to significantly lower compliance. However, a similar experiment reported by Alm, *et al.* (1995), which also used student subjects, found that increasing the income tax rate increased tax compliance. This result was also found by Beck, *et al.* (1991) who considered reporting behaviour under income uncertainty. The experiments were carried out with 112 students, whose risk preferences were controlled by mapping their after-tax disposable income on to the probability of winning a cash price in a lottery.

Collins and Plumlee (1991) examined the effect of the tax rate both on under declaring and effort (labour supply) in an experiment involving 120 students. Subjects obtained income by performing a decoding exercise. The results show that increasing the tax rate increased underreporting, but that there was no significant effect of the tax rate upon effort.

Whilst results are somewhat mixed, the majority of previous experimental work indicates that increases in the tax rate would lead to a greater amount of underreporting.

Income

The 'theory' of income tax evasion predicts that evasion would increase as income rose, provided that individuals have decreasing absolute risk aversion. However, it is not clear, in theory at least, how evasion as a fraction of income would vary with income. Several studies have investigated the effect of income upon income tax evasion, but no clear overall conclusion emerges.

Spicer and Becker (1980), in an experiment involving 57 student subjects, the main aim of which was to analyse the effect of feelings of inequitable treatment upon tax evasion, found that actual income did not have a significant effect on the *percentage of taxes evaded*. Baldry (1987) found that an increase in true income increased the amount of tax evasion, but had no effect on the decision to evade. On the other hand, Alm *et al.* (1992a) found that an increase in true income leads to higher compliance, a finding that is contrary to income tax evasion theory. They state that '...declared income is a normal good with an income elasticity (approximately 0.7) that is significantly less than one' (p. 110). A similar result is reported by Witte and Woodbury (1985) and Dubin, *et al.* (1987).

Becker, *et al.* (1987) conducted two identical experiments in which subjects earned income by completing a number of tasks. Two dependent variables were used in the analysis. These were the propensity to evade taxes (i.e. whether tax evasion occurred or not) and the extent of taxes evaded, if tax evasion occurred. It was found that the propensity to evade taxes increased with income, but no significant effect of income on the extent of tax evasion could be found.

Deterrence Factors

The basic theory of income tax evasion concludes that increasing expected punishment (by raising the audit rate, the fine multiplier or both) should increase tax compliance. Much of the experimental literature has been devoted to an investigation of the strength of these relationships.

Becker *et al.* (1987) found that the auditing probability had a negative effect on both the propensity to evade taxes and percentage of taxes evaded. However, work by Spicer and Thomas (1982) found that a deterrent effect of audit only existed when participants were fully informed. Their experiment involved 54 student subjects and the audit probability was set at three different levels. One third of the subjects received precise information, whilst another one third were told merely that the audit rate would be low, high or medium. The remaining one third of subjects were given no information concerning the audit rate. The investigators found that the percentage of taxes evaded was negatively and significantly related to the audit rate only for subjects who received precise information. Friedland (1982) has also examined the effect of imperfect information concerning the probability of audit and the fine rate. Contrary to Spicer and Thomas, he found that the precision of the information about the fine rate and the probability of audit had no effect upon the percentage of income reported. However, vague information about the audit probability strengthened the deterrent effect of low probability audits and increased the deterrent power of low fines.

Spicer and Hero (1985), in an experiment involving 36 students, found that the number of audits had a negative and statistically significant effect on tax evasion in the last round. However, Webley *et al.* (1991) report a number of experiments, the majority of which were unable to find any significant effect of audit occurrence on the number of periods of tax evasion. Alm *et al.* (1992b) observed that when the audit rate increased, then so did compliance. Also, they observed that when the audit probability was low there was much more compliance than expected utility theory would lead one to predict. For example, even when the audit probability was zero, the average group compliance was 20 per cent. In addition, when the audit probability was high, subjects evaded more than would be predicted by expected utility theory.

Collins and Plumlee (1991) examined the effect of three different audit schemes, which were a random audit scheme, a cut-off audit scheme (the 20 per cent of subjects who declared the lowest level of income were audited), and a conditional audit scheme. It was found that the highest underdeclaring occurred under the random audit scheme and the lowest under the conditional audit scheme. However, the difference between them was not statistically significant. Their results also indicated that the effect of fine rate on underreporting was not significant.

The main conclusion of Friedland *et al*. (1978) was that a large fine combined with a low probability of audit was a more effective deterrent than a mathematically equivalent penalty of a small fine with a high probability of audit. Webley, *et al*. (1991) report a study, carried out with 46 students, which attempted to replicate the findings of Friedland *et al*. (1978). The main difference was that Webley *et al*. (1991) tried to obscure the purpose of the experiment by using a complex business simulation. They found that the fine rate did not have a significant effect on either the percentage of taxes evaded or the number of occasions that tax was evaded, but that the audit probability had a positive effect on the amount of declared income (although not on the number of periods that tax was evaded). Moreover, contrary to the findings of Friedland *et al*., there was no evidence that a large fine with a small probability of detection was a more effective deterrent than a small fine with a high probability of detection.

In conclusion, a number of experimental studies have found a negative relationship between tax evasion and the audit rate, although sometimes the link is not straightforward. However, there is less evidence of an effect of the fine rate upon evasion. In some cases this may be attributable to deficiencies in experimental design, but it may also reflect the rather complex relationship which may exist between the variables.

The Study

Most previous experiments have been conducted using students as subjects. This may be problematic for a number of reasons. Robben *et al*. (1990) reported that students were more likely to underreport their income than nonstudent subjects. Students are less experienced in filing tax returns and in tax matters generally, than are members of the public. Therefore, the use of only student subjects may limit the generality of the results obtained. This study has been carried out using participants from a variety of occupations, as well as groups of students. In addition, many of the previous experiments have involved small numbers of participants, typically fewer than 50, and sometimes as few as 15-20. A larger number of subjects may increase the reliability of the experimental findings. In this study there is a total of seven experiments, involving about 270 participants, which makes it one of the largest tax evasion experiments undertaken.

Finally, often experiments in this area have been conducted in a 'laboratory' situation. In order to make the experiments closer to the actual tax assessment procedure, and also to protect privacy by giving participants the opportunity to complete the tax forms in their own homes, five of the experiments were conducted over a longer time period. The tax forms were distributed to participants at the beginning of a day. At some point during the day, participants decided how much of their income to declare on the tax form, and the forms were collected following day. The experiments continued in this manner for several days. The values of variables used in the experiments were chosen to be consistent with the actual policy parameters in Turkey. In most of the previous experiments, these parameters have been set without regard to their realistic values and have been changed in large, discreet jumps. Finally prizes were given to participants in order to encourage them to take the experiments seriously. Often these were in cash form and typically had a value in Turkish Lira equivalent to between £30 and £70. Average household earnings of subjects involved in the study are about £340 per month, so that a typical prize was equivalent to several days' pay.

Design of the Experiments

In total seven experiments were conducted. The first was carried out with thirty-four doctors, two dentists and one nurse at the University Hospital in Manisa. The second experiment was conducted with 52 participants in Adana, where participants were mostly lawyers, although it included some secretaries, cleaners, lecturers, businessmen and shop owners. Experiment three was conducted in Adana with judges, lecturers and businessmen. In total there were 42 participants. In the first experiment the prize was a medical textbook valued at £50, whilst in the second and third experiments a cash prize of £70 was given to the participant who had the highest net income at the end of experiment. A fourth experiment was undertaken with 24 participants who were mainly architects or engineers in Mugla. Here, the money prize was £25. The participants in the fifth experiment were 60 students in the fourth year undergraduate management course at the Middle East Technical University in Ankara. This experiment took place in a lecture room and lasted for one hour. The prize for the participant who had the maximum net income was a cash sum of about £30. However, since ten students had the same maximum net income the prize was divided amongst them. The sixth experiment was carried out in Leicester and involved 20 Turkish subjects who were mostly post-graduate students. The method and the parameters used were the same as for the first four experiments. A cash prize of £20 was given. The last experiment took place in Istanbul with 38 participants who were mostly self-employed business people or teachers.

In the final experiment each participant was paid according to his or her net income in the experiment (the lowest payout was about £7.50, whilst the highest was £18). The payment method was changed here in order to discover whether paying each subject would make any difference to the findings (not discussed here). In each round the subject's net income (minus fines) was calculated. One of the eight rounds was selected for payment and each participant was paid one per cent of the selected round's net income minus any fines. In addition, in order to make the experiment closer to the real tax assessment procedure each participant was told that if net income was negative in the round selected for payment, they would have to pay that amount from their own pocket.

The methodological approach, which underlies the experiments, is broadly similar to that adopted by Friedland *et al.* (1978), except that the participants were not told that they should aim to maximise net income. The instructions (see Appendix A) were read to the subjects, who were assured of confidentiality and anonymity. It was explained that the study was for the purpose of academic research. The instructions explained that each subject would receive salary slips for each round of ten months and there would be four rounds altogether. Terms such as 'taxable income', 'audit probability' and 'penalty' were used in the experiments and these terms were explained to participants if they were unfamiliar with them. For each 'month', participants had to decide how much of their taxable income to report to the tax authority and they paid tax on the income that they declared. Audits were conducted randomly according to a predetermined frequency, of which the subjects were informed. When the subjects were audited and their income was found to be underreported, a fine (a predetermined and announced multiple of evaded tax) was imposed.

Envelopes containing the instructions and the tax table for each round were given to each of the participants at the beginning of one day and collected on the following day. The tax table told them what their income was for each month in that round. Each individual's income for each month was different in order to find any income effect and to make the experiment more interesting for the participants. For the first round, the tax rate was 25 per cent, the fine magnitude was three times the tax evaded, and audit rate was ten per cent for each month. In subsequent rounds these parameters were varied. The chosen values were written at the top of the tax tables for each round (see Appendix B). Participants entered their 'declared income', the amount of 'income tax' and 'net income' (gross income – income tax) in the appropriate columns of the form. Audit selection was performed upon the receipt of the completed forms for each round, by drawing numbered chips from a container, with one chip for each subject. The columns headed 'audited', 'fine', and 'net income less fine' were completed by the investigator and the completed forms for each round were returned to the participants along with tax tables for the next round. The experiment continued in this fashion for four rounds. At the end of the experiment participants were asked to complete a small questionnaire, which provided information about, amongst other things, their age, sex, marital status, occupation, number of children, and attitudes to risk.

Model Specification

To motivate the analysis, consider the following simple theoretical framework, which is a slight extension of that discussed by Pyle (1989, section 5.1). Individuals are expected utility maximisers, who care about two things: their financial gain; and the stigma or shame that arises when caught evading tax.[2] The utility function is therefore $u = U(y, \xi)$ where y is financial gain and $\xi = 1$ if the individual chooses to evade and 0 otherwise. If I is taxable income, f is the fine rate, p is the probability of tax audit and θ is the proportion of income declared, then expected utility is:

No evasion: $\quad EU = U((1-t)I, 0)$

Evasion: $\quad EU = pU\big((1 - t\theta - ft(1-\theta))I, 1\big) + (1-p)U\big((1-t\theta)I, 0\big)$

Maximisation of expected utility can lead to two different types of optimum: a corner solution at $\theta = 1$ and an interior solution at some $\theta < 1$. The former will be observed whenever

$$U\big((1-t)I, 0\big) > \sup_{\theta < 1}\big\{ pU\big((1-t\theta - ft(1-\theta))I, 1\big) + (1-p)U\big((1-t\theta)I, 0\big)\big\},$$

which is likely to happen particularly when the stigma/shame effect is large. For the interior optimum, the first-order condition is:

$$\frac{\partial EU}{\partial \theta} = tI[(f-1)pU_y((1-t\theta - ft(1-\theta))I,1)$$
$$-(1-p)U_y((1-t\theta)I,0)] = 0 \tag{13.1}$$

where $U_y = \partial U(y,\xi)/\partial y$. Thus the optimal degree of income reporting can be written in the general form:

$$\theta = \tilde{\theta}(p,t,f,I) \tag{13.2}$$

Note that if marginal utility is homogeneous in y, the solution for θ does not involve income at all. For example, if utility takes the form $U(y,\xi) = y^\sigma - \phi\xi$,[3] the solution is:

$$\tilde{\theta} = \frac{1-A(1-ft)}{t(1-A(1-f))} \tag{13.3}$$

where $A = ((f-1)p/(1-p))^{1/(\sigma-1)}$.

We do not use any specific functional form for utility in our empirical work, but instead use simple linear approximations in the following four variables: tax rate, t; expected penalty as a proportion of tax due, pf; probability of audit, p; and log experimental income, $\ln(I)$, so that all four variables are in dimensionless form.

In addition to these four 'economic' variables, we include a number of other explanatory variables intended to capture two effects. The first of these is variation in preferences stemming from differences in characteristics such as age, gender and economic circumstances as reflected by occupation and actual (rather than experimental) income. The second extension to the simple theoretical model is to allow for learning or experimental fatigue effects, which we do by including dummy variables to capture shifts in behaviour between experimental rounds and the occurrence in earlier rounds of a fine for evasion.

The two types of solution for the expected utility maximisation problem give rise naturally to a two-part econometric model, analysing the corner and interior solutions separately. Thus we estimate the following conditional distributions, using conventional econometric forms for both:

$$\Pr(\tilde{\theta} = 1 | p,t,f,I,z) \tag{13.4}$$

$$f\left(\tilde{\theta}\,\middle|\,\tilde{\theta} < 1, p, t, f, I, z\right)$$ (13.5)

where z represents all observable characteristics of the individual that may affect the form of preferences, together with variables representing learning and fatigue effects. For the discrete probability (13.4) we use the logit model as an approximation, and for the conditional density (13.5) we use a regression approximation.

In estimating these two components of the behavioural relation, it is important to take into account the fact that there may be some important unobservable psychological characteristics affecting behaviour, besides the measurable attributes such as age and gender included in z. To allow for these individual-specific attributes, we assume them to remain constant across all experiments the individual takes part in. These individual effects can then be accommodated in a variety of ways. We use Chamberlain's (1980) conditional logit technique to estimate (13.4), and standard fixed and random-effects regression as alternative estimators of (13.5). These methods are described below, and the results of applying them to our experimental data are summarised in Table 13.1.

The Conditional Logit Technique

The fixed-effects logit model is as follows:

$$\Pr(y_{ij} = 1 \mid x_{ij}) = \frac{\exp(x_{ij}\alpha + u_i)}{1 + \exp(x_{ij}\alpha + u_i)}$$ (13.6)

where $i = 1...n$ indexes individual experimental subjects and $j = 1...J_i$ indexes the experiments. The dependent variable $y_{ij} = 1$ if the outcome involves evasion and 0 otherwise; the row vector of explanatory variables is $x_{ij} = \{1, j, p, t, f, \ln(I)\}$. Note that the fixed effects u_i can capture the preference shifters z_i which are constant through all experiments for a given subject. Chamberlain (1980) first noted that it was possible to estimate panel data logit models consistently in the presence of fixed effects, using an appropriate conditioning argument. This approach maximises a likelihood function constructed from the conditional sample distribution: $\Pr(y_{i1} \cdots y_{iJ_i} \mid \sum_j y_{ij})$.

However, note that this conditional probability is identically equal to 1 for individuals with no variation in their experimental responses, and that the conditioning variable Σy_{ij} contains potentially important sample information. Consequently, there may be a considerable sacrifice of efficiency, as the price paid for the robustness of this approach.

Fixed- and Random-Effects Regression

For interior values of the evasion rate θ, we use a panel-data regression model in which the degree of evasion practised by tax evader i in the jth experiment is:

$$\theta_{ij} = w_{ij}\beta + v_i + \varepsilon_{ij} \tag{13.7}$$

In this model, the row vector of observable explanatory variables is w_{ij}, unobservable personal characteristics are represented by the individual-effects v_i and ε_{ij} represents all other random factors affecting any particular experimental outcome. Note that the coefficients β appearing in the regression model (13.7) should be comparable in sign, but not in scale, with the logit coefficients α.

We estimate the model (13.7) in two alternative ways. One is by means of fixed-effects (or within-group) regression, in which the v_i are treated as arbitrary unknown constants and eliminated by the within-group transform. This entails applying standard multiple regression to the following equation:

$$(\theta_{ij} - \overline{\theta}_i) = (w_{ij} - \overline{w}_i)\beta_i + (\varepsilon_{ij} - \overline{\varepsilon}_i) \tag{13.8}$$

where $\overline{w}_i$ etc. denotes the mean of a variable over all experiments undertaken by individual i. Note that this within-group transform eliminates both the unobservable effects v_i and all observable variables which have no variation over experiments (for example age and gender).

The second alternative method of estimating the model (13.7) is to use random-effects regression, which is based on the assumption that the individual effects v_i vary randomly across individuals, independently of all observed variables. Under these circumstances, the model can be estimated efficiently by means of two-step generalised least squares. Note, however, that the assumption of independence is a strong one, and it is important to test its validity, which we do by means of a Hausman test. This involves a comparison of the fixed effects estimates of β (which do not require the independence assumption) with the random-effects estimates (which do). A statistically significant difference implies the rejection of the independence assumption, and suggests that the random effects estimates may be biased.

Results

The theoretical model outlined above implies a behavioural relation that entails separate impacts for the variables t, p and f (or pf). However, attempts to estimate models involving all three variables were unsuccessful, in the sense that the estimates (particularly for the coefficient of p) displayed very poor statistical precision. Instead, Table 13.1 gives results for models with p excluded as a separate variable. Thus the joint effect of p and f is captured through the single variable pf. These restricted models do not fit the data significantly worse than the analogous unrestricted models, and their economic implications are similar.

The first column of Table 13.1 gives the Conditional Logit estimates. Note that there are no estimates for coefficients of variables which are constant across experiments for a given individual. Thus we cannot draw inferences about the impact of age, gender, occupation etc. However, there is strongly significant evidence of a positive influence of the tax rate on the probability of evasion, and weaker evidence of a negative impact of the expected penalty imposed by the tax authority. This corresponds well with economic intuition and with much previous experimental evidence. The experimentally-assigned income has a clear positive impact on the evasion probability. There is also significant evidence here of a degree of adaptation as the sequence of experiments proceeds. The probability of evasion is reduced by experience from a previous round of a tax audit leading to a fine and there is also weaker evidence of a decrease over time in the propensity to evade.

The fixed- and random-effects regression results are given in the next pair of columns in Table 13.1. They are computed using the set of experiments in which the degree of evasion (θ) is positive, and thus represent the distribution of θ conditional on evasion. They are broadly in line with the logit estimates, with the exception of the income response, which is small but significantly negative. Thus a high assigned income tends to reduce the degree of evasion, whilst simultaneously increasing the probability that evasion will occur. Although it is possible to generate such an outcome from a suitably-specified theoretical model, this is a surprising finding that merits further research. The strong incentive effect of high tax rates is confirmed by these regression results, but there is no significant evidence of an effect of the severity of tax audits on the amount (rather than incidence) of evasion. Thus, while there is some evidence that punishment operates as a disincentive to becoming a tax-evader, there is no evidence of an impact of the amount of tax evaded by those who do decide to evade.

The Hausman test, which compares the fixed- and random-effects results, turns out to be significant (with a p-value of around two percent). Thus the independence assumption which underlies the random-effects model is rejected, but not by a huge margin. Thus, whilst bearing in mind that there is a possibility of bias, it seems reasonable to pay some attention to the qualitative pattern of the coefficients of the explanatory variables which are constant across experiments within individuals. These coefficients suggest that the groups which are most likely to evade are: the young; males; the wealthy; and those for whom actual income data could not be obtained. The skilled occupational group (including technicians, architects, etc.) appears significantly more law-abiding than other groups.

Table 13.1 Logit and regression estimates (continued over)*

Covariate	Fixed-effects logit	Regression on sub-sample of tax evaders ($\theta > 0$)		Full sample regression	
		Fixed effects	Random effects	Fixed effects	Random effects
Tax rate (t)	14.927	1.097	1.339	1.212	1.337
	(6.410)	(0.692)	(0.690)	(0.610)	(0.612)
Expected penalty rate (pf)	-9.946	0.008	-0.650	-0.430	-0.740
	(6.434)	(0.370)	(0.314)	(0.214)	(0.203)
ln(experimental income)	0.531	-0.048	-0.047	-0.006	-0.008
	(0.172)	(0.010)	(0.010)	(0.009)	(0.009)
Previously fined	-0.791	-0.021	-0.020	-0.002	0.004
	(0.171)	(0.010)	(0.009)	(0.009)	(0.009)
Round 1	2.375	0.088	0.200	0.166	0.222
	(1.842)	(0.180)	(0.178)	(0.155)	(0.155)
Round 2	2.665	0.151	0.214	0.201	0.233
	(1.611)	(0.173)	(0.173)	(0.153)	(0.153)
Round 3	0.618	-0.034	0.015	0.003	0.024
	(0.490)	(0.028)	(0.024)	(0.016)	(0.015)
Age	-	-	-0.004	-	-0.007
			(0.002)		(0.002)
Male	-	-	0.062	-	0.085
			(0.035)		(0.035)
Married	-	-	0.069	-	0.063
			(0.042)		(0.045)
ln(actual Income)	-	-	0.092	-	0.029
			(0.043)		(0.044)
Missing income data	-	-	0.364	-	0.205
			(0.168)		(0.172)
Student	-	-	0.048	-	0.101
			(0.137)		(0.136)
White collar	-	-	0.244	-	0.212
			(0.166)		(0.189)

* standard errors in parentheses.

Table 13.1 Logit and regression estimates (continued)*

Covariate	Fixed-effects logit	Regression on sub-sample of tax evaders ($\theta > 0$)		Full sample regression	
		Fixed effects	Random effects	Fixed effects	Random effects
Skilled	-	-	-0.134	-	-0.050
			(0.060)		(0.066)
Business person	-	-	-0.038	-	0.059
			(0.073)		(0.077)
No. subjects	97	177		229	
Experiments per subject	38.9	28.2		32.6	
Hausman test	-	$\chi^2(7) = 22.2$		$\chi^2(8) = 135.0$	

* standard errors in parentheses.

As a check on the robustness of these results, we have also used a single regression model, estimated in fixed and random-effects form, covering all experiments. This therefore ignores the qualitative distinction between evaders ($\theta > 0$) and non-evaders ($\theta = 0$) and is not a fully appropriate estimation approach. Nevertheless, the broad character of the results is similar, apart from the clearer negative impact of the expected penalty rate, and the lack of any significant income effect. The random-effects estimates of the coefficients of observable personal characteristics are very similar to those obtained for the sub-sample of tax-evaders, despite the highly significant Hausman test result which rejects the independence assumption. This robustness of the estimates suggests that the coefficient biases in the random-effects models may not be of much practical concern for explanatory variables like age, gender, etc.

Conclusions

In this chapter we have reported the results of a series of tax 'experiments' that were undertaken with various groups of people in Turkey in 1998. In total more than 270 individuals participated in the experiments. The objective of the exercise was to gather information with which to test the effect of certain variables upon (i) the decision to evade income taxes and

(ii) the amount of income tax evasion. Unlike most previous experiments in this field we have included participants other than students as part of the sample. Also, we conducted the experiments outside of the classroom/laboratory environment. We believe that these changes make the decisions made by the participants more credible. In order to encourage the participants to take the 'games' seriously, we offered a substantial money prize to the person in each experiment who achieved the highest net income.

Our results indicate a very strong positive effect of tax rates upon both the decision to evade income tax and upon the amount of income tax evasion, once individuals have decided to evade. In other words, higher income tax rates encourage individuals to become tax evaders and further encourage existing evaders to increase the extent of their evasion. The effect of expected punishment is less clear. Whilst it has its expected deterrent effect upon the decision to evade, there would appear to be no discernible effect upon the amount of evasion undertaken by those who have decided to evade. One can find an intuitive, psychological explanation for such behaviour, which might be as follows. Individuals prefer to declare their income to the tax authority and the threat of punishment helps to reinforce that behaviour. However, those who have overcome any qualms they might feel about evasion have crossed a significant boundary between acceptable and unacceptable behaviour. Any marginal increase in expected punishment for this group has little or no effect upon the amount that they declare to the income tax authority. In such circumstances it may require a substantial change in punishment to bring their behaviour back into line.

Likewise, the influence of income appears to be complicated, having a different effect upon the decision to evade (where an increase in income encourages evasion, as economic theory would predict) from its impact upon the amount of evasion (increasing income leads to a fall in the amount of undeclared income). Finally, there is some evidence of differences between different groups in their willingness to evade, with young men most likely to engage in evasion.

Our results also suggest that the behaviour of individuals changes over time, as their experience of experiments increases. Whether this behaviour mimics real life is debatable, but may be worth further exploration. It is reassuring to find that our results do not indicate that student subjects behave in these experiments in ways that are substantially different from employed people of the same age.

Finally, the experiments reported in this chapter were set up in such a way that it was always financially worthwhile for participants to engage in tax evasion and yet a substantial number of them declared the whole of their allotted income in each round of the experiment. This behaviour is worthy of further analysis. It may be that these individuals did not understand the nature of the experiment or that they had a remarkable degree of risk aversion. However, these are unlikely to be explanations for subjects' behaviour. A more plausible explanation is that the simple economic model of income tax evasion (following Allingham and Sandmo, 1972) needs to be recast in order to explain this kind of behaviour more readily. One way of doing this has been outlined in both this and the preceding chapter and involves incorporating stigma (or conscience) into the formal economic model of taxpayer behaviour.

Notes

1. Net income is defined as gross income minus taxes and penalties.
2. A similar model was presented in Chapter Twelve. However, in that model stigma was related to the amount of undeclared income. In other words, individuals suffered pangs of conscience if they failed to be good citizens, i.e. if they did not contribute their share to the common pot. The more income they failed to declare, the more remorse they suffered. In the model presented here individuals only suffer if they get caught for evasion and are exposed as cheats. Clearly this is a more cynical view of human nature.
3. This is similar to the structure of the utility function employed in Chapter Twelve and by Gordon (1989).

References

Allingham, M.G. and Sandmo, A. (1972), 'Income Tax Evasion: A Theoretical Analysis', *Journal of Public Economics*, vol. 1, pp. 323-38.

Alm, J., Jackson, B R. and McKee, M. (1992a), 'Estimating The Determinants of Taxpayer Compliance with Experimental Data', *National Tax Journal*, vol. 45, pp. 107-14.

Alm, J., McClelland, G. H. and Schulze, W. D. (1992b), 'Why Do People Pay Taxes?', *Journal of Public Economics*, vol. 48, pp. 21-38.

Alm, J., Sanchez, I. and Dejuan, A. (1995), 'Economic and Noneconomic Factors in Tax Compliance', *Kyklos*, vol. 48, pp. 3-18.

Baldry, J.C. (1987), 'Income Tax Evasion and The Tax Schedule: Some Experimental Results', *Public Finance*, vol. 42, pp. 357-83.

Beck, P.J., Davis, J.S. and Jung, W. (1991), 'Experimental Evidence on Taxpayer Reporting Under Uncertainty', *The Accounting Review*, vol. 66, pp. 535-58.

Becker, W., Büchner, H. and Sleeking, S. (1987), 'The Impact of Public Transfer Expenditures on Tax Evasion: An Experimental Approach', *Journal of Public Economics*, vol. 34, pp. 243-52.

Chamberlain, G. (1980), 'Analysis of Covariance with Qualitative Data', *Review of Economic Studies*, 47, pp. 225-38.

Clotfelter, C. (1983), 'Tax Evasion and Tax Rates: An Analysis of Individual Returns', *Review of Economics and Statistics*, vol. 65, pp 363-73.

Collins, J.H. and Plumlee R.D. (1991), 'The Taxpayer's Labor and Reporting Decision: The Effect of Audit Schemes', *The Accounting Review*, vol. 66, pp. 559-76.

Davis, J.S. and Swenson, C.W. (1988), 'The Role of Experimental Economics in Tax Policy Research', *The Journal of American Taxation Association*, vol. 10, pp. 40-59.

Dubin, J.A., Graetz, M.J. and Wilde, L.L. (1987), 'Are We a Nation of Tax Cheaters? New Econometric Evidence on Tax Compliance', *American Economic Review*, vol 77, pp. 240-45.

Elffers, H., Weigel, R.H. and Hessing, D.J. (1987) 'The Consequences of Different Strategies for Measuring Tax Evasion Behavior', *Journal of Economic Psychology*, vol. 8, pp. 311-37.

Friedland, N. (1982), ' A Note on Tax Evasion as a Function of the Quality of Information about the Magnitude and Credibility of Threatened Fines: Some Preliminary Research', *Journal of Applied Social Psychology*, vol. 12, pp. 54-59.

Friedland, N., Maital, S. and Rutenberg, A. (1978), 'A Simulation Study of Income Tax Evasion', *Journal of Public Economics*, vol.10, pp. 107-16.

Gordon, J.P.F. (1989), 'Individual Morality and Reputation Costs as Deterrents to Tax Evasion', *European Economic Review*, vol. 33, pp. 797-805.

Hessing, D.J., Elffers, H. and Weigel, R.H. (1988a), 'Exploring the Limits of Self-Reports and Reasoned Action: An Investigation of Psychology of Tax Evasion Behaviour', *Journal of Personality and Social Psychology*, vol. 54, pp. 405-13.

Hessing, D.J., Kinsey, K.A., Elffers, H. and Weigel, R.H. (1988b), 'Tax Evasion Research: Measurement Strategies and Theoretical Models', in W.F. van Raaij, G.M. van Veldhoven and K.E. Wärneryd (eds), *Handbook of Economic Psychology*, Kluwer Academic Publishers, Dordrecht, Netherlands.

Kinsey, K.A. (1986), 'Theories and Models of Tax Cheating', *Criminal Justice Abstract*, vol. 18, pp. 403-25.

Long, S.B. and Swingen, J.A. (1991), 'Taxpayer Compliance: Setting New Agendas for Research', *Law and Society Review*, vol. 25, no. 3, pp. 637-83.

Pyle, D.J. (1989), *Tax Evasion and The Black Economy*, MacMillan, Basingstoke.

Pyle, D.J. (1991), 'The Economics of Taxpayer Compliance', *Journal of Economic Surveys*, vol. 5, pp. 163-98.

Robben, H.S.J., Webley, P., Weigel, R.H., Warneryd, K., Kinsey, K.A.., Hessing, D.J., Martin, F A., Elffers, H., Wahlund, R., van Langenhove, L., Long, S.B. and Scholz, J.T. (1990), 'Decision Frame and Opportunity As Determinants of Tax Cheating: An International Experimental Study', *Journal of Economic Psychology*, vol. 11, pp. 341-64.

Spicer, M.W. and Becker, L.A. (1980), 'Fiscal Inequity and Tax Evasion: An Experimental Approach', *National Tax Journal*, vol. 33, pp. 171-75.

Spicer, M.W. and Hero, R.E. (1985), 'Tax Evasion and Heuristics', *Journal of Public Economics*, vol. 26, pp. 263-67.

Spicer, M.W. and Thomas, J.E. (1982), 'Audit Probabilities and The Tax Evasion Decision: An Experimental Approach', *Journal of Economic Psychology*, vol. 2, pp.241-45.

Webley, P. and Halstead, S. (1986), 'Tax Evasion on the Micro: Significant Simulations or Expedient Experiments?', *Journal of Interdisciplinary Economics*, vol. 1, pp. 87-100.

Webley, P., Robben, H., Elffers, H. and Hessing, D. (1991), *Tax Evasion: An Experimental Approach*, Cambridge University Press, Cambridge.

Witte, A.D. and Woodbury, D.F. (1985), 'The Effect of Tax Laws and Tax Administration on Tax Compliance: The Case of the US Individual Income Tax', *National Tax Journal*, vol. 38, pp. 1-13.

Yitzhaki, S. (1974), 'A Note on Income Tax Evasion: A Theoretical Analysis', *Journal of Public Economics*, vol. 3, pp. 201-02.

APPENDIX 13.1

Instructions for Experiment Subjects

Thank you for agreeing to participate in this experiment, which is conducted for the purposes of academic research. You do not need to give your name and we can assure you of anonymity. Each one of you will receive a notional gross income for each of the next ten 'months'. This will be repeated four times. For each month you have to decide how much of your gross income, which is taxable, to report to the tax authority. You will pay tax on the income that you declare. Audits will be conducted randomly according to a given rate. If you are drawn in the random sample, you will be audited and if you have failed to report all of your income, a fine will be imposed on any tax evaded. At the end of the experiment, everybody's net income (i.e.gross income minus taxes paid and any fines imposed) will be calculated and a prize will be given to the person with the highest net income (the exact prize and its monetary value was specified in each experiment).

Now look at the second page. In the first column you will see ten 'months' are listed and the gross income you will receive for each month has been entered. Starting from January consider carefully how much of your gross income you want to declare. This is the income upon which you will pay income tax. Write the amount in the column headed 'Declared Income'. Calculate your income tax liability using the appropriate tax rate that is given at the top of the table. For example, if you have reported an income of 40 million Turkish Lira and the tax rate is 25 per cent for this month, you will pay income tax of TL10 million. Write this sum in the column headed 'Tax Paid'. Deduct this sum from your gross income (not from your reported income), and write the result in the column headed 'net income'. Please leave blank the columns headed audited, fine, and net income minus fine.

After you have completed the tax table, the papers will be collected. Then a random audit will be conducted according to the audit rate that is given at the top of the table. If for some month, you come up in the draw, then for this month only we will check whether you have underreported your income, and if you did, you will be fined a multiple of the tax you have not paid. The fine multiplier is also given at the top of the table. For example, if you have not paid TL five million of income tax, which you should have paid and the fine multiplier is three, then if you are discovered you will pay a fine of TL 15 million. After the four rounds total net income for each person will be calculated and the prize will be paid to the person with the highest aggregate net income over the whole experiment.

APPENDIX 13.2

Table 13.A.1   Tax table, first round

Tax rate: 25 percent; Fine multiplier: 3; Audit rate: 10 per cent

Months	Gross Income	Declared Income	Tax Paid	Net Income	Audited	Fine	Net Income Minus Fine
Jan.							
Feb.							
March							
April							
May							
June							
July							
August							
Sep.							
Oct.							

Table 13.A.2   Parameters used in experiments one to four, and six

	Tax Rate	Fine Magnitude	Audit Rate
Round One	25%	3	10%
Round Two	25%	1.5	15%
Round Three	50%	3	10%
Round Four	50%	1.5	15%

Table 13.A.3   Parameters used in experiment five

	Tax Rate	Fine Magnitude	Audit Rate
Round One	25%	3	5%
Round Two	25%	1.5	10%
Round Three	50%	3	5%
Round Four	50%	1.5	10%

Table 13.A.4   Parameters used in experiment seven

	Tax Rate	Fine Magnitude	Audit Rate
Round One	25%	3	10%
Round Two	25%	3	10%
Round Three	25%	3	15%
Round Four	25%	3	10%
Round Five	25%	1.5	15%
Round Six	25%	1.5	10%
Round Seven	50%	3	10%
Round Eight	50%	1.5	15%